THE
JEWISH CONTRIBUTION
TO CIVILIZATION

This book IS PUBLISHED
FROM THE PROCEEDS OF
THE LUDWIG VOGELSTEIN
MEMORIAL FUND

 *The* JEWISH
CONTRIBUTION
to CIVILIZATION

By CECIL ROTH

THE UNION OF AMERICAN HEBREW
CONGREGATIONS · *Cincinnati*

MCMXL

Fourth Printing

COPYRIGHT, 1940 BY

CECIL ROTH

PRINTED IN U. S. OF AMERICA

TO
MY BROTHER
LEON ROTH

'Tra cotanto senno'
(INFERNO, IV. 102)

EDITOR'S INTRODUCTION

For many years Jewish teachers and the average Jewish layman have sought a book that would give them an authoritative account of the contribution of the Jew to civilization. Young people, in particular, in these days when Jews are challenged throughout the world, feel the need of knowing what share their own people has had in the story of mankind.

That the Greeks contributed art, that the Romans contributed law, that the Hebrews contributed religion to the sum total of our Western civilization is well known even to the general reader. However, what more specific influence did the Hebraic heritage have upon the world? What cultural influences did the Jewish people exercise? Have we made any contribution to the fields of art, music, drama, and letters? Have we in any way helped in the progress of science? These and other questions naturally agitate the thinking Jew of today. And to all of these questions, as well as to many others, he will find an answer in this book.

There is another more practical value to this work coming as it does at a time of crisis in the Jewish world. Psychologists have pointed out the danger of giving a child a bad name. If he is called by it often enough he may begin to believe he deserves it. Our enemies and detractors so often accuse us of being middlemen who do nothing productive, that our own people begin to believe it. It is important therefore that our people, especially our young people, learn the truth about their past.

To find out, as the reader will in this book, that not only in science, art, music, and letters, but even in such a field as maritime discovery, we have played a significant part, may have a wholesome effect on the minds of our persecuted and discouraged people.

In issuing this book, we feel the Union of American Hebrew Congregations is making a significant contribution to the literature of Jewish education. We hope it will receive the widespread reading it deserves and will help to revive in many of our fellow Jews the moral courage of our ancestors to live a life devoted to truth and to the improvement of the fate of our people and of mankind.

EMANUEL GAMORAN

PREFACE

THIS work is intended as a contribution towards the settlement of a discussion of long standing, which is now once again attracting attention. It is alleged by modern anti-Semites, in order to justify a prejudice which, in these ostensibly tolerant times, they hesitate to base on theological grounds, that the Jew is essentially a middleman, who has produced nothing; that he is an alien excrescence on Western life; and that the influence which he has had on the world's culture, during the past two thousand years, has been entirely negative, if not deleterious. Such a criticism demands an analysis based not on theory but on fact; and this is what I have endeavored to provide. I have set out to write this book as objectively as possible. I am making no attempt to evaluate the Jewish genius or even to decide whether such a thing exists. Perhaps, on the basis of the material collected in this volume, it may be possible to come to some conclusion upon these problems in the future. My task has been a comparatively simple, if laborious, one. I have tried to assemble and set down in this volume a representative selection of the contributions made to the civilization, the culture, and the amenities of the western world by persons of Jewish lineage.

There has been in this no question of a theological test of any sort. Today, as has been indicated, the assault upon the Jew is made on "racial," not religious grounds. Persons in whose veins there runs the blood [1] of a single Jew as far as three generations back—of one traceable Jewish great-grandparent, that is—are ferociously persecuted today in Germany on the plea that their stock is alien, and *ipso facto* harmful to German, "Nordic," and European cultural life. The Jewish people, moreover, is consistently blamed for the actions of persons of Jewish origin, who not only have cut themselves off from Jewish life, but who even have professed markedly anti-Jewish sentiments, which they have not scrupled to translate into action. Hence, one is justified in attempting to evaluate the Jewish contribution in terms of Jews and not of Judaism alone by taking into account those contributions made by persons of traceable Jewish ancestry, whatever their religious affiliation or sympathies.

I must confess, however, that normally, in the absence of such a religious distinction, I would find it difficult to define precisely what a Jew is. I have no intention to enter into any of the current controversies on "race" and "blood," nationality and religion. I can only state, as an historical fact, that how-

---

[1] This term in the present connotation is of course based on an ancient and exploded embryological theory. To make use of it, as in the present instance, is sometimes convenient; to draw further implications (and still more to make it the basis of a political theory or policy) is absurd to a degree. So also the terms "Aryan" and "Non-Aryan," while occasionally convenient in use, are a scientific monstrosity. It is one of the most regrettable features in contemporary intellectual life that an imposing pseudo-scientific structure—sometimes dominating public affairs—can be erected on the basis of a linguistic misusage.

ever distinct the Jews may have been from their
neighbors ethnologically at the beginning of their
settlement in Europe, this distinction has been progressively modified. For countless generations every
European country (not excluding Germany) pursued as a point of principle the policy of encouraging
conversions from Judaism to the dominant faith by
every means which lay in its power, fair or foul.
There were baptisms from conviction. There were
baptisms from material interest. There were forced
baptisms, on an enormous scale, in more countries than
one. If this violent pressure has been relaxed during
the last century and a half, the tendency toward leaving the Jewish fold has been maintained by the constant procession of those converted from conviction or
from convenience, or those who have drifted insensibly
into the majority by the gradual process of assimilation.

On the other hand, even at the darkest hour of
degradation, there were Christians who saw fresh
spiritual potentialities in Judaism and became inte-
grated in the Jewish community as "children of Abraham the Patriarch." The numbers in question were
never great, but a process of this sort, continued for
a period of two thousand years, necessarily modified
whatever purity of stock may originally have existed.
To this must be added the illicit admixture which was
inevitable on either side, the result of scenes of violence or interludes of romance.

It is impossible to escape the conclusion that the
much-discussed "racial" differentiation between the

Jews and their neighbors, especially in those countries like Germany, in which their settlement is of oldest date, is largely artificial. The amount of Jewish blood traceable among non-Jews is surprisingly great, even if one goes back for only a single century. *Vice versa,* few Jews can fail to have (whether they realize it or no) some tincture of non-Jewish blood in their veins. To quote the words of the late Lucien Wolf (which gather new weight in the light of these facts), "the Jew who emerged from the Ghetto was no longer a Palestinian Semite but an essentially modern European, who differed from his Christian fellow-countrymen only in that his religion was of the older Semitic form and that his physical type had become sharply defined through a slightly more rigid exclusiveness in the matter of marriages than that practiced by Protestants and Roman Catholics."

My use of the term "Jew" in the following pages hence denotes a person whose immediate ancestors professed the Jewish religion.

The differentiation is clearly to some extent an artificial one. The background and the upbringing of the Jewish and non-Jewish elements are in many instances identical. In the case of persons of mixed ancestry, the fifty or twenty-five per cent of Jewish blood cannot be proved the decisive factor in the determination of the particular genius of a poet or playwright or philanthropist. No more is it, of course, in the determination of the character of a criminal, a decadent, or a revolutionary. If the Jewish people is to receive a full measure of blame for the one cate-

gory, it is justified in claiming some measure of credit
for the other.

It must be realized that the author has no intention
of giving here anything in the nature of a connected
account of those subjects on which he touches. Those
who may be interested in "Jewish art" or "Jewish
medicine" must be referred to the specialized works
devoted to those questions. It would have been beyond the power of a single man to give a satisfactory
survey of the many fields of human activity of which
this book treats; and the author will have served his
purpose if he has indicated, by mentioning some outstanding names, how Jews have collaborated in each
sphere. The psychological and philosophical nature
of the contribution he is not in a position to judge,
nor can he agree with what is generally so confidently
asserted on these subjects. The Jew is distinguished,
perhaps, by a slightly greater degree of intellectualization; possibly by a freshness of outlook, natural in
one whose approach tends to be external; and, in
consequence, by a faculty for synthesis and for introducing new ideas. He is apt to show, in fact, certain
characteristics inevitable in persons who belong,
through the circumstances of their history, to a single
sociological group. To say more is hazardous.

The outcome of my enquiry has been more than a
little surprising, even to myself. There is no branch of
human culture or civilization which Jews have not
touched and enriched. In some branches, the contribution has been more significant than in others. But,
whether we consider literature or medicine or science

or exploration or humanitarianism or art, the Jew has
been prominent. That he has not produced giants in
all these branches is of course true; for the same is
the case with every other fraction of humanity. England has produced only one Shakespeare, Germany
only one Goethe; and who will say that these stand
on a higher level, whether as thinkers or as masters
of the written word, than the Prophet Isaiah? England
gave birth to no philosopher on the same plane as
Spinoza; no musician who excels Mendelssohn; no
contemporary painter, perhaps, of the calibre of Pissarro or Liebermann. In the fields of medicine and
science, moreover, the Jewish contribution during the
past century can well stand comparison with that of
any country of the world without exception—and
that notwithstanding the fact that emancipated Jewry
numbered until a few years ago far less than the population of one of the Balkan or Scandinavian states.

Certain assertions made in this volume may appear
to some readers extravagant. I can only plead that I
have taken the utmost pains to verify my statements
and have included nothing for which I was unable to
find reliable authority. Many will doubtless be surprised, for example, to discover the extent of the
participation of the Jews in the maritime discoveries
of the fifteenth century. But the data are indubitably
as I have stated them; my account cannot claim even
the merit of originality. It must be borne in mind, after
all, that general ignorance of a fact does not necessarily impair its validity.

I am certain, moreover, that any baseless claims

which may have been made, notwithstanding my
caution, are far outnumbered by omissions, whether
due to ignorance or to the obvious impossibility of
being able to ascertain the precise antecedents of every
individual. Nothing has been further from my mind
than any sort of Jewish chauvinism. A man or a group
of men does not deserve particular merit for having
performed his or their duty. Only when the fact is
impugned does proof become necessary.

My indebtedness in the composition of a work of
such complexity is too great to permit detailed ac-
knowledgment to all who have assisted me. I must,
however, express my deep gratitude at least to Dr.
Charles Singer, who revised the chapters on the Jew
in Medicine and kindred branches in the light of his
vast knowledge; to my brother, Professor Leon Roth,
of the University of Jerusalem, for contributing the
essential part of the section on Philosophy; and to my
wife, who with heroic application compiled the Index.
In adapting the work to the requirements of the American reader, I have had also the invaluable assistance of
Dr. Emanuel Gamoran and a group of his friends, Dr.
James G. Heller of Cincinnati, Mr. Reuben Leaf of
New York, and Mr. Abraham H. Friedland of Cleveland.

CECIL ROTH

CONTENTS

THE
JEWISH CONTRIBUTION
TO CIVILIZATION

CHAPTER I. *The Hebraic Heritage*

I

JEWISH history is approximately divided into two
nearly equal periods, the dividing line between them
falling, whether one adopts the theological or the
political standpoint, at the age of Jesus of Nazareth,
or the destruction of Jerusalem by the Romans a
generation after his death. During the early period,
roughly coinciding with the nineteen centuries before
the beginning of the Christian Era, the Jews—or rather
as they are better termed over most of this period,
the Israelites—constituted one of the many lesser
nationalities of the Near East. They were distinguished from their neighbors principally by their
religious beliefs and by the superior ethical code
which resulted therefrom. During the latter period,
roughly coinciding with the nineteen centuries of
the Christian Era, they have been a people scattered
throughout the world, in all continents and in almost
every land, still adhering to their distinctive religious
system but exercising their influence as individuals
rather than as a group.

It is with the latter period, more properly the
"Jewish," that this work will in the main deal. But

it would be misleading to omit all reference to the
Heritage of Israel, which, taken over by Christianity
(in a somewhat modified or expanded form, as Jew
and Christian respectively hold) has left an ineradi-
cable influence upon the structure of the modern
world.

It is a commonplace that modern civilization is an
amalgam of three elements. From Rome, we have received our conception of law and, to some extent, of
politics. From Greece, operating sometimes through
Rome, we have our philosophy, as well as our aesthetic
standards, whether in literature or in the other arts.
And to Israel, the Western World owes its religion and
its ethics.[1]

The basis of the Hebraic contribution to Western
civilization and the Hebrew's greatest gift to humanity is the ideal of the One God, Creator of Heaven
and Earth. According to the biblical account, this conception, familiar to the Patriarchs, was reaffirmed to
their descendants at the foot of Mount Sinai; according to the critical view, it was a gradual discovery,
fully realized only some centuries later. In any case,
it is fundamental to a consideration of the Hebraic
element in modern life. Greek and Indian thinkers
may have had a glimmering of the same truth. Only
the Hebrew proclaimed it aloud, adhered to it through

[1] To this conventional triple division may be added the modern
contribution of technical efficiency, which constitutes the outward
shell (too often confused with the substance) of present-day civilization. In this, Jews, as individuals, have played a noteworthy part,
which will be considered in detail in later chapters of this book.

persecution and vilification, yielded up his life for its sake, and made it central to his whole existence. The Jews of today, adhering to the monotheistic tradition of their fathers, number some sixteen million souls. But, through Jesus and Paul, the Hebraic teaching, in a modified form, yet basically identical, passed to Europe, and is now cherished by 650,000,000 Christians throughout the world. Six centuries later, it was reiterated in Arabia with desert sternness by Mohammed and is now the creed of 220,000,000 Moslems. The kernel of both religions is the terse declaration which the Hebrews believed to be uttered by the Deity Himself from Sinai: *I am the Lord thy God. . . . Thou shalt have no other gods before Me.*

There is, of course, more in monotheism than this dogmatic self-affirmation of Deity. The most unfettered thinker of today who steadfastly refuses to subscribe to any theological dictum owes, nevertheless, to Hebraism the breaking of the shackles of polytheism—the worship of animals and images, of the stars and planets, of a plurality of deities such as those in the Hellenic pantheon with their human appetites and lusts and failings. There was in this a degrading and demoralizing effect, which cannot escape the notice of any student of ancient history. The commanding part taken by the moral code in the biblical religious system is too familiar to require any amplification here. But the ideas of the value of human life, the sanctity of the home, and the dignity of the marital relationship, which nominally prevail at the present time, are essentially a biblical heritage. For the religion of the ancient Hebrews was not circumscribed in its application. As has been remarked by a modern thinker, the struggle for justice and the struggle against other gods in the biblical age, instead of being two separate movements, are logically one and the same. Even at the present time, when the conception of mediation between man and his Creator and the institution of hagiolatry sometimes tend to obscure among the ignorant the monotheistic basis of Western spiritual life, the clarion voice of the Hebrew prophets is an ever-present reminder of that underlying principle of Unity to which every Church adheres.

The monotheistic idea had, moreover, a far-reaching influence on Western thought even in its least theological aspects. We usually connect Hebraism with morals, and we are apt to think that we have thereby exhausted its significance. But Hebraism has significance for science, too. Science is the search for regularity. It is the attempt to find order and system. But regularity, order, and system are only derivatives from the unity postulated in the Hebraic conception of God. The modern reaction against "Laws of Nature" need blind us no more than the modern reaction against Puritanism to the immense scientific significance, both historical [1] and actual, of monotheism. The triumphs of modern science have been made possible only by the "superb and unshaken confidence in the rationality of the Universe," which is one of the ultimate bequests of the Hebrew prophets to hu-

[1] The point is made by Whitehead, *Science and the Modern World*, Chap. i.

manity at large. If Duty, with the capital D of traditional morality, is the "stern daughter of the voice of
God," the Law of Science is that voice itself.

A necessary extension of the idea of the Divine
Unity is that of the equality of *all* before the One
God. Out of the same seed which gave birth to the
conception of the Chosen People, there developed
ultimately in the Hebrew prophets and in the Talmud
the idea of the brotherhood of all peoples. The brotherhood of peoples makes abhorrent the idea of inter-
necine war. All the dreams of universal peace that
have stirred mankind down to our own day are to be
traced back to that Messianic vision of the Prophet
Isaiah, of an age when "people shall not lift up
its sword against people, nor shall they learn war
any more." To us today it may seem trite, but there
was an epoch-making originality in this idea in an age
when conquest was regarded as the natural right of
the stronger, and a victorious war the ideal of every
powerful state. Contemporary developments have
given the Hebraic attitude new force and value, and
today it is no exaggeration to say that the future of
civilization depends upon the renewal of the prophetic
dream.

The God of Israel was, moreover, a God of righteousness. This overwhelming passion for righteousness
is insisted upon in the Bible almost as much as the
monotheistic idea, for the one is the concrete expression of the other. Here was no impersonal deity, indifferent to men's affairs, nor yet a selfish one, swayed
by flattery and bribes; but a God Who loved good-

ness, Who abhorred oppression, Who laid down positive standards of conduct between man and his fellow, Who insisted on justice, truth, and morality. The ideals of social justice, which Western reformers are endeavoring to carry into practice in our own day, are the ideals taught by Isaiah, Amos, and Micah, now part of the common heritage of mankind. It would be absurd to claim that the affirmation of righteousness as a fundamental principle in the conduct of human affairs is peculiar to the Hebrew; it is to be found in the teachings of Buddha, of Confucius, and of the Greek philosophers. These, however, made their protest against superstition and their plea for righteousness, almost simultaneously, some two hundred years after Amos and Hosea had sounded the call in Palestine, in the eighth century B.C.—and this, according to the traditional view, was nearly a thousand years after those same ideas had been proclaimed at Sinai. Moreover, the non-Hebrew thinkers, in effect, made ethics a substitute for religion. It is the enduring glory of the Hebrews that they made ethics central in religion—the ideal to which the Western World pays at least lip-service. Nor is there any comparison between the academic reasoning of Plato and the burning hunger for righteousness which is characteristic of the prophets.

The Old Testament is herein no less potent a force in the modern world than the New. But it is impossible to neglect in this connection the essential Hebraic content of the Gospels. Jesus was a Jew not only by birth, but also by upbringing; and some of his most

striking sayings were part and parcel of the rabbinic
teaching of his day. The Lord's Prayer and the Sermon
on the Mount are paralleled in the Talmud, verse for
verse and phrase for phrase. The Golden Rule, "Do
unto thy neighbor as thou wouldst be done by," is
only a paraphrase of the recommendation of Jeṣus'
older contemporary, Hillel, who died when the
founder of Christianity was only ten years old. Hillel
taught, "What is distasteful to thee, do not to thy
neighbor." The Rabbis of the age of Jesus joined with
him, too, in averring that the pentateuchal injunction,
"Love thy neighbor as thyself" (Lev. 19:18), was a
fundamental principle of religion. As this same Hillel
declared, "This is the whole Law; the rest is but commentary."

2

When the Christian believer goes to church to pray,
he does not realize that he is making use of another
Jewish innovation. In ancient times the basic element
of public worship was animal, sometimes human, sacrifice. So, too, with the primitive Hebrews. But, at an
early date, this method of worship was restricted since
it was forbidden to offer up sacrifice outside the central
sanctuary which was ultimately situated in Jerusalem.
Thus, even in remote times, pious believers in the more
distant parts of the country had perforce dispensed
with sacrifice when they poured out their hearts to
God; and the prophets, with their bitter denunciation
of formalism without piety, strengthened this tendency. During the Babylonian Exile, when Jerusalem

and the Temple lay in ashes, the nation dispensed altogether with sacrifice. To this period probably belongs
the origin of the *Beth ha-Keneseth* or Synagogue—the
"place of assembly," where the reading of God's law
was accompanied by prayer. Hence, in the period of
the Second Temple, a synagogue was to be found in
every city and township of Palestine, and this manner
of worship became familiar to the non-Jewish world
by the erection of similar institutions in all the principal centers of the Diaspora.

Thus, after the destruction of Jerusalem in 70 A.D.,
no irreparable blow was felt by Judaism as a religious
system. Its spiritual potentialities, indeed, were
strengthened. The synagogues continued to function
regularly, prayer taking permanently the place of sacrifice.[1] That which was considered, at the time, the most
bitter element in the national disaster, subsequently
came to be regarded by the Jew, earlier than any other
branch of the human family, the natural mode of worship.

When Christianity began to expand through the
world, under the aegis of Paul and his companions, the
first centers of missionary activity were the synagogues, found in all the most important cities of the
Roman Empire. These, rather than the pagan temples,
formed the model and the ideal of the new sect. First,
the Christian missionaries attempted to convert the

---

[1] It is not generally realized how long the traces of animal sacrifice, on the pagan model, remained in the church. Thus, for example, it was customary to slaughter a stag in St. Paul's Cathedral
in London each Christmas until long after the Reformation—nearly
fifteen centuries after the Jews had abandoned such practices.

Jewish congregations to their own way of belief; in case of failure, they set up their own sectarian synagogues. In either circumstance, it was the Jewish, not the Pagan system which was followed. That which to us is so natural and so obvious must have appeared to some contemporaries, a remarkable innovation, but, in the long run, it carried the day. And, some six centuries later, when Islam began its triumphant march, the Mosque, too, with its sternly Puritan procedure, was modeled upon the spiritualized places of worship of the two Peoples of the Book,[1] Jews and Christians.

The Church, of course, owes much more to the Synagogue than this, though this is the essential. Its structure and "orientation" copy the Synagogue, in which worship was directed towards Jerusalem, that is, in much of Europe, to the East. The stoup at the door, for holy water, seems to reproduce the laver at the entrance of the older (and, to this day, the Italian) synagogues, which enabled worshippers to precede their godliness by cleanliness, in accordance with the dictates of the rabbis. The light before the high altar is a reminiscence of the perpetual lamp, which (following the example set in the Temple in Jerusalem) burned day and night in the "lesser sanctuaries" which replaced it. The use of incense followed Old Testament prescription, revered though not practiced by the Jews after the destruction of Jerusalem. The separation of the sexes in public worship, which Jewish reformers have almost abolished in recent years, was

[1] The very term Mosque is apparently derived from the Judæo-Aramaic *masgeda*.

frequently practiced by the Church even after the Reformation. And, when the ecstatic Christian revivalist cries *Hallelujah*, or the devout worshipper pronounces *Amen*, he is using a Hebrew term familiar in synagogal worship long before the Church came into being.

So, too, with ceremonial. Christian baptism may be traced back to the symbolic bath which the proselyte to Judaism had to undergo. The communion service was modeled upon the *Seder* meal of Passover Eve. Theologians dispute the exact degree of interdependence, yet it is clear that Jesus' last "supper" constituted the prototype, and his words the specific injunction, which lay at the bottom of this all-important Christian institution, while the elements recall the ceremonial breaking of bread and benediction of wine on the eve of Sabbaths and festivals. The lectionaries of the Church continue the tradition of the cycle of the public reading of the Law in the synagogues. This, again, was not so obvious a procedure as centuries of usage have made it appear to us; but it was rendered essential in ancient Judea in order to familiarize the people with the regulations of Jewish religious and social life embodied in the Pentateuch, and for that reason had been a regular practice ever since the fifth century B.C. As time went on, it became customary to read a section from the Prophets, containing a passage related to the section in the Pentateuch; this has its echo in the Second Lesson of the Church. Much of Christian worship is made up of the Psalms of David, while many original hymns are based upon these so closely as to be in certain cases (e.g. the English "O God, our Help in Ages Past") mere paraphrases.

3

Though the influence of the Bible is greatest in the Western World on the theological and ethical side, it is discernible also in the field of politics. This does not imply that the Jews enjoyed a very high political development, as is true of the Greek city-states and the Roman republic. Nevertheless, it has been suggested that the "people of the land," at the time of the Hebrew monarchy, constituted a sort of democratic assembly, and in the time of the Maccabees and the Last Commonwealth there certainly existed a popular Council, whose assent was considered necessary for any constitutional change.

The importance of Hebraism in the political heritage of modern Europe, however, does not lie in exterior details, but in the spirit. The Hebrew monarchy came into existence under the influence of a conception, to be found nowhere else in antiquity, which regarded the constitution as the result of a tripartite agreement or covenant between the people, the ruler, and the Deity. This may sound elementary. But, if the Deity is the embodiment of justice and righteousness, it follows that the monarchy is dependent on the maintenance not only of certain religious but also of human values. We see this conception in the story of the oldest Hebrew monarch, Saul; it reaches its highest development in the career of David. It underlies the outline of the ideal monarchy which is given in the

Mosaic Code. And, above all, it is implicit in the whole course of subsequent Hebrew history, when prophet after prophet dared to admonish the ruler for his breach of the fundamental laws, for his callousness to human misery, for his oppression of the poor. It is remarkable that in almost all cases the prophet's reproofs were heard with forbearance, as though to acknowledge his right to criticize and the essential justice of his claim. A remarkable phrase occurs in the description of the king's prerogatives in the Pentateuch (Deut. 27:20) which sums up the Hebraic ideal of the monarchy: "that his heart be not lifted up *above his brethren.*"

In the course of the sixteenth and seventeenth centuries, when the study of the Bible in the vernacular was popular in Western Europe, these stories received new life. In every land, but especially in the English-speaking countries, pious Christians identified themselves with the Israelites of old, people with people and tyrant with tyrant. When a nation thinks in this way, absolutism cannot be condoned. In just the same manner as the oppression of Israel by the Court of Samaria had been against God's expressed will, so, the Puritans thought they were fulfilling the desire of God when they fought against arbitrary government. Elijah's reproof of the tyranny of Ahab applied no less, they thought, to the unconstitutional attempts of Charles I. They read an indictment of the Star Chamber in the thunderings of Amos and found that ship money was condemned implicitly in the episode of Naboth's vineyard. The Bible, moreover, was in diametrical opposition to the idea of the divine descent of kings, which was one of the basic principles of primitive absolutism.

Hence the Hebraic conception of the tripartite agreement between God, His people, and the ruler, a breach of which might forfeit the latter's throne, lay at the basis of the reaffirmation of constitutional government in England. This, in turn, was taken over by the fathers of the American Revolution, who were inspired at every turn by the ideas of the Bible, its teachings and language, as well as by the theory and the practice of their Bible-intoxicated precursors on both sides of the ocean, one hundred and fifty years before. The Pilgrim Fathers and founders of the North American colonies had been devoted students of the Bible— it had been for the sake of interpreting it as they desired that some of them had left their original homes— and in numerous cases were themselves Hebraists. The "Pilgrim Code" of Plymouth Colony (1636) and the "Body of Liberties" of Massachusetts (1647) were confessedly based on the Hebrew scriptures, and the leaders of the American Revolution, from Benjamin Franklin downwards, were imbued with Hebrew conceptions.

It was Hebraic mortar (in Lecky's famous phrase) that cemented the foundations of the republic; and not without reason did its first seal depict the overthrow of Pharaoh in the Red Sea, with the motto: "Rebellion to tyrants is obedience to God." A few years later this same conception was adopted to some extent, though with a different philosophical back-

ground, in France. Imitated in the course of the nineteenth century in almost every other country of the
Western World, it is thus intimately connected with
the conception of constitutional government such as
we knew it until yesterday.

4

The literary influence of the Hebrew scriptures has
been vast. In a score of European languages the Bible
was the first book to be translated and among so many
peoples it first set a literary tradition, establishing the
standard of orthography, composition, and style. For
the whole of Europe, but especially for the so-called
"Nordic" peoples, the Scriptures continued to play an
almost dominant literary role. This was not the case
only in the Dark Ages or with unimportant tribes. It
was Luther's translation of the Bible into High German which rendered that particular dialect supreme
and first demonstrated the force and malleability of
the German language. It hence marks the beginning
of modern German literature. The greatest German
orator of today, when he holds his thousands of hearers
spellbound by his command of language, apparently
does not realize that he is making use of an instrument
which became what it is today only through the force
of the Hebrew scriptures.

In England and in other English-speaking countries,
the stimulus of biblical literature, in the incomparable
version "authorized" by King James in 1611, has been
incalculable. Generation after generation of Englishmen heard the Bible read in church and studied it at

home. In many cases it was the only book; in all, it was the principal book. At last its cadences, its music, its phraseology, sank into his mind and became part of his being. He quoted it, intentionally, more frequently than modern taste approves; more often still, he quoted it unwittingly. Hence by slow degrees his daily speech was not merely enriched, but to some extent moulded by its influence. Phrase after phrase, figure after figure, became current in the English language, which would be a strangely denuded thing if all these Semitic influences were removed.

Few people can realize today to what an extent their ordinary conversation is colored by the Hebrew Scriptures. When a man escapes by the skin of his teeth, when he goes down to the sea in ships, when he enquires whether a leopard can change its spots, when he threatens to make his enemy lick the dust, he is using biblical phrases which have become an inseparable part of his language. The way of a man with a maid, the tale that is told, the multitude of counselors, the crown of her husband, the pride that goes before a fall, the bread of idleness, the way of an eagle, the apple of the eye, the wife of a man's bosom, coals of fire, all these phrases became naturalized in English through familiarity with the Proverbs of Solomon. In chapters xxx and xxxi of that work alone, it is possible to enumerate no fewer than twenty-four passages which are familiar to every English-speaking person. Even so unecclesiastical a conception as "a thirsty soul" (not necessarily used today in its original meaning) is based on Prov. 25:25. "He who runs may read" is a mere mistranslation of Habakkuk 2:2 (the correct rendering is "He who reads may run"). . . . The list could be protracted indefinitely. Similarly, we owe many phrases to the earlier Prayer-book version of the Psalms, based upon Coverdale's rendering. There is only one work the influence of which on the English language is comparable to that of the Bible—the plays of William Shakespeare. But, as has recently been demonstrated, Shakespeare's use of the Bible was itself extensive, and its stimulus may be traced throughout his writings.

This biblical inspiration is not necessarily direct. English prose of the heroic period is saturated with biblical atmosphere. Bunyan's *Pilgrim's Progress*, for example, is so imbued with this sentiment that both in conception and in language it is a direct continuation of the same tradition. Through this and similar works the Hebraic influence was refracted, the original radiance appearing from a dozen different directions and in as many different forms. It is difficult in fact to imagine what the English language and English literature would now be but for the influence of the Scriptures—the influence, that is, of the ancestors of the Jewish people of today, as expressed in and through their literary heritage. Moreover, the Hebraic faculty for associating moral ideas with the name of things (bread, wine, and so on) and sublimating them into a call to virtuous living has contributed to the general background of the Anglo-Saxon mind and affected the thought and style of generations of writers.

Apart from this literary influence, which English and German illustrate to such a remarkable degree, every language of Europe has been enriched by various Hebrew words which have now become wholly naturalized: *Jubilee, Satan, Paradise, Cherub, Armageddon,* and numerous others. Moreover, all Western tongues contain words which are now reserved for conveying certain specifically Hebrew conceptions. The Greek ἄγγελος means a messenger—by no means the same thing as our "angel." The Latin *benedicere,* to commend, is far removed from the conception now universally found in European languages, to bless—that is, to pronounce a formula conveying spiritual beneficence. To adore is very different from to pray—the meaning of the Latin *adorare.* The case is identical with terms such as "The Lord," "Prophet," etc. The words may be derived from the Greek or Latin, but their "semantic" meaning is essentially Hebraic. This is not a point of mere philological interest. It must be realized that the reason why the words in question had to be borrowed by the European tongues from the Hebrew, or else to have their original meanings modified, is because no conceptions of the sort or words to express them existed hitherto. They are, therefore, yet another indication of the extent to which the spiritual and ethical life of Europe has been enriched by the Hebraic heritage.

Even from the point of view of literary form, the biblical influence has been a potent one. The Book of Ruth is as perfect an idyll as literature can provide; the story of Susannah is an admirable detective tale;

the Book of Tobit has provided the direct model for
a novel of our own day. Moreover, the Old Testament may be said to have provided the world with the
pattern of its present historiography. According to
the Russian thinker, Berdyaev, the Jews were the first
people to contribute the concept of "historical" to
world history, "thereby discharging the essence of
their specific mission." The Chronicles of Kings and
relations of individual episodes are a general phenomenon in ancient literature. But the grandiose biblical
conception, starting with the creation of the universe
and continuing through the centuries to almost contemporary events, was essentially different. The Hebrew was brought by it to a realization of his own
relative position in the scheme of things—as the heir to
the ages but neither their author nor their cause. Particular significance from this point of view attaches to
the Book of Daniel, perhaps the first expression of the
true philosophy of history. "In it," writes Berdyaev,
"we are made to feel dramatically that mankind is
engaged in a process that tends towards a definite
goal." And in Daniel's interpretation of Nebuchad-
nezzar's dream, this thinker sees the earliest attempt to
attribute a design to history, an attempt which was
later to be repeated and developed in Christian philosophy.

The Bible, moreover, was only incidentally interested in dynastic history. The people is central
throughout, and the modern type of history, which
centers its attention upon the ordinary man, neglecting
the kings and the captains, found its prototype in

biblical narrative. It was not until after a lapse of many centuries that an audacious pioneer of our own day was able to revert more closely to the biblical conception, attempting a universal history which should trace the record, not of a few centuries or groups only, but of the whole evolution of mankind.

5

The outcome of what has been stated above may be summed up very briefly. The Jewish people is largely a product of the Bible, under the influence of some thirty-five centuries of history, seldom uneventful and frequently tragic. On the peoples of the Western World, the biblical influence has not been quite so direct or so protracted. Yet, for a period of between ten and twenty centuries, it has been an integral part of their background, modifying their religion, their thought, their conceptions—to some extent, even their politics and their language. Deprive modern Europe and America of the Hebraic heritage, and the result would be barely recognizable. It would be a different, and it would be a poorer thing. In Woodrow Wilson's expressive words, "if we could but have the eyes to see the subtle elements of thought which constitute the gross substance of our present habit, both as regards the sphere of private life and as regards the action of the state, we should easily discover how very much besides religion we owe to the Jew."

CHAPTER II. *The Process of Degradation*

I

THE Jew's association with the European world began
far back in classical times. There are indications that
even during the biblical period he was known in the
Greek isles. Aristotle encountered one, who is reported
to have given him much information, during his travels
with Alexander the Great. Jews were very numerous
in Alexandria, long the center of Hellenistic culture,
from the time of its foundation, and they were found
in Greece itself, at least from the third century B.C.,
when the classical glories had barely departed from
Athens and from Corinth. In Rome and elsewhere in
Italy, they were numerous from the second century
B.C.; and Italian Jews may still be encountered whose
families trace their descent, according to legend, from
the nobles of Judea taken into captivity by Titus after
the fall of Jerusalem.

In Spain, Jews were present in some numbers at
least as early as the beginning of the Christian era,
centuries before the Visigoths had absorbed the Romans, or the Arabs had displaced the Visigoths, or the
Christians had driven out the Arabs. They were to be
found in France from the first century onwards, well

before the Franks arrived from beyond the Rhine to give their name to the country. Inscriptions and literary evidence attest their presence in Hungary, in the Balkan states, and in South Russia in the classical period, many years before the barbarian incursions and the arrival of the peoples who were to give those regions their present ethnic character. Even in the remote border-province which stretched along the Rhine, Jews were familiar in the Roman period, as a number of venerable relics serve to show. By the beginning of the fourth century, a Jewish community, fully organized and with the customary religious and lay leaders, flourished at Cologne. In 321, Constantine the Great issued an edict curtailing certain privileges formerly enjoyed by the Jews of this city, and ten years later he exempted the "rabbis, heads of synagogues, elders, etc.," from various onerous personal obligations. It was 150 years after this that the Germans first permanently crossed the Rhine and established themselves in the Roman province. The aliens today, therefore, are not the Jews, the only representatives perhaps in the Rhineland of its inhabitants of sixteen centuries ago. As a modern authority has phrased it, "the Jews had settled in Western Europe before many of its most typical inhabitants had emerged from Asia, and before others had crossed the Central European plain or had traversed the North Sea to invade the West."

There was still, indeed, a considerable Jewish nucleus in the East; but it was henceforth a diminishing group. From the late classical period on, Jewish history, Jewish literature, Jewish thought, and the

predominant part of the Jewish people, have been inseparably associated with Europe and the Western
World.

Yet it was in Europe that the Jews' lot was the
hardest. This is not the place to trace the progress and
development of Jewish persecution or to attempt to
place the responsibility for it. It is enough to sum up
the result. There were isolated corners where something of the spirit of freedom long persisted. Before
the clouds gathered to their fullest extent over the old-
established Jewish centers of the Mediterranean, Jews
had begun to migrate to the new centers on the Atlantic seaboard. But, taking Europe as a whole, it may
be said that from the period of the Christianization of
the Roman Empire down to the French Revolution,
the Jew was subject to a systematic degradation, an
exclusion from opportunity, a warping of his natural
bent, and a distortion of his normal position. The
history of the Jews in the Western World, during the
last 150 years, is the record of their gradual recovery
and their return to a more or less balanced existence,
socially and economically—a process which began
with prodigious rapidity but which, before it could be
fully accomplished, was reversed in that country
where it had achieved its most remarkable progress.

2

During the first half of their history, the Jews had been
a normally-constituted people, rooted in the soil as
peasant proprietors. Their economic development was
retrograde, rather than advanced; trade was in the

hands of non-Israelitish traders to such an extent indeed that the words "Canaanite" (that is, it is to be presumed, Phoenician) and "merchant" were used interchangeably. The mercantile colonies in the towns of Palestine, in the biblical period, were largely composed of strangers, and the great commercial *entrepôts* lay on the coastal plain, in non-Israelitish hands. After the return from the Babylonian captivity, conditions were much the same. It was in the Greek cities, not in the strongly Jewish uplands, that trade was centered. It is significant that no money was coined by any Jewish ruler until shortly before the beginning of the Christian Era. "Ours is not a maritime country," wrote Josephus (*Contra Apionem*, I. xii) in the first century of the Christian Era. "Neither commerce nor the intercourse which it promotes with the outside world has any attraction for us."

This natural balance was inevitably disturbed when, owing to the circumstances of their defeat by the Romans, the Jews were forced to leave their former country and were scattered throughout the Western World. Emigrants, even from an agricultural country, tend to abandon agricultural life (the United States today provides an illustration of this fact). Yet, for a long time after their Diaspora began, the Jews resisted this temptation. The great Jewish settlements in Mesopotamia, where Jewish life flourished as it did nowhere else outside Palestine, were predominantly agricultural: the most detailed picture of the methods of farming which obtained here in the first centuries of the Christian Era is preserved in the Babylonian Talmud.

In other centers, perhaps, there was greater variety; but everywhere, in Egypt, Cyrenaica, Greece, Italy, Spain, even France and Germany, there was in early times a solid nucleus of Jews settled on the land, earning their livelihood by tilling the soil.

It was first in Europe, and in Christian Europe especially, that the Jew was compelled to abandon his predominantly agricultural interests. This was partly the result of circumstances, for it is the trader rather than the farmer who travels, and the immigrant to a land already occupied must perforce congregate in towns and engage in urban occupations. But, in addition to this, the growing religious prejudice and the consequent insecurity made it unsafe for individuals who did not belong to the dominant faith to live in rural isolation. With the passage of years and the increase of fanaticism the life of the isolated Jewish agriculturalist became more and more dangerous. Frequent persecutions uprooted him time after time and drove him into a strange country where there was no room for him on the soil, and he was compelled to join his fellow-Jews in the towns. Successive Church Councils forbade him to work in the fields on Sunday, notwithstanding the fact that he rested on Saturday. Finally, the feudal idea made land-holding dependent upon military service, from which the Jew was generally excluded (the English *Assize of Arms* of 1181, for example, specifically forbade him to possess any weapons).[1] Thus, he was prevented both from holding land

---

[1] The Jews did not entirely lose their martial qualities, even under these circumstances. They frequently served in Spain both

and tilling it, a Jewish farmer being almost as curious an anomaly, in Northern Europe at least, as a Jewish monk would have been.

In the towns, the Jews were at the beginning mainly artisans, as they have remained to the present day in those countries where fewer restrictions have been placed upon their economic life. In Roman Egypt, the boatmen were predominantly Jews. In Sicily (as in Salonica, down to our own day) they were the porters and stevedores. In Germany and Northern Italy, they were expert miners. In Imperial Rome they were represented in all walks of life, from painting to peddling. Throughout the Middle Ages, we find Jewish craftsmen and Jewish trade-guilds—those of the weavers, carpenters, dyers, blacksmiths, and so on—sometimes maintaining their own guild-halls and even their own synagogues. Many, of course, were engaged in trade, selling, above all, imports adventurously brought from distant countries, as will be shown in another chapter.

In time, this, too, was restricted. Gradually, religious

---

in the Christian and in the Moorish forces; they assisted in the defence of Naples in 537, of Worms in 1201, of Pernambuco in 1654, etc.

With the removal of medieval disabilities, professional Jewish soldiers appeared. Fifteen Jewish officers served under Wellington at Waterloo; and many Jewish soldiers have since attained high rank (e.g., General Giuseppe Ottolenghi, Italian Minister of War in 1902–3, or General Sir John Monash, who commanded the Australian forces in France during their smashing victories in 1918). In France alone there have been, up to 1939, no less than 50 Jewish generals. Jews have served in all the wars of the American Republic since the very beginning—some 2500, for example, in the Civil War, of whom nine became generals.

disabilities were extended until they excluded the Jew from almost every form of normal economic activity. The cities became organized on a new corporate basis, with civic control over manufacture and commerce; and the new prejudices prevented the Jew from being a citizen. The craft guilds claimed a monopoly in the various branches of manufacture, but these bodies were united in a quasi-religious brotherhood in which the unbeliever could generally find no place. The guild merchant extended the same idea to trade; and the Jew would normally have been excluded, even had he been able to pray or feast with the rest. The frequency of attack, massacre, and pillage compelled him to discover a walk of life in which his property could be easily concealed and, above all, easily transferred. And, as chance would have it, just at this period a re-adjustment in the economic organization of Europe provided such an opening, into which he was reluctantly forced.

In remote times, the Jew had shown no proclivity toward finance. Rather, indeed, the reverse, as the passage quoted above from Josephus clearly shows. In Egypt only, where Jews were actively engaged in every branch of commercial life, do we meet with Jewish bankers and financiers from the beginning of the Christian Era. With this exception, there is no mention of Jews in financial pursuits until the sixth century, when they are encountered in France. This was, of course, not unnatural, for the Jews in France at this period played an important role in commercial life, and the transition from wholesale trade to finance

is in most cases very slight. The impetus which ruined
the Jewish economic and social balance came from
without.

As the Middle Ages advanced, the Church had begun to set its face sternly against lending money at
interest, on the ground that this was prohibited not
only by the Old Testament (Deut. 23:19), but also
by the Sermon on the Mount (Luke 6:35, in its current mistranslation), and according to Aristotle by
nature itself, which did not intend to make money
breed by the ordinary processes of reproduction. The
prohibition was an impracticable one (as was soon discovered); for in a money-economy any man may be
reduced to momentary necessity, and thus have ur-
gent need of a loan in order to carry on his business, to
prepare for the harvest, or sometimes even to live.

The situation would have been an impossible one
but for the presence of the Jew, who, precisely as he
found himself excluded from other methods of gaining a livelihood, was forced into this most unhonored
profession. The non-Jewish capitalists lent to kings
and magnates, under the cover of various devices (such
as making out the bond for a larger amount than the
sum lent, or euphemistically calling the interest by
some other name). The more open, least lucrative, and
most unpopular branches of the profession, such as
lending on pledge for a short period to the artisan and
tradesman, were forced upon the Jew. Thus, for example, in the heroic days of Florence, when a great
part of the city ultimately depended for its livelihood
upon large-scale financial operations abroad, the Jews

were summoned to the city for the purpose of administering to the requirements of the populace, to save Christians from being contaminated by the sin of usury! [1]

In medieval England, the Jews were invariably, or almost invariably, moneylenders. But why? Because they were admitted to England for this very purpose. Why, therefore, did they not leave? The answer is that they were not allowed to, that they applied for permission to do so on more than one occasion, but were refused. The Crown, in fact, insisted on retaining them, so as to fleece them at incredibly frequent intervals for the benefit of the Exchequer, thus becoming the silent partner and ultimate beneficiary of all their transactions. "No Jew may remain in England unless he do the King service," ran the opening words of a notorious Edict of Henry III of 1253, "and from the hour of his birth every Jew, whether male or female, shall serve us in some way."

But the Jew, as has been indicated, was not the only usurer during the Middle Ages, though he was the only one of whom the Church did not overwhelmingly disapprove. Italians (known under the generic name of Lombards) and South Frenchmen (generally called Cahorsins) had a particularly bad reputation for their remorseless activities in this field; and, among the former the Paduans were especially notorious, Dante

---

[1] For a fuller and consecutive account of the subject treated in this chapter, reference may be made to the present author's *Bird's-Eye View of Jewish History*, Cincinnati, 1935. See also below, Chap. X.

in his *Inferno* singling them out for exemplary punishment. The fact that the center of the money market in London to this day is in "Lombard" Street is an eloquent reminder of that period. Sometimes, pitiless usurious activities were carried on in the shadow of the Papal *curia* itself. So remorseless were the Christian usurers that St. Bernard of Clairvaux called attention to the fact that they far exceeded the Jews. Similarly, when the Jews were expelled from France in 1306, the chroniclers deplored their departure, as it left the people in the hands of much less reasonable Christian competitors. The notorious Gianfigliazzi family of Florence who lent money in Languedoc at the preposterous rate of 266⅔ per cent is only one example.[1] In Italy, indeed, one reason why the Jews were often summoned to open a loan-bank was that the local moneylenders had become too extortionate. Thus the Jews were admitted to Todi, in Umbria, only when the normal rate of interest had reached a shattering figure. In Brindisi, the poor burghers had good reason to rejoice when the Jews were authorized to lend money at the rate of 40 per cent, as otherwise they "would have been forced to sell their belongings at vile price"; and after their expulsion, the rate of interest charged by the Christian usurers rose to 240 per cent.

[1] The author may be excused for quoting once more the expressive words of Geoffrey of Paris:

"For the Jews were debonair,
Greatly more, in this affair,
Than now the Christians are."

Sometimes, it was notorious that the Jews were mere decoys, acting for Christian capitalists behind the scenes. Joseph Sessa, an anti-Semitic Italian jurist of the eighteenth century, gives reluctant testimony to this fact. He writes: "A majority of the sums lent by the Jews to Christians at an interest of 18 per cent, whether on security or otherwise, are advanced to the Jews themselves by Christians. The latter ordinarily retain the pledge, in order to safeguard themselves, sharing in the Jewish usury to the extent of eight, ten, or even twelve per cent. These facts have often been laid bare, and continue to be daily." [1] An even more astonishing commentary upon the state of affairs is provided by contemporary documents from Italy, from Poland, and from the south of France, which demonstrate that the poverty-stricken Jewish communities were forced to borrow money, at an extremely high rate of interest, from Christian religious houses.[2]

3

Other than moneylending, there was one calling only, or at the most two, which the Jew was normally per-

[1] So too at Nuremberg, over the period 1304–7, we find the Christian firm of Holzschuher lending money to Jews at a virulent rate of interest, apparently going as high as 220 per cent.

[2] The story of Shylock, the prototype of the Jewish usurer of legend, is symptomatic of the manner in which fantasy has been allowed to travesty fact. The story of the pitiless creditor and the pound of flesh first appears in relation to an historical event of the sixteenth century, with a Roman Jew, Samson Cesena, as victim and a Christian merchant, Paolo Secchi, as his persecutor. In *The Merchant of Venice*, the incident is reproduced, but the roles are reversed!

mitted to practice in Christian Europe. In order to prevent any competition with non-Jewish merchants, closely organized in guilds to which he was not admitted, the Jew was in most cases rigorously excluded from ordinary trade—that is, purchasing from the manufacturer or producer, and selling to the consumer. But this restriction did not extend to second-hand commodities. Accordingly the Jew was the universal ragman and old-clothes dealer. Attempts were made to exclude him even from this unenviable walk of life (in Venice, for example, the guild of *strazzaiuoli* periodically voiced its indignation and begged that this concession should be withdrawn), but generally speaking, no difficulties were raised. Finally, though prohibited from opening a shop, the Jew was usually allowed to sell unimportant trifles, sometimes of home manufacture, in the countryside, if not in the towns. Throughout Western Europe, the "Jew Peddler," pack on back, was a familiar figure in the seventeenth, eighteenth, and early nineteenth centuries.

These three callings, moneylending, old-clothes dealing, and peddling, were the only ones which were universally permitted to Jews in Europe down to the period of the French Revolution. Here and there were exceptions, more generous opportunities being conceded either to individuals or to the whole body. But nowhere was there complete freedom of vocation and movement. In England, for example, it was not until 1831 that Jews were able to open shops for retail trade in London; yet the English policy was particularly liberal in comparison with that which prevailed on the

Continent. These regulations, moreover, were enforced with the utmost ruthlessness. Thus, in various
German and Italian cities the Jews were allowed to
exist only for the purpose of moneylending. Once
their utility in this direction had disappeared, they
would be expelled; while any individual who attempted to gain his livelihood in a more dignified manner was treated as a criminal.

In Venice, for example, down to the close of the
eighteenth century, the Jewish community was only
tolerated on the express condition that it maintain
in the Ghetto four loan-banks (a more polite term for
pawnbroking establishments) for the benefit of the
poor. The only other professions legally permitted
there were old-clothes dealing and the wholesale export trade to the Levant, which did not compete with
Christian traders. The same was the case in the cities of
the *terra firma*. This ignominious condition of affairs
was sternly enforced, and any attempt on the part of
the Jews to broaden their economic status, or to place
it on a slightly more dignified plane, was systematically
blocked. Even as late as 1777, the Venetian government
closed down all the factories owned by Jews throughout its possessions—including the silk-looms at Padua,
where the industry had been established and developed
by the Jews; and thousands of hands were thrown out
of work. In this same place the Jews were not even allowed to work as turners and carpenters and to sell the
products of their industry to their fellow-townsmen.
As late as the middle of the nineteenth century, the
Roman Jews (still restricted almost completely to old-

clothes dealing) were compelled to close the shops opened outside the Ghetto. In Russia, similar regulations existed, at least outside the rigorously restricted Pale of Settlement, down to the War of 1914–18.

4

Though the channels of livelihood which were left open to the Jew were so few and so ignoble, levies were made upon him as though he were the sole capitalist. He contributed to all ordinary taxes. In addition to this, there were dozens of other imposts. The Jewish community, as such, had to pay heavily for the privilege of toleration—so heavily, indeed, that in the eighteenth century many ancient congregations were reduced to insolvency. Their ordinary tolls and market-dues were double what the Christian had to pay. There was a tax on Jewish weddings, a tax on the Sabbath candles, a tax on the citron used at the Feast of Tabernacles, a dice-tax which could be levied by every ruffian encountered on the high-road. A special poll-tax, similar to that levied on animals and included in the same list of tolls, had to be paid in Germany at the entrance to every town and state. Even on the dead, there was a special toll to be paid at the city boundary as the body was escorted to its last home. In Frankfort, no less than thirty-eight different imposts were levied upon the Jews, mostly additional to those imposed on the ordinary townsfolk.

Much is sometimes said about the influence of the Jewish moneyed dynasties in the Middle Ages. This is generally pure invention, as there were very few cases in which the medieval Jew, however wealthy, was able to transmit his fortune to his heirs (see below, pp. 265–266). Legally, indeed, his property reverted to the Crown; though the reality was seldom so severe, and in most cases the Treasury restricted its claims to one-half the dead man's property, returning the rest to his legal heirs so that they might accumulate further profits for the royal benefit. Yet even at the end of the Middle Ages, and after the former conception of royal rights was modified, the actual result was frequently identical. Thus Samuel Oppenheimer, the Court Factor at Vienna at the period of the War of Spanish Succession, was forced into bankruptcy because of an unpaid debt from the Imperial Treasury amounting to 6,000,000 florins. A more astonishing case still was that of Mordecai Meisel, the Jewish philanthropist, who built a synagogue which is still among the sights of Prague. The story is best related in the words of the writer of a Fugger News Letter who can hardly be described as pro-Jewish:

From Prague, the 5th day of April, 1601: A short time ago there died here the Jew Meisel. Notwithstanding that he had left His Imperial Majesty ten thousand florins, and much cash also to the Hospital for poor Christians and Jews, His Imperial Majesty on the following Saturday, viz., the Sabbath of the Jews, ordered Herr von Sternberg, at that time President of the Bohemian Chamber, to enter the Jew's house forcibly and to seize everything there was. The widow of Meisel handed this over willingly, for she had already set aside and hidden the best part of the treasure. That which was taken away came to forty-five thousand florins in cash, promissory notes, jewels, clothes and all kinds of coins. After this, however, the President, against whom the Jewess and the sons of the two brothers of Meisel had raised a strong protest to the privy councillors, was not satisfied with all this money and booty, and, no doubt at the command of His Majesty, once more broke into the house at night. The son of one of the brothers was taken prisoner, secretly led away and tortured.

Apart from such episodes, there was no limit to the indignities, deprivations, and restrictions from which the Jews suffered in their long Middle Ages. They were compelled to live together in a separate quarter of the town, known as the Ghetto, which was generally unhealthy and rarely large enough to accommodate them without the most appalling overcrowding. The Ghetto gates were closed every night, and, until they were opened again in the morning, no Jew might show his face outside and no Gentile might venture within. On the days of the great solemnities of the Christian Church and during Easter, the entrances were barred and the Jews treated virtually as prisoners. In the streets, sometimes in the Ghetto, too, the Jew had to be distinguished by an ugly badge of shame, a yellow circle worn on the outer garment above the heart in Germany, a yellow or crimson hat or kerchief in Italy. The number of weddings was restricted, in Germany at least, and only one member of each family was permitted to set up his own household. The remainder were compelled either to emigrate or to remain unmarried; yet, at the same time, association with non-Jewish women was punished by the most drastic penalties, including death.

In the courts of law, a special oath had to be taken *more judaico*, to the accompaniment of a degrading ceremonial. Each Sabbath the Jews were forced to attend conversionist sermons, where they were compelled to hear long tirades against Judaism. Their children might be seized and forcibly baptized, after which, uncanonical though it was, there was no redress, and they were brought up in Christian surroundings, sedulously removed from any possibility of contact with their parents. Jews were not allowed to employ Christian servants or even to enlist the service of Christian neighbors for the purpose of kindling fires on the Sabbath. Christian midwives and Christian wet-nurses were not allowed to lend assistance in time of need. Jews were not allowed to ride in coaches, or to be addressed with the customary courteous prefixes, or to be called by names which were not characteristically Jewish, or to wear ordinary clothing. On Good Friday, in many places, they were stoned by the rabble and buffeted by the authorities, sometimes with fatal results. They were not allowed to erect tombstones over their dead or to escort them to their last resting-place with the prescribed religious dirges.[1]

---

[1] It may be remarked that in present-day Germany a large number of these prohibitions are closely paralleled, some even exceeded.

They were harried with absurd accusations, such as that of the ritual murder of Christian children (repeatedly condemned by the Popes) and the even more absurd charge of desecrating the Host, which caused the loss of thousands of lives from the thirteenth century onwards.

So many restrictions, in fact, were placed upon the Jew that life would have been impossible for him had he obeyed them all. Evasion was necessary, if he were to exist. Thus, for example, in places where the Jews were restricted to dealing in old clothes, tears were deliberately made sometimes in new articles so as to render them technically second-hand. Where the Jew was excluded from manufacture, a fictitious Gentile partner was occasionally acquired in whose name the business was carried on. If taxation became too crushing, it was not surprising that the victim attempted to minimize his apparent profits. Restrictions on residence and occupation might perhaps be overlooked, if the police authorities received a gift. . . . There was, in fact, the same experience that modern theories suggest: that laws, in order to be obeyed, must be reasonable; that a ridiculous rigor defeats its own object, penalizing the law-abiding at the expense of the less responsible elements; that the multiplicity of restrictions tends to bring the fundamental laws of security and government into disrepute. This generalization applies all the more when the restrictions are of a definitely unethical character, as were so many of those from which the Jew suffered. The result was what might have been expected—evasion, sharp practice, petty deceit, a perpetual state of suspicion and grievance against those responsible for the hard lot of the victim, a feeling of contempt for the laws which they enacted. This sentiment continued in some unhappy cases after the justification had passed. But the wonder is that in the majority of instances it should have disappeared so rapidly.[1]

5

Yet the relations which prevailed between the Jews and their neighbors were friendly enough when no outside pressure was brought to bear, and their services were appreciated in the most unlikely quarters. Here are two or three examples. In the eleventh century, Rüdiger, Bishop of Speyer, ambitious for the expansion of his episcopal seat, invited the Jews to the town, endowed them with lavish privileges and provided them with a special quarter within the walls of the city. "Wishing to make of Speyer a city," he boasted, "I thought to increase its honor a thousandfold by bringing in the Jews." He was by no means alone in holding such ideas. At the end of the Middle Ages, in 1569, the city of Orange, in the south of

[1] On the other side, it is possible to adduce instances of an exaggerated scrupulousness. The story is told, for example, of a saintly Russian rabbi of the last century, who made a practice of destroying a postage-stamp every time he sent a note by hand, as the post was a government monopoly! Such in fact was the general delicacy of feeling that no man was admitted to pray with the congregation on the Day of Atonement until he had been formally absolved from ill-considered vows which he had hastily taken on himself during the year and which were clearly impossible of fulfilment. This is the origin of the much-maligned *Kol Nidrei* formula.

France, was in the depths of depression, its wealth dwindling and its commerce languishing. There were at that time no Jews in the city and the Town Council recommended as one of the measures for restoring prosperity that "two hundred Jewish households" should be invited to settle. So, also, when the position of the Jews at Neustettin was menaced, the guilds appealed almost unanimously to the King of Poland to leave them undisturbed.[1]

Or take another scene—one of the most tragic of this period. When the Jews were expelled from Spain, in 1492, the overseas possessions of the Crown of Aragon, particularly Sardinia and Sicily, were included in the Edict. In vain the Council of the latter kingdom protested, pointing out the loss which the people as a whole would, and indeed did suffer in consequence of this measure. On January 12th, 1493, the last Jews left Palermo. It is on record that, as long as the vessels which bore them were in sight, the inhabitants stood on the housetops and waved farewell

[1] It must not be imagined that these instances are isolated. In Lindau, when the interest on loans made by Christian merchants rose to 216 per cent, the citizens begged for the admission of the Jews to the town as their only salvation. In 1544, and again in 1550, when the Emperor Charles V issued a decree expelling the crypto-Jews from Antwerp, the magistrates of the city protested on the grounds that such action would spell ruin to the city and the state. The new oppressive legislation enacted by the Venetian Government at the close of the eighteenth century elicited protests from the municipalities of Verona and Ceneda. In 1781, the civil authorities at Avignon testified that the Jewish community contributed greatly to its welfare, and gave no cause for complaint by their conduct as regards morality, religion, or commercial life. Similar illustrations can be multiplied.

to their old neighbors, who had lived in their midst in peace and amity almost as long as Sicily had a history. They had, indeed, good cause. It was not long after, at the beginning of the sixteenth century, that Aragonese intolerance drove the Jews likewise from the neighboring mainland. A recent learned work shows that Calabria has not yet recovered from the blow. Or, again, we have the delightful episode of the romantic lady in medieval Worms who was so impressed by the ceremony of the Rejoicing of the Law and the beauty of one of the male participants that she bequeathed a parcel of ground to the Jewish community for use as a public garden.

6

Notwithstanding his physical degradation, there were certain specific values which the Jew succeeded in keeping alive even amid the squalor of the Ghetto. There was, in the first place, the idea of the family. His home life, in the Middle Ages, was generally on a plane distinctly higher than that of his neighbors. Marriage was regarded as a natural and praiseworthy state, not, as in the Church, a concession to human weakness. The monogamous ideal, though formally accepted by the Jews of Northern Europe only about the year 1000,[1] had already long been the general rule. It was, moreover, considered more seriously than among the European Christians, for concubinage, adultery, and

[1] It will be recalled that legalized bigamy was practiced in Europe as late as the sixteenth century, this being one of the suggested solutions to the marital quandary of Henry VIII of England.

prostitution were rare phenomena in the *Judengasse* at a time when sexual life without was at its lowest level. In the twelfth and thirteenth centuries, when wife-beating was not only customary among all classes but expressly permitted by Canon Law and by the statutes of some small towns, Rabbis declared: "This is a thing not done in Israel." The practice was, indeed, regarded in the Codes as justifiable ground for divorce.

As a corollary to the purity of the home, drunkenness was rare, instead of being considered a natural pastime. The warmth of domestic life extended till it embraced outsiders, even utter strangers. The visitor from a distant Ghetto could always count upon a welcome, hospitality, and assistance. There was a highly-developed system of charity, in advance of modern ideas in that it showed the utmost delicacy for the feelings of the recipient, besides trying to substitute self-support for pauperization (see below, p. 330).

Furthermore, education was considered a religious duty. Illiteracy was almost unknown among the Jews, and even the illiterate had the profoundest respect for learning. A universal system of education had existed in Palestine since the first or second century B.C., and Josephus had explicitly avowed that "our principal care of all is this: to educate our children well." That early ideal was never lost sight of. Hence in the Ghetto period there existed, in the smallest Jewish community, an educational system of a breadth and universality which the most advanced state in modern Europe or America has even now barely equalled, and certainly not surpassed. Enrollment for either sex was free. The number of pupils in each class was regulated. The elements of the vernacular were taught as well as of Hebrew. Meals were given to those who required them. Boots and clothing were distributed to the most needy in winter. A community of less than 1,000 souls in eighteenth-century Italy would maintain a school of this type with no less than six teachers and assistants. Compare this with the provision which would have been made in a contemporary English or American village! Or one may take another criterion. In 1861, there were no less than 54.5 illiterates in each hundred Italians above the age of ten years; among their Jewish fellow-citizens, only 5.8!

Arrival at adolescence did not mark the end of education. Every synagogue had attached to it voluntary associations for the purpose of study, which would assemble after the morning and evening service. Wealthy enthusiasts would establish regular courses of instruction in their own houses. In Poland, in the seventeenth century, we are told, "there was hardly a single house in which they did not study. Either the householder himself was a scholar, or else his son or his son-in-law studied perpetually, or, at the very least, he gave hospitality to some young student." Adult education was thus taken as a matter of course among Jews, centuries before the conception had begun to penetrate the outside world.

The scheme of education was not restricted, as might be imagined, to quasi theological studies, but by reason of the wide humanity of Judaism was extended to every field of human interest. When Germany, for example, had hardly emerged from barbarism, there were Jewish schools in the Rhineland, to which students streamed from every part of the world, and which were hardly distinguishable from the primitive universities which Christian Europe was beginning to develop at this period. It was not until these academies had already been in existence for centuries that the first German university—destined to have an ephemeral existence—was started at Erfurt (1379). Not long after this, in 1466, the handful of Jews living in Sicily, numbering at the most not more than 100,000, received formal license from the king to open their own university, with faculties of medicine, law, and presumably the humanities. Twenty-four years later, the idea was revived in Northern Italy. These facts are in themselves sufficient to show the profound Jewish veneration for scholarship, quite apart from the Rabbinic disciplines, even in this remote period.

As a natural consequence, there was in the Ghetto and the *Judengasse* a spirit of free inquiry which was elsewhere rare, if not unknown. In this fact, perhaps, lay the greatest service of the medieval Jew to mankind. It was a period when authority was triumphant in the intellectual sphere, when thought was circumscribed even more than practice, when uniformity had established itself, not as an accident but as a principle, throughout European life. Had this state of affairs continued unchallenged, progress—scientific as well as philosophical—would have been impossible. The mere fact that the Jew existed, and that he preserved the habit of independent thought, helped to save the world from this menace. It was impossible even for the least original mind to fail to realize that in the Jewish quarter there existed a class as intelligent at least as other men were, who yet did not believe as other men, who possessed literature and beliefs and practices which were not like those of the rest of the world, and who refused to pay even lip-service to the prevailing ideas. This very fact saved the world from accepting uniformity finally as a natural thing. It stimulated students and thinkers to realize the existence of other spheres to conquer, over and above those which were delineated from the pulpit. And, if from time to time, Europe shook off its lethargy and began to re-examine for itself the wells of human thought, the propinquity of the Jew was in part responsible.

7

The Age of Degradation lasted, roughly speaking, up to the time of the French Revolution. In England, Holland, and America, there had been a considerable measure of social emancipation even before this time; in Central and Eastern Europe notable relics of the old system continued long after. But in general it may be said that it was the French Revolution which broke down the gates of the Ghetto and permitted its downtrodden inhabitants to enjoy for the first time the same rights and opportunities as their neighbors.

The consequences were remarkable. A section of the European population, of at least normal intelligence, with their wits sharpened by generations of intensive Talmudical study, were suddenly allowed after centuries of repression to emerge into the world, and given a natural outlet for the first time. The inevitable happened. Jews began to find their own level. The grandchildren of the petty Ghetto traders and usurers became leaders of business, of thought, of society. Those whose intelligence qualified them, rose in a remarkable manner in the circles to which they were at last admitted. It was, of course, no more than what might have been expected. The Jew of the Ghetto period was not a usurer, a petty trader and so on, by choice. His intellectual interests were at least as wide and as varied as those of the patrician or citizen of the outside world. It was not, therefore, that his descendants rose above their level; it was that after a lapse of centuries they at last found their level.

In what direction could these newly-emerged scions of the Ghetto seek an outlet? The centuries of repression could not fail to leave their trace. It was impossible for those who during long generations had been restricted to the more degraded forms of business life to become immediately farmers or artisans, simply because the statute-book no longer forbade these occupations. It was inevitable that they found expression in the more dignified forms of business and the so-called "professions," for which their artificially stimulated intellect perhaps gave them special qualifications. They could not fail to be attracted particularly to those callings where there were no vested interests to discourage or exclude them. They thus tended to engage in activities in which personality and personal ability were important, or in newly-opened fields where family connection and tradition counted for little. In Central Europe, moreover, Jews were still excluded, with considerable rigor, from the civil service and from commissioned rank in the army and navy, fields of activity in which elsewhere, too, much prejudice yet prevailed. This stimulated a yet more disproportionate concentration in those professions still left open.

This is the reason why, in the nineteenth century, the progress of the Jews in certain spheres appeared to be so rapid. Answering their natural bent for study, they seized the opportunity of entering the professions of law, medicine, literature, and journalism. In the economic world, they were primarily attracted by the new businesses which the industrial revolution had created, or those which were calling for new blood, new ideas, and new methods. We thus find them figuring, in more than their due proportion, in banking in the nineteenth century, in the entertainment industry in the twentieth.

Like a cork released under water, they forced their way to the surface after having been artificially depressed for so long. Like water spilled on uneven ground, they followed the contours of the soil, took advantage of every opening, and flowed irresistibly into every gap. But the analogy may be pursued a little further. After a time the water is absorbed by the soil. Its moisture has been drunk in with beneficial results. The earth on which it fell has to some extent been fertilized. Yet in the process, the water has ceased to have an independent existence. So, too, in the phenomenon which we are attempting to examine. It was seldom long before these Jewish pioneers of the nineteenth and twentieth centuries lost their specific Jewish characteristics, in many cases even their Jewish loyalties. The fertilizing impetus and enthusiasms which they had brought became absorbed into the common store and enriched the common life, but their distinctiveness passed away. On the other hand, the new ideas and methods were by now universal property. Hence in many callings in which the Jews were thought to have a dominant position, their influence dwindled progressively as the nineteenth century advanced and the twentieth began, though in many instances the legend outlived the actuality.[1]

It was natural that the older a Jewish center was, the more rapid was the rise of its children, for on

---

[1] A fact which tended to obscure this phenomenon was that the Jews did not emerge from their repressed condition simultaneously. In some places, emancipation was retarded; in many families, the influence of conservatism was stronger; sometimes, the adjustment took longer. The impression might thus be given of a continuous advance. Actually, this did not take place. In more than one generation, there was a fresh exodus (though on a scale which was unimportant); but by this time the earlier wave had reached its climax or even begun to recede. The initial impetus, indeed, seldom lasted for more than one generation, or two at the most; for the transmission of outstanding ability from generation to generation is as rare among Jews as among their neighbors. The children of the Ghetto prodigy, who dazzled the eyes of his contemporaries, generally developed into Englishmen or Frenchmen or Germans of normal tastes, normal interests, and normal ability, indistinguishable from their neighbors except through a diminishing family tradition.

emergence from the Ghetto they did not have the problem of acclimatization added to that of emancipation. This is perhaps the explanation of the disproportionate distinction attained in so many fields by the Jews of Germany, who had lived there since the fourth century, or by those of Italy, who were already acclimatized at the time of the birth of Jesus. In England and in France, where the settlements were less ancient, the number of important names is smaller by far, and it is noteworthy that in these countries the majority of outstanding Jews probably belonged to the oldest strata.

The following pages present a number of examples to illustrate these generalizations. The process is in most cases identical. There was consistent collaboration between the Jews and their neighbors in every field of endeavor, from the beginning of their settlement in Europe and throughout the Middle Ages, so far as was permitted. The long night of the Ghetto put an end to this tradition, save in a few exceptional instances. With the downfall of the system of restrictions, the collaboration was resumed with an intensity naturally heightened by the previous unnatural repression. In new fields of endeavor, especially, Jewish names begin to figure with unusual frequency. But in most cases the lessons which they taught and the stimulus which they provided were rapidly assimilated. Activities which owed their origin to Jews became part of the common stock. There is everywhere a tendency for this participation to recede to its natural proportion, modified perhaps only by an hereditary proclivity in favor of intellectual activities and an enforced tendency to urban life.

Even before the Ghetto walls were effectively established, however, Jews played a vital part in the intellectual process to which the modern world owes its birth.

CHAPTER III. *The Revival of Learning*

I

FROM the point of view of intellectual history, the modern world began with the Renaissance, that rediscovery of the treasures of antiquity, which deeply stirred the man of the Middle Ages and brought about a "new birth." The old conception that this reawakening began with the rediscovery of Greek literature in the fifteenth century is misleading. Long before that period, the classical heritage was opened up to Western Europe—not, indeed, in the Greek originals, for few men could read or understand Greek, but in Latin versions. The texts in question were inelegant, and often inaccurate, but the conceptions of the originals were conveyed faithfully enough. The result was sufficient to open up new horizons before the wondering eyes of students. It was of this revival—the "Latin" Renaissance—that Dante, Chaucer, and Petrarch were born.

The part played by the Jews in this process was of the utmost importance. It may be said, indeed, that it could not have come about as it did but for their assistance; and that without them, the revival of the fifteenth century would have been retarded or assumed a different form. The story is familiar how in the Dark Ages and after, when the Hellenic tradition was entirely lost to Christian Europe, it was nurtured and further developed in Moslem Spain. It was here that the wisdom of Hippocrates, the astronomical records of Ptolemy, and above all the philosophy of Aristotle, continued to be revered, studied, and commented upon. The original texts, indeed, were inaccessible; the studies centered around Arabic translations, in many cases made from the Syriac. The matter, however, was the same, and from the eleventh century onwards, when the breath of intellectual interest had begun to stir again in Europe, it was to the Mohammedan sages of Andalusia that eager Christian students looked for some notion of the wisdom of ancient Hellas. Of course, it was not only the Greek authorities that were revered and sought after. Their Arabic exponents, Averroes, Avicenna, and the rest, enjoyed almost equal prestige; and if Christian Europe imagined that the former provided a gate to wisdom, it was no less convinced that the latter owned the key.

The Mediterranean world at this time was divided culturally and politically, it may be said, into three sections. There were the Greeks, possessing the treasures of antiquity, yet hardly aware of their value; the Arabs, studying them in vernacular versions in their schools, particularly in Southern Spain; and the Latins, painfully conscious of their inferiority, yet for linguistic reasons unable to obtain access to the sources for which they thirsted. All these three sections were cut off from one another by differences of language,

religion, and tradition. The gulf would have been un-
bridgeable, but for one element which was to be found
in all. From the truly catholic point of view, the Jews
were the only real Europeans, whose purview extended beyond the boundaries of the Latin world, to
the Greek on the one hand and to the Arab on the
other. They possessed a common language, Hebrew,
which was understood, in certain circles at least, the
whole world over and could thus form a medium of
intercourse; they were so endowed with linguistic
knowledge that they could travel from land to land
without great difficulty and could generally find some
co-religionist who could read and speak the most difficult foreign tongue.

The Jews were, therefore, peculiarly qualified to
serve as a bridge between these mutually exclusive
and mutually intolerant worlds. The Jews of Spain
shared the intellectual heritage of their Moslem neighbors—some, indeed (such as Maimonides or Israeli [1]),
were reckoned among its greatest adornments. But the
Hebraic heritage was available to Jews throughout the
world. The humblest Jewish scholar in Italy or Provence thus had access to intellectual resources of which
his most erudite Christian neighbors were ignorant.
It was, therefore, to the Jews, in most instances, that
Christian students had recourse for the intellectual
achievements of the Arabs and even the ideas of the
sages of ancient Greece.[2]

[1] See *infra*, pp. 184–6, 216, 222–5.
[2] The best account of this available in English is to be found in
Joseph Jacobs' *Jewish Contributions to Civilization*—a work of

Many hundreds of translations made by Jews in the medieval period, illustrating their intense interest and their fruitful participation in every branch of intellectual activity, have been preserved. It was the resultant Latin versions of the Greek classics and of their Moslem exponents (whether made directly from the Arabic, or through the medium of Hebrew versions prepared by Jews for their own use) which penetrated Europe from the eleventh century onwards with such far-reaching results.

This intellectual, scientific, and philosophical system, based upon the encyclopedic teachings of Aristotle as preserved and developed by the Moors and Jews, was accepted unquestioningly throughout Europe, and was embodied by Dante almost in its entirety in that greatest literary monument of the Middle Ages, his *Divine Comedy*. Thus Dante's entire cosmic system, enveloped within the *Primum Mobile* rests on a conception of the world immediately derived from Arabic and Jewish thinkers.

It is symptomatic that Aristotle ("The Master of those who know" as Dante calls him) has in his train in the Inferno, Averroes "who made the Great Commentary." In the famous pictorial representation of the Middle Ages, in the Spanish Chapel in Florence, vanquished philosophy is represented by turbaned figures, typifying its legendary association with the Moslem world. But though the system was expounded

---

studied moderation—and in the chapters by Charles and Dorothea Singer in *The Legacy of Israel*. I have drawn heavily on both books in this and the following chapters.

by Mohammedan thinkers (with the aid of Jews and persons of Jewish origin), it was mainly through Jews that it was transmitted from the Moslem to the Christian world.[1]

The importance of this process in European thought, science, and civilization was incalculable. To it is to be traced the origin of mathematical study in Europe, the ultimate basis of all technical progress. It was the foundation of medieval medicine, which, though long superseded, is nevertheless the basis of our own. It enriched medieval Europe with fresh literary concepts and forms. It formed the basis of astronomical investigation, which was all-important at the period of the great discoveries. Arabic and, indeed, medieval science in general are today no longer of more than academic importance, but it is upon them that our modern thought and science depend.

Before we leave this subject, a point referred to cursorily above must be accentuated. Just as the Jews played a part of vast significance as intermediaries in the transmission of Islamic culture to the Latin world, so they contributed in no small measure to the evolution of that culture. To an anonymous Jew is due, for example, the introduction into Europe from the East (below, p. 194) of the Indian work, *Kalilah and Dim-*

[1] Joseph Jacobs, in his *Jewish Contributions to Civilization*, draws a distinction between the philosophical texts, which according to him were for the most part derived by the Latin world direct from the Arabic, and the scientific, which in many cases were transmitted *via* Hebrew. The opposite thesis is maintained most brilliantly by Renan in *Averroës et l'Averroïsme*. But in any case the indubitable collaboration of Jews with Christian translators (e.g., Michael the Scot, *below*, p. 62) must be taken into account.

nah, or Fables of Bidpai (subsequently translated into 38 languages, in 112 different versions) on which so much of the lighter literature of the Middle Ages, including at least one-tenth of the fairy-tales familiar today, ultimately depends.

Again, in 680, a Basran Jew named Masurjuwaik translated a handbook of medicine from Syriac to Arabic, and wrote original treatises on the benefits and evils of foodstuffs and drugs. The Jewish scientist, Mashaala (pp. 142, 323), was a figure of great significance in the intellectual life of the Moslem world in the eighth century. Other names of considerable importance will be mentioned later on from time to time. Some historians go so far as to suggest that the greatest philosophers and physicians of Moslem Spain were of Jewish, when they were not of Christian, extraction. This, though clearly an exaggeration, contains in it the germ, at least, of a truth which should not be overlooked.

2

There were three main centers for the fruitful activity of the Jews, as interpreters of Graeco-Arab science to Europe. One was Toledo, at the court of the kings of Castile. Another was Naples, under the auspices of the House of Anjou. The third was Provence, the bridge between France and Spain, where the local Jewish scholars, particularly of the family of Ibn Tibbon, translated large numbers of texts from the Arabic of their native Spain into Hebrew for the benefit of their co-religionists north of the Pyrenees. These were frequently rendered into Latin at the request of Christian savants. Connected with this family was Jacob ben Makhir [1] (p. 78), a prolific translator in all branches of knowledge, whose original contributions to science were also of the utmost importance. But even in Northern Europe the process was repeated. Thus, in 1273–4 a Jew named Vives translated into French in the house of Henri Bate, at Malines, several books by the Spanish Jewish globe-trotter, exegete, and philosopher, Abraham ibn Ezra. These works were subsequently used by Bate to good effect in his own writings.

The contemporary appreciation of this activity may be conveyed by an enumeration of the patrons under whom these Jewish translators worked, many of whom were normally far from friendly towards the Jews—men like Raymund, Archbishop of Toledo in the twelfth century, the Emperor Frederick II, Manfred of Sicily, Charles of Naples, and Alfonso the Wise of Castile in the thirteenth, Robert of Naples and Pedro III of Aragon in the fourteenth.

The case of Alfonso the Wise was particularly interesting. He was not himself conspicuously pro-Jewish; indeed, the legislation contained in his famous code, the *Siete Partidas*, was notably intolerant. But he realized how backward his kingdom was in intellectual matters, as compared with the high standard

[1] The vital dates of persons mentioned in this work will be given in the text only when it is necessary for understanding the chronological setting. In other cases reference should be made to the Index.

of civilization which still prevailed in the remnants of
the Moorish principalities of the South. Accordingly,
he deliberately set himself to adapt the masterpieces
of Arabic science and literature into Spanish, incidentally creating thereby the Spanish language as we
know it today. Naturally, and inevitably, it was to
the Jews that he had recourse—the Jews, who were
at home both under Moslem and Christian rule and
piously retained some knowledge of the Arabic language even in Northern Spain and beyond. The first
task undertaken was the translation of a curious work
known as the *Lapidario*, a discourse upon the property
of metals and precious stones. One of the authors of
this work, incidentally, had himself been a Jew, one
Abolays. This version was completed in 1256 by the
royal physician, Rabbi Judah ben Moses. Then followed a long series of similar translations of astronomical, philosophical, and scientific works; treatises
on the quadrant, the candle-clock, and quick-silver;
literary exercises and philosophical disquisitions. Much
of this literature was subsequently translated into
Latin; all of it formed henceforth part of the general
European heritage.

Similar activity, if not quite so systematic, was
carried on under the auspices of the Holy Roman
Emperor, Frederick II. Of the Jewish savants under his
patronage the most important was Rabbi Jacob Anatoli, whom he invited to Naples, where he had not
long before established a University. Anatoli was the
first to translate the philosophy of Averroes from the
original Arabic. His version was in Hebrew, but the

Latin texts of the great Cordovan philosopher, which were current in the Middle Ages and as late as the seventeenth century in some important European centers, were based upon his translation. In his original work, which was of portentous bulk, he mentions with respect various suggestions of the Emperor himself.

When the Hohenstaufen were ejected from Southern Italy, their intellectual interests were maintained by their successors of the House of Anjou. Charles of Anjou in particular turned to Jews to assist him in acclimatizing, in the Christian portion of his dominions, the lore of the Arabs still numerous in Sicily. For this purpose, he employed Faraj ben Salim of Girgenti, the first of the professional translators of the Middle Ages, whose *magnum opus* was a version of the enormous medical compendium of Rhazes, the *Liber continens*. Another translator who worked under the same auspices was Moses of Palermo, specially instructed in Latin by the king's order, to whom we owe a Latin version of a work on the diseases of horses, ascribed to Hippocrates. This was one of the earliest veterinary treatises and constituted the basis of almost all those current in Europe, until the close of the sixteenth century.

The Jews were not solely responsible for many of the translations. In many cases, no doubt, one has to imagine the Jews reading from the Semitic original, which they would translate extemporaneously into the vernacular—Castilian or Italian—which some eager Christian student sitting by their side would write down in monkish Latin. In addition, there were a number of converted Jews who played a prominent role in this activity. Such were Petrus Alphonsi, an important figure in the history of literature, who brought an echo of the revival into England; or Constantine the African, a convert either from Islam or from Judaism, who translated many works of Jewish origin and who was greatly utilized by the English thinker, Adelard of Bath; or Jacob of Capua, who worked at Padua. Most important of all was John of Seville (Avendeath), a baptized member of the Ibn Daud family, who played a particularly prominent part in this activity, working in collaboration with such men as Plato of Tivoli. No medieval translator, with the exception of the indefatigable Gerard of Cremona, produced a greater bulk of work. He translated Avicenna, al-Gazali, and "Avicebron" among the philosophers, as well as many works in all branches of science. He was responsible for the introduction to Europe of the *Secretum Secretorum* ascribed to Aristotle, one of the most popular works of the Middle Ages, which has not entirely lost its vogue even today. He may be said, indeed, to have provided a large proportion of the scientific equipment of the average medieval library.

Similarly, in astronomy the Jews played a most significant role in transferring the Arabic knowledge of the stars, and Graeco-Arabic astronomy in general, from Islam to Christendom. All the more valuable astronomical tables of the Middle Ages were either translated or compiled with Jewish aid. This, as we shall see, was to be of the utmost importance for its bearing upon the progress of maritime exploration. It

was John of Seville who translated into Latin the
works of al-Battani and al-Farghani, the two chief
Arabic writers on astronomy. The latter, under the
name Alfergano, is cited by Dante; various passages
in the *Convito* and the *Vita Nuova* are based upon
his theories. Al-Kindi's treatise of the Stations of the
Moon was translated for Robert of Anjou by Kalonymos ben Kalonymos ("Maestro Calo"). Al-Heitham's
astronomical compendium was translated from Arabic
into Spanish by a Jew named Abraham at the request
of Alfonso X; Jacob ben Makhir translated al-Hazen's
Astronomy and the works of Autolycus and Menelaus
on the Sphere.

While working at the court of Frederick II, Jacob
Anatoli came into contact with the great Michael the
Scot, one of the outstanding figures in the intellectual
life of the Middle Ages, whose name is still a byword
for supernatural knowledge. It was he who was sent
by the Emperor on a mission to the Universities of
Europe to communicate to them the versions of Aristotle which he and others had made. This mission
makes him one of the most important figures in the
Latin Renaissance. It is highly probable that he is to
be identified with a certain remarkable Christian sage
whom Anatoli often cites cryptically though with the
utmost respect. Whether this is so or not, it is certain
that Jews were very closely associated in his work.
For this we have for instance the evidence of Roger
Bacon, who informs us categorically that a Jew named
Andrew was principally responsible for those translations from the Arabic which are bound up with the

name of Michael the Scot, as well as with those ascribed to Herman the German, Alfred the Englishman, and William the Fleming.

Bacon implies that Michael was ignorant of Arabic; in which case the aid of Andrew, who has been conjecturally identified with Anatoli himself, must have been all important. This evidence confirms and illustrates in a remarkable fashion the fact that the Jewish share in the early revival of learning was of the utmost significance.

3

The participation of the Jews in European intellectual currents knew no intermission, continuing, though with abated force, owing to the growth of persecution, through the period of the Italian Renaissance. Down to the middle of the sixteenth century, Jewish savants, such as Jacob Mantino, one-time physician to the Pope at Rome and to the Doge at Venice, or Abraham de Balmes, medical attendant on the Cardinal Grimaldi, continued to carry on the work of translation. Translations were now made in elegant Latin, and not, as hitherto, into the "barbarous" medieval scholastic dialect. By this time the original Greek sources were being made available to the world with increasing rapidity, and the work of translation became less important. The Jew, excluded with growing rigor from academic life, henceforth played a less important part than he had in the earliest stage of the Renaissance. Yet it was far from a negligible one; for, notwithstanding all the difficulties in his way, his intellectual interests could not be suppressed, and his collaboration is to be traced in almost every facet of the Renewal of Learning. It is thus no coincidence that the countries which led in the revival of the fifteenth century were those which still contained considerable Jewish settlements. A king of Portugal, successor and namesake of the ruler who was responsible for the peculiarly brutal expulsion of the Jews from that country in 1497 (in fact a universal forced conversion: below, p. 230), recorded his own conviction that "the Renaissance found Portugal ready to receive its impetus because the way had already been prepared partly by the learned Portuguese Jews."

It was symptomatic that one of the many Greek scholars who streamed westward after the fall of Constantinople in 1453, and brought the revival of letters to flower, was a Jew, Elijah del Medigo, of Crete. This savant was regarded in his day as one of the foremost, if not the foremost, exponent of Aristotelian philosophy, as distinct from the fashionable Platonism then gaining ground. In 1480, he was summoned to Padua as referee in a dispute in University circles. Here he made the acquaintance of Giovanni Pico della Mirandola, who invited him to Florence to act as his tutor. Pico, that knight-errant of the Renaissance, was himself deeply interested in Hebrew studies and particularly in the Cabbala, which he first introduced to the Christian world; but it was in philosophy that he desired Del Medigo's guidance. The latter thus became a familiar figure in humanistic circles in Florence. He was depicted in Gozzoli's famous fresco in the Medici Palace in the Via Larga, and there can be little doubt that he was among the brilliant company which assembled to discuss philosophical problems in the Orti Oricellai. Nor was he the only Jewish savant who figured in the cosmopolitan body of scholars which the Medici attracted to Florence. There was, for example, Johanan Alemanno, an expert in Greek and Arabic philosophy as well as Hebrew literature, in whose writings there is a penetrating delineation of Lorenzo the Magnificent and his surroundings; or again, Abraham Farisol, the cosmographer, who informs us how he saw at the court of the Medici a giraffe sent by the Sultan of Egypt. The influence of these Jewish savants on the Florentine thinkers, such as Marsilio Ficino as well as Pico himself, cannot be overlooked.

Other Jewish participants in the new birth in Italy illustrate the great breadth of their interests, co-extensive with that of the Renaissance as a whole. Among those who enjoyed Lorenzo the Magnificent's patronage in Florence was Guglielmo da Pesaro, author of one of the earliest extant treatises on the art of dancing, which had a considerable vogue in Italian society during the fifteenth and sixteenth centuries; Giovanni Maria, the musician, who subsequently became converted and was raised by Leo X to the dignity of Count of Verocchio; and more than one other.

This activity was not, of course, restricted to Florence. Benvenuto Cellini had as one of his masters Graziadio the Jew, of Bologna; and the metal-worker

Salamone da Sessa (subsequently converted, as Ercole de' Fedeli) worked at the courts of Mantua and Ferrara, as well as for that most discriminating patron, Cesare Borgia. There were lesser artists all over Italy, of whom Moses da Castellazzo is best remembered in Jewish annals. In the seventeenth century, Joseph Levi and Angelo de' Rossi of Verona enjoyed a high reputation. Their productions are still sought after by collectors. And at the court of Mantua, when it was one of the centers of Italian intellectual life, the Jews played a part of real importance, in their corporate capacity in the development of the nascent drama.

Much of the activity of the Italian Jews at the period of the Renaissance will be dealt with in connection with different topics later on. As an illustration, however, of the extent of their interests, one may take a single humble instance, the handkerchief. Further research is still required on the early history of this indispensable article. In England, it does not appear to be very ancient, for the Oxford English Dictionary does not record the use of the word previous to 1530. But Italian Jews were familiar with the handkerchief long before then. In the writings of a certain rabbi named Isaiah of Trani, who died in the first half of the fourteenth century, we find a detailed description of "the piece of cloth used for cleansing the nose" which he called by its Italian name, *fazzoletto*. This is certainly one of the earliest mentions of the object. To assume on the basis of this that the Jews invented it would be too much. But we are justified in deducing that they soon adopted it widely before it was in general use in any but the highest circles, and certainly before it was familiar in England.

As it happens, this record may be carried a little further. At the beginning of the sixteenth century a French student named François Tissard visited Italy, and took the opportunity to study local Jewish life. His observations are embodied in the preface to the Hebrew and Greek Grammar which he published shortly after his return home, *Grammatica Hebraica et Graeca* (Paris, 1508). This is the earliest surviving work printed in France in which Hebrew type was used. Among other matters, he calls particular attention to what he considered the disgusting habit of one of his Jewish teachers at Ferrara, who used to carry a piece of cloth about with him and would put it to his mouth to remove his spittle, instead of expectorating on the ground like a decent Christian! "I began to abhor this fellow for this to such an extent," observes Tissard naïvely, "that I must make an example of him."

This Jewish anticipation of what is now regarded as an elementary piece of hygiene, ridiculed by non-Jewish observers, has its parallel in a practice to which attention was drawn by Rammazzini, the great Italian physician of the seventeenth century and originator of the study of occupational diseases. He mentions, among the outstanding unsanitary habits of the Jews of Venice, their practice of keeping the windows open, day and night! The Italian physician's attitude is in striking contrast to the prescriptions of Moses Maimonides, who five centuries before had recommended air and sunlight as being among the most important safeguards of health (see below p. 227).[1]

Or, as a final example, a public bath was regarded an essential institution of the Jewish quarter (it was better for a Jew to live in a town without a synagogue than in one which lacked a public bath, the rabbis had taught), and systematic ablutions were part of the recognized system of religious hygiene. Hence John Locke, in urging the benefits of cold water on his fellow-countrymen, appealed to the example of the Jews:—

"If the rivers of Italy are warmer, those of Germany and Poland are much colder than any in this our country; and yet in these the Jews, both men and women, bathe all over, at all seasons of the year, without any prejudice to their health."—*Some Thoughts Concerning Education.* (1690) §7

4

The revival of learning would have remained the prerogative of a comparatively small class had it not been for the invention of printing. The Jews were quick to realize the potentialities of this new art. As early as 1444—six years, that is, before the date generally assigned to the beginning of Gutenberg's activity

[1] A modern parallel may be adduced. In the lavatories in New York restaurants, a card is prominently displayed requesting employees to wash their hands after using the toilet, in accordance with a recent municipal regulation. This hygienic practice has been universal among Jews for twenty centuries, as a quasi-religious prescription.

—an agreement for the cutting of a Hebrew font "according to the art of writing artificially," was entered into at Avignon between a wandering German craftsman and a member of the local community. No specimens of this earliest Hebrew press, unfortunately, have survived; for the persecution of Hebrew literature was hardly less ruthless in its day than the persecution of the Jews themselves. But before long, Hebrew presses were active in more than one part of the Jewish world, and in several places the Jews were pioneers, anticipating the other local craftsmen by some years. Thus, in Portugal Hebrew printing began in 1478, and non-Hebrew seven years later, when the first Latin book appeared (no work in the Portuguese language earlier than 1495 is known).[1] Indeed, of the twenty-four known books printed in Portugal before 1500, the first eleven are in Hebrew.

When the Jews were driven out of this country in 1497, they took their skill and their equipment with them, and various Hebrew works, printed at Fez shortly after, are extant, notably an edition of the liturgical guide, *Abudrahim*. This is the earliest book printed on the African continent. Similarly, the first book printed in the Balkans was the Hebrew Code of Rabbi Jacob ben Asher (Constantinople, 1493); and the earliest work printed by the European method in Asia is a commentary on the Book of Esther, published at Safed, in Palestine, in 1577. At Cairo, where a Euro-

[1] There is, indeed, a vague and probably inaccurate reference to a book of 1490, but even this is some time after the initiative had come from the Jews.

pean press was not started until 1798 during Napo-
leon's expedition, a Hebrew press had been active
since 1557.

It was not only in Hebrew printing that Jews were
active. Notwithstanding the efforts made to exclude
them from honorable walks of life, a few managed to
become engaged in secular work. Thus, Abraham
Zacuto's Almanac and astronomical tables were published by Abraham d'Orta at Leiria in 1496 in two
editions, Latin and Spanish. The latter is noteworthy,
as it is the only incunabulum printed in Portugal with
the text neither Latin, nor Portuguese, nor Hebrew.
At the beginning of the following century, Girolamo
Soncino was active as a publisher in Northern Italy,
mainly in Latin and Italian. He took pains to search
out manuscripts in order to establish the best texts, his
edition of Petrarch being particularly noteworthy.
Moreover, he contests with the great Aldo the credit
for first realizing the potentialities of the so-called
Italic type.[1] Similarly the most famous Portuguese romance of the sixteenth century, Ribeiro's *Menina e
Moça*, was first published by the Jew, Usque, at Ferrara in 1554.

Perhaps the most important factor in the popularization of learning, without which the newly-invented
printing-press would have remained little more than a
toy, was the replacement of parchment—always ex-

---

[1] It is interesting to note that bilingual typographic activity was
not confined to Western Europe. The first Turkish press, founded
at Constantinople in 1729 (over two hundred years after the first
Hebrew press in that city, set up in 1503) was carried on with the
help of a Jew named Jonas.

pensive, and necessarily restricted in quantity—by paper, of which the supply was unlimited. The Chinese had long ago made paper from silk and other materials. The Arabs had learned to manufacture it from cotton, but it was not until comparatively late that Western Europe mastered the art, and began to make linen paper. The Jews once again were among the pioneers, and the earliest known paper factory in Europe was that which they established in the thirteenth century at Jativa, near Valencia.

5

The Renaissance, when it crossed the Alps from Italy to Germany, took on a different complexion. The serious, introspective Germanic spirit took into consideration various questions which the light-hearted Italians had preferred not to raise, or the answers to which they had taken for granted. The spirit of inquiry, which had been fostered by a re-examination of medieval science, was now applied to medieval religion. Literary criticism, developed in order to cope with the texts of classical literature, was applied to that of the Latin Bible. The new-found passion for going back to the sources was applied to the Catholic tradition, and the same spirit which had questioned authority in philosophy began to question it in matters of faith. The Renaissance, in fact, developed in its northern form into the Reformation. This in turn had its repercussions south of the Alps in the Catholic Reaction, or Counter-Reformation. In the end, the religious life of Europe, whether it titularly retained the old faith or embraced the new form, was revolutionized.

The Jews' part in bringing about the Reformation is frequently exaggerated, and generally misunderstood. The Reformation, like all Christian reform movements before and after, implied a return to the Scriptures. All agitators for reform necessarily went to the Bible for support, and occasionally approximated biblical practice in one matter or the other. It was hence natural that one of the commonest terms of ecclesiastical vituperation in the Middle Ages was "Judaizer"—an epithet which recurs in the controversial works of the period with wearisome frequency.

But in fact it was seldom justified. The Jew, as such, had no interest in the dispute, one way or the other. There was little for him to choose, theologically speaking, between the Reformed and Catholic forms of Christianity. Nor was there any material reason why he should prefer one to the other. It was true that Martin Luther, at the outset of his career, had referred to the Church's atrocious treatment of the Jews as an additional argument against it. Yet later he reversed his opinion, and inveighed against the Jews with a virulence which surpassed the worst precedent that the Middle Ages could provide. For many years to come, the treatment of the Jews by Catholic and Protestant Europe was much the same; and, if the latter subsequently changed its policy, this was due to economics and expediency rather than to abstract, disinterested toleration.

It is thus misleading to speak of a direct Jewish influence upon the Reformation.[1] Yet the influence of Jewish scholarship, and hence of individual Jewish scholars, was far from negligible. As has been pointed out, the Reformation was based upon the rejection of Catholic tradition in favor of the authority of the Bible and the removal from the latter of the glosses by means of which (as the Reformers claimed) the Church of the Middle Ages had attempted to maintain its ascendancy over religious thought. But the Bible was available to the Western World only in its official Catholic version, the Vulgate; it was the Jews alone who possessed the Hebrew original and the key to its interpretation. Hence, just as Italian savants applied to Greek scholars for guidance in their researches into Plato, so German theologians applied to Jewish Rabbis for assistance in understanding the Hebrew Scriptures. It was only a coincidence, perhaps, that the intellectual clash in Germany began with an attempt on the part of the Dominicans to suppress the Talmud, which was doughtily championed by Johannes von Reuchlin; yet it was symptomatic of the trend of events. All the great leaders of reform—Luther, Zwingli, Melanchthon, Tyndale, Servetus, and so on—studied Hebrew. Many of them, too, had Jewish scholars to teach them.

[1] An exception is to be made only as regards the Marranos, or crypto-Jews of Spain and Portugal. Compulsorily converted to Catholicism, they could not be expected to appreciate its spirituality; yet in many cases they entirely lacked Jewish knowledge and loyalties. They were hence a particularly favorable soil for the Reform doctrine, and played an important part in its propagation in Flanders. Thus Marc Perez, the Calvinist leader at Antwerp in the middle of the sixteenth century, was of Jewish extraction, as were many others.

Reuchlin, for example, had been instructed by Jacob Loans (physician to the Emperor Frederick III) in Germany and by Obadiah Sforno in Italy; these two savants have been reckoned, for that reason, among the fathers of the Protestant Reformation.

The newly aroused interest did not end with the Hebrew text of the Bible. In order to understand the Scriptures, it was necessary to have recourse to rabbinical literature, so as to discover what was the Jewish tradition on the subject. From this period dates the real beginning of Christian-Hebrew scholarship, the establishment of effective chairs of Hebrew at the principal European universities and the emergence of a class of Christian Hebraists of real ability, whose contributions to Jewish scholarship have sometimes been of the utmost value.

The recourse to Jewish tradition was fruitful and left a permanent mark. The writings of the great medieval Franco-Jewish biblical commentators, Solomon ben Isaac of Troyes (Rashi) and David Kimchi of Narbonne, were of the highest importance; for it was upon them that the new translations of the Bible, the foundation of the Reformation, depended. Luther, indeed, relied principally upon Nicholas de Lyra, the fourteenth century Franciscan exegete, said to have been a Jew by birth. His critics indeed sneered at him on that account. Had Lyra not lyred, they said, Luther could never have danced. But Lyra himself depended to an overwhelming extent on the writings of Rashi, whose interpretations in many instances he simply adapted, giving them a Christian tinge. Subsequently,

Lyra's writings were furnished with an important supplement (likewise used by Luther) by Paul de Santa Maria, Bishop of Burgos, who had formerly been Rabbi Solomon Levi and naturally derived to a great extent from Jewish sources. Kimchi's commentary was used in a large degree by successive generations of Christian exegetes, particularly in the preparation of the English "Authorized Version" of 1611. To such an extent was this so, that, it has been aptly said, though no Jews were tolerated in England at the time when this magnificent achievement was being produced, Rabbi David Kimchi was present at Westminster in spirit.

Hence, just as Jewish collaborators assisted in the labor of translation of secular and scientific texts into Latin, which marked the beginning of the revival of learning, so the Hebraic spirit, Jewish learning, and individual Jewish scholars participated to a marked extent in its latest phase—the biblical research and re-examination of doctrine which accompanied the revival of religion.

CHAPTER IV. *The Great Voyages of Discovery*

"THE greatest event which has happened since the creation of the world (leaving aside the incarnation and death of Him who made it) is the discovery of the Indies" wrote a sixteenth century Spaniard, Francisco Lopez de Gomara, in dedicating his *Hispania Felix* to the Emperor Charles V. There was less exaggeration in this statement than was customary in such effusions, for the discovery of the sea-route to India and the existence of the vast American Continent was among the most epoch-making events in all recorded history. The succession of maritime discoveries at the close of the fifteenth century suddenly enlarged men's horizons, showing them the existence of a new world, other than that known to their fathers and fathers' fathers before them. This widening of perspective provided humanity with a new universe to conquer. It shifted the balance of power from the Mediterranean to the countries of the Atlantic coast. It laid the foundation of the world of today.

The discovery of America and of the Indies was not, to be sure, a sudden stroke of genius or of luck, but the culmination of a gradual movement spread over many generations. The earth had from antiquity been regarded as a sphere of which only a small part was known. Already in the thirteenth century, the English friar, Roger Bacon, had offered as proof the authority of Hebrew writers to show that Asia could be reached by sailing west from Europe. Indeed, the rabbis had made some astonishing guesses about the structure of the universe, which by coincidence were near enough to the truth. The so-called "Jerusalem" Talmud (*Aboda Zara*, 42c.) boldly states that the world is in the form of a globe. The *Zohar* (Lev. 1:3) goes even further, asserting that the earth rotates on its axis like a ball; thus, when it is day in one half of the globe, the other half is plunged in darkness, and those living below have their heads in the opposite direction to those above. This statement, accepted by many medieval scholars,[1] familiarized in wide circles among the Jews the conjecture of antipodean conditions which, from the sixth century on, had been treated with general derision.

The progress of maritime discovery at the close of the Middle Ages was bound up with certain technical improvements. Ships were small, knowledge was limited, mechanical aids almost non-existent. Even after the introduction of the compass, it was impossible to estimate the position of a ship at sea. The starting-point in the history of modern exploration began when ships could sail out boldly into uncharted seas instead of hugging the coast or steering in a direction which

---

[1] Like the thirteenth-century author of the *Mashal haKadmoni*, Isaac Sahulla.

would bring them in sight of known land within a few hours.

In the development and perfection of the instruments and tables by means of which this became possible, Jewish savants, who were deeply interested in astronomy, played a part of the utmost importance. As a result their names are inseparably associated with the whole story of maritime discovery.

The nautical instruments used in the Middle Ages were almost without exception based on Arab models. These in turn depended on Greek science. Their prototypes were introduced to the Moslem world by that remarkable Jewish genius of the eighth century, Mashaala, "the phoenix of his age," who first adapted the Greek treatise on the astrolabe for the use of the Arabic-speaking world. Throughout the Middle Ages, Jewish scholars, in particular, continued to work on this indispensable instrument, as we shall see later.

Apart from the astrolabe, the most important nautical instrument in the early days was the quadrant for the determination of the right ascension of the sun and stars, and hence the relative position of the vessel at any given moment. For a long time the quadrant in general use was one devised by that twelfth century genius known as Robert the Englishman, first translator of the Koran into any European language. His invention held the field for many generations until it was superseded by the improved instrument of Rabbi Jacob ben Makhir, compiler, incidentally, of the calendar used by Dante. This was known after him as the *Quadrans Judaicus*. The importance of Jacob ben

Makhir's work was universally recognized, for he was read and quoted with respect by the founders of modern astronomy, Copernicus and Kepler, long after his day.

A more important invention was due to Rabbi Levi ben Gershom of Bagnols, in South France, the most eminent Jewish philosopher and exegete of the fourteenth century. His *magnum opus* was a philosophical work, *The Wars of the Lord*, which covered also a considerable part of the field of natural science. An entire section, comprising no less than 136 chapters out of a total of 237, is devoted to astronomy. The reputation which the author enjoyed was so great that almost as soon as the book was put into circulation, Pope Clement VI had the astronomical portion translated into Latin. This was indeed fortunate since, when the original Hebrew was published, that part was not considered to be of sufficient theological importance to warrant inclusion. In this treatise the author described an improved quadrant which he had invented, and which could be handled more easily than the cumbersome old affair. The great Regiomontanus, reading this account, was so impressed that he constructed an instrument according to the Rabbi's recommendations, which he named *Jacob's Staff*. This was the instrument which accompanied all the great explorers of the Renaissance, Vasco da Gama, Magellan, even Christopher Columbus, on their travels. It remained in use for approximately three centuries, and was not given up until John Hadley's reflecting quadrant was adopted by the British Admiralty in 1734. Even after that it continued to be used by surveyors for land measurements.[1]

The quadrant, used alone, was inadequate as an aid in navigation. In the heyday of the Portuguese maritime activity at the close of the fifteenth century, the scientists at the Court of King João II of Portugal advised him to find out whether it was possible to extend the scope of the mechanical devices hitherto employed, by adapting to nautical use the old planispheric astrolabe known to the Greeks. The King entrusted this task to a commission of three scientists. One of them was Martin Behaim (that is "the Bohemian"), said by some authorities to have been a Jew. The other two were the King's two Jewish physicians, Master Rodrigo and Master Joseph Vecinho. The three savants set to work methodically. The result was the manufacture of an improved astrolabe, which, used in conjunction with tables of the solar declination which

---

[1] The "Jacob's Staff" consisted of a long central bar marked with a scale and provided with a movable cross-bar (or four of varying sizes, used alternatively). One end was placed to the eye and the traversal was adjusted until one end was in line with the sun and the other with the horizon. By calculating the length of the cross-piece and its distance from the eye, the angle between the sun and the horizon could easily be calculated. With the aid of this instrument, it was thus possible to prick the chart while at sea, instead of landing (as had hitherto been necessary) each time the position was to be determined. A representation of the instrument is constantly before our eyes in the picture of the Jack of Diamonds, as it is to be found in any ordinary pack of playing-cards. Under the name "sun-glass," it continued to be used by Suffolk sailors within living memory. From Marlowe's *Tamburlaine the Great*, II. iii. 3, it seems that, besides being used for navigation, Jacob's Staff was the earliest form of range-finder.

they prepared, made it possible to navigate by observation of the sun. Portuguese historians record this discovery with pride, for now oceanic navigation in its complete sense became possible.

Navigation necessarily required one other aid without which the instruments were useless—reliable astronomical tables, essential in all work based on solar or sidereal observation.[1] All the more important astronomical tables of the Middle Ages, without exception, were at least translated or compiled with the help of Jews; in the most important cases they were entirely of Jewish authorship.

Shortly before the capture of Toledo by the Christian forces in 1085, a series of astronomical tables had been drawn up in that city—the swan-song, as it were, of Arab science in the old capital. In the compilation of these, the Toledo Tables, a number of Jewish astronomers had assisted. Some time later, in the thirteenth century, Alfonso the Wise, King of Castile, in his endeavor to naturalize Moslem science in his dominions, set about having these adapted for the use of non-Moslem scholars and brought up to date. Among those to whom he applied with this object in view were Judah ben Moses Cohen, a Jewish physician, and Isaac ben Sid, *hazan* or reader in a Toledo synagogue. These two in collaboration with other Jewish savants

[1] What follows is based upon Joseph Jacobs' admirable summary in his *Jewish Contributions to Civilization*—a superb achievement which, had he been spared to complete it, would have rendered a great part of the present work unnecessary. Much use has been made in this section also of the chapter in *The Legacy of Israel* on "The Jewish Factor in Mediaeval Thought."

were the authors of the famous "Alfonsine Tables," which they themselves translated into Spanish and which continued in great repute for centuries. They are found in innumerable manuscripts and were published time after time long after the invention of printing. The last edition which appeared for practical use was that of Madrid in 1641. As late as the seventeenth century they were still being consulted by Kepler and even Galileo.

The Alfonsine Tables in their turn were adapted by Isaac Israeli of Toledo for his contemporaries in 1310. They became classical throughout Europe, and were utilized by Scaliger, the sixteenth century founder of the modern science of chronology, and by Petavius. Further astronomical tables formerly in general use were compiled by Joseph ibn Wakkar at Toledo in 1396, and in Aragon by various Jewish savants for Pedro III (IV). Other calculations were made by Emanuel ben Jacob, known to the outside world as Bonfils de Tarascon. These were shortly afterwards translated into Latin from the original Hebrew and were extensively used by many European scholars of the age of the Renaissance, especially by Pico della Mirandola and Peiresc.[1]

---

[1] It is interesting to note that even the points of the compass, as they were known to mariners of old, owed their nomenclature to Jews. It is in the *Sepher Asaph* of the ninth (?) century that we first find these mentioned by the names current in the Middle Ages—*Graecum, Scirrocum, Garbinum, Magistrum*. These terms were taken over by the Latin world and were crystallized by mention in the *Treasure*, composed by Brunetto Latini between 1260 and 1269.

2

One of the principal centers of activity in the period of preparation which led up to the great maritime discoveries of the late Middle Ages was Majorca. The island lies midway between Europe and Africa. It inherited the traditions of Islamic civilization, of which it was one of the last European refuges, as well as of Latin culture; its inhabitants, many of whom were Jews, were from necessity skilled navigators, as much at home on the high seas as in their own sea-girt birthplace. In consequence, they were quite familiar with the art of navigation, the coastline, and geographical knowledge in general. By degrees their reputation extended. In the end they came to be the cartographers *par excellence* of Christendom, and they were called upon when new maps were required—especially by the princes and rulers of the Spanish mainland. Their productions may be said to sum up geography so far as it was known in the later Middle Ages and to have served as the point of departure for subsequent discoveries.

So much is more or less familiar. But what is not so generally realized is the fact that these Majorcan cartographers, upon whom Europe relied for its geographical knowledge, were for the most part Jews. At their head was the Crescas family. Abraham Crescas was so highly esteemed that he was appointed by the Infant Juan of Aragon as "Master of Maps and Compasses," a dignity for which he was paid, apparently, by an authorization to establish a public bath for his coreligionists at Palma. On one occasion the Infant Juan of Aragon wrote to the authorities on the island stating that he wanted a complete chart which would represent the Straits of Gibraltar, the Atlantic coasts and the mysterious ocean beyond. It was natural that the task was entrusted to Abraham Crescas and his son Jahuda. They worked on it for two years (1376-7), and the result was their famous *mapamundi*—"that is to say, an image of the world and of the various states of the world and of the regions which are on the earth and of the divers manners of people which inhabit it." This, now famous as the Catalan Atlas, is one of the most remarkable monuments of medieval science that have come down to us. "Never have we seen so fair a map," cried Don Juan when he saw it. The sources from which Crescas obtained his information cannot be ascertained, but it is certain that he must have made use of the experiences of Joseph the physician, or Yuceff Faquin, a Barcelona Jew who had settled in Majorca and who was reported to have sailed the entire known world.

The sequel was remarkable. In 1381, Charles VI of France wrote the Infant Juan, informing him of his desire to possess an atlas of the world executed by the cartographers of Majorca, who enjoyed so high a reputation for their care and precision. The other replied that he knew of no *mapamundi* better than that recently executed by his Jewish subjects. This he generously dispatched with his letter with careful instructions as to its transport. It remained a prized possession of the Royal Library in Paris and is now among the treasures of the Bibliothèque Nationale. Much has been written about it and in recent times it has twice been reproduced in facsimile. This work marks a real epoch in European map-making, inasmuch as it added for the first time the discoveries of Marco Polo to the conventional map-drawing which had continued almost unchanged for centuries.

Abraham Crescas continued to work unremittingly under the patronage of the Aragonese Court until 1387. On his death in that year, his son, Jahuda, the Compass or Map Jew, as he was popularly called, inherited his reputation and his clientele, and we find his former patron, now King of Aragon, commissioning from him a new *mapamundi* to replace that sent to France.

In the wave of forced baptisms which swept through Spain in 1391, Jahuda Crescas was compelled to change his religion. Henceforth, he was called Jayme Ribes. But he was too useful to be allowed to change his occupation, and he was summoned to Barcelona to conduct his work nearer the Court. On the death of his patron and of the latter's successor, Martin I, who had continued his scientific interests, Jayme Ribes was invited by Prince Henry the Navigator to Portugal. He was known as Maestre Jacomo de Majorca and was the first director of the famous nautical observatory at Sagres, cradle of the Portuguese discoveries. Here the expeditions were organized which resulted in the rounding of the Cape of Good Hope and the discovery of the sea route to India.

Another Jewish cartographer of Majorca, believed to belong to Abraham Crescas' family, was Haym ibn

Risch. He, too, became converted at the time of the persecutions in 1391, adopting the name of Juan de Vallsecha. He was probably the father of the Gabriel de Vallsecha, who executed in 1439 another famous *mapamundi*—now one of the treasures of the Institute of Catalan Studies in Barcelona, for it belonged to Amerigo Vespucci. In this map the meridian of the Azores is used for the first time in the history of cartography. Still another Majorcan cartographer of Jewish birth was Mecia de Viladestes. One of his maps, dated 1413, is preserved in the Bibliothèque Nationale in Paris.

It is significant that the anti-Jewish persecutions marked the end of the glories of the Majorcan school of cartography. The little group of *conversos* continued the Jewish tradition for another generation; thereafter, there was a rapid decadence. One incident illustrates this very clearly. The Jewish map-makers with their widespread connections had known and indicated all that was possible about the cities, the trade-routes, and the oases of the Sahara. Their successors forgot it all. Pedro Roselli, in his planisphere of 1465, seventy-five years after the outbreak of persecution, marked only four localities to the south of the Atlas range; his successors knew only one.[1]

[1] It was not only by providing maps that the Jewish scientists of Majorca contributed to geographical discovery. They also excelled as manufacturers of nautical instruments. Two were especially famous. The physician, Isaac Nafuci, was a favorite of Pedro IV of Aragon, who called him "the celebrated Jew of Majorca" and never tired of singing his praises. In 1359, the king chose him "to make the clocks and quadrants that we desire," and

3

With regard to the ancestors of Christopher Columbus, a certain degree of mystery, largely of his own
making, still prevails. This is chiefly due to the fact
that, in his anxiety to claim a noble origin, he spoke as
little and as confusedly as possible about his parentage.
There are certain obvious discrepancies, moreover, between his own account of his career and what we
know from documentary sources of that of Cristofer
Colombo, son of the Genoese weaver, with whom he
is generally identified.

Spanish scholars, such as Jose M. Erugo, C. Garcia
de la Riega, Otero Sanchez, Nicholas Diaz Perez, etc.,[1]
in order to claim him for their own country, have put
forward the hypothesis that he was of Marrano extraction, and therefore obliged to be secretive about
his origin. It is certain that the name of Colombo, or
Colon, is by no means unknown among Jews, that
Christopher left a small legacy to a Jew living by the
gate of the Jews' Street in Lisbon, that he shows a

---

in 1365, at a critical moment of the war with Castile, he ordered
payment to be made to him for a silver quadrant which he had
provided. Nafuci worked in conjunction with the Majorcan Jewish scientist Ephraim Bellshom (to whom, incidentally, a contemporary rabbi turned to discover the area of a globe, in connection with the construction of a ritual bath). The two
collaborated in the manufacture of an astrolabe for the use of
the Infant Juan, together with a translation into Catalan of an
astronomical work of the famous al-Farghani.

[1] The hypothesis now (1939) has the support of Salvador de
Madariaga.

particularly strong biblical influence in his writings, that his somewhat mysterious signature is capable of Hebraic interpretations and that his son states categorically that his father's progenitors were of the royal blood of Jerusalem—*a phraseology consistently used by Spanish Jews of the period when they desired to boast their aristocratic origin.* "The theory that Columbus was born at Pontevedra . . . cannot lightly be brushed aside," asserts André, in his biography. "On the other hand, there is perhaps equal reason for believing him born in Aragon, *the son of converted Jews.*"

Whatever the truth may be, it is incontestable that the great explorer had a penchant for Jewish society, and that Jews were intimately associated with his enterprise from the beginning.

Discouraged by his failure in Portugal, where he had first applied for assistance, Columbus had made his way to Spain. Here, too, he met with rebuff after rebuff. The only persons who took him seriously were a little group, all or nearly all of whom were either Jews or of Jewish descent belonging to Marrano families which converted to Christianity by force during the persecutions at the close of the fourteenth century, still remained at heart, in most instances, faithful to the religion of their fathers. The most prominent was the learned Diego de Deza, later Inquisitor General, who, notwithstanding his Christian zeal, belonged to a family which originated in the *juderia;* the latter introduced Columbus to Abraham Zacuto, the astronomer (below, pp. 92–94), whose discoveries were utilized to good effect by the explorer later on. A striking contrast to Deza was Don Isaac Abravanel, the last scholar-statesman of Spanish Jewry, who occupied an important position in the financial administration of the country, yet devoted all his leisure to Jewish studies. His associate, Abraham Senior, last Crown Rabbi of Castile, was likewise a staunch supporter of the explorer. More influential still was Luis de Santangel, Chancellor and Comptroller of the Royal Household, a great-grandson of the Jew Noah Chinillo of Calatayud. Gabriel Sanchez, another of the most fervent supporters of the expedition, was also of Jewish origin, being the son of a *converso* couple and nephew of Alazar Ussuf, of Saragossa. Among the other patrons of Columbus were Alfonso de la Caballeria, member of a famous Marrano family and Vice-Chancellor of Aragon, and Juan Cabrero, the Royal Chamberlain. Indeed, the only high official intimately concerned with the genesis of the expedition belonging to an "Old Christian" house was the royal secretary, Juan de Coloma, whose wife was, however, descended from the Jewish clan of De la Caballeria.

It was this group which rallied round Columbus when, faced with failure, he was preparing to leave Spain for good. Santangel secured him an audience with the Queen and, representing to her the advantages which would accrue to the Crown and to Spain from the discovery of the sea-route to the Indies, persuaded her to neglect the adverse views of the pedants upon whom she had previously relied. When at last she acquiesced, the question of finance remained. Once more Santangel came forward, advancing without interest no less than 1,140,000 maravedis towards the expenses of the expedition. A certain amount was still needed; this was provided by Don Isaac Abravanel. The story that the queen pawned her crown jewels for the purpose of financing the expedition is a pious invention.

Preparations for the expedition were now pushed forward. Columbus' crew consisted of some ninety men all told. Among the few of these whose names have been preserved, persons of known Jewish origin are prominent. One was Alonso de la Calle, whose very name indicated that he had been born in the Jewish quarter. Roderigo Sanchez, a relative of the High Treasurer, joined the expedition at the personal request of the queen. A New Christian named Marco was ship's surgeon; while Mestre Bernal, the ship's physician, had been punished a couple of years previously by the Inquisition as a judaizer. Land was first sighted by the Marrano sailor, Rodrigo de Triana; and Luis de Torres, the interpreter, who had been baptized only a few days before the expedition sailed, was the first European to set foot in the New World. The expedition, moreover, was equipped with the astronomical tables and instruments of Abraham Zacuto and other Jewish scientists. On his return to Europe, the famous letters in which Columbus first announced the news of his discoveries were addressed to his Marrano patrons, Luis de Santangel and Gabriel Sanchez. In view of all this evidence it may be stated without exaggeration that the discovery of the New World as early

as 1492 would have been unlikely but for the assistance
of persons of Jewish origin.[1]

4

The Jewish scientific activity of the later Middle Ages
culminated in the work of Abraham Zacuto, one of the
most remarkable savants of the fifteenth century,
whose work was of the utmost importance in the
period of the great maritime discoveries. The most
capable astronomer, perhaps, of his day, he had taught
that subject, informally, as appears from the latest researches on the subject, at the University of Salamanca,
where he met and was consulted by Columbus. On
the expulsion of the Jews from Spain in 1492, he made
his way to Portugal, where he received appointment
almost immediately as Astronomer-Royal; and, when
persecutions followed in that country in 1497, he managed to escape to North Africa, where he compiled
the well-known chronicle, Sepher Juhasin, which
made his name memorable in the annals of Jewish
literature.

While at Salamanca, he compiled a series of astronomical tables, based on the work of his predecessors

[1] It is an ironic consideration that, notwithstanding the assistance which the Marranos had given in the discovery of the New
World, they were not safe from persecution even here. As early
as 1515 the Inquisition started its operations, bringing persons
suspected of judaizing back to Europe for trial; and before the
end of the century autos da fé were familiar spectacles in every
part of the Spanish dominions overseas. Among the earliest victims of the Inquisition in the New World was Hernando Alonso,
who had followed Cortes to Mexico as one of the conquistadores;
he was burned at the stake, with another judaizer, in 1528.

but considerably improved, which immediately obtained general recognition. His pupil, Joseph Vecinho (pp. 94 ff.), translated them into Latin and Spanish, and had them published at the press of the Jewish printer, Abraham d'Orta, at Leiria in 1496. So highly esteemed was this work that before the end of the century it was twice republished at Venice, the classical center of the maritime art.[1] This compilation continued to be cited in Portugal long after the author had been driven out; thus, in the *Reportorio dos Tempos*, Lisbon, 1518, there are to be found tables of the declination of the sun, "punctually taken from Zacuto by the honest Gaspar Nicolas."

The tables of Zacuto were carried in the fleets of Vasco da Gama, Cabral, João da Nova, and Albuquerque, but are most important for the use made of them by Christopher Columbus. In his writings the latter mentions how he consulted the "Almanack" on his voyages and how on one occasion he saved himself and his companions from a difficult position by predicting an eclipse with its aid. It is pretty obvious that it was Zacuto's tables to which he referred. In any case, it is certain that he took them with him on his later voyages, for there is preserved at Seville a copy of the Leiria edition which belonged to the great explorer. It has been conjectured that it was presented to him by the author or translator, and bears manuscript annotations from Columbus' own pen.

[1] There were other editions here in 1500, 1502, 1525 and 1528, and the work has been reproduced more than once in facsimile. See, most recently, A. Fontoura da Costa, *L' Almanach Perpetuum de Abraham Zacuto* (1934, 1935).

It was in Portugal that Zacuto's activity reached its zenith. Here he devised a new astrolabe, which he manufactured of iron instead of wood as was previously usual, thus making that cumbrous instrument available for ordinary use. The assistance which he gave to Vasco da Gama before he set out on the voyage which resulted in the discovery of the sea-route to India was of the utmost importance. The Court asked his opinion before the expedition was authorized. The ships were equipped with his improved astrolabe, and in contemporary records we find reference to lessons in its use being given to the navigators before they put out to sea. So great was the impression that this new experiment created that it is referred to by Camoens in his *Lusiads*, the greatest Portuguese epic poem in flowing verses.

The ultimate object of the great medieval voyages of discovery was to find a more convenient route to India. While Bartholomew Diaz with his two tiny caravels was ploughing his way south by sea towards the Cape of Good Hope, two other audacious pioneers, João Perez of Covilhã and Alfonso de Paiva, were dispatched eastward to investigate the overland route; among their equipment were maps made by Behaim's two Jewish collaborators. Subsequently, two Jews followed—Joseph Çapateiro of Lamego, who had great experience in Eastern travel and had presented the King a report on Ormuz, the emporium of the Indian spice-trade, and Rabbi Abraham of Beja, whose knowledge of languages was considered remarkable. At Cairo, they met João Perez, now on his way back from India; his companion had died meanwhile, leaving his last instructions to a faithful Jew who had accompanied him in his travels.

Rabbi Abraham remained with Perez, going as far as Ormuz and then returning by the caravan route *via* Damascus and Aleppo. Joseph, on the other hand, was sent back to Lisbon immediately. He brought information amassed from Arabian and Indian pilots which indicated a sea-route to the Far East. Armed with this information, with the Majorcan maps, with Vecinho's tables, and with Zacuto's improved astrolabe, Vasco da Gama set out on the epoch-making voyage which was to result in the discovery of the sea-route to India.

Before sailing from Lisbon on July 8th, 1497, Da Gama conferred publicly with Zacuto and affectionately bade him good-bye in the presence of the whole crew. On his arrival at Anchediva, not far from Goa, the explorer was greeted by a tall European with a flowing white beard, a Jew from Posen, who had found his way to India after remarkable adventures. He had risen to the rank of Admiral to the Viceroy of Goa, whom he had persuaded to treat the strangers kindly. Da Gama's conduct towards the old man was most ungrateful, even according to brutal fifteenth-century standards. He had him seized and tortured until he consented to be baptized and to pilot the Portuguese flotilla in Indian waters. Gaspard da Gama, as he was henceforth known, subsequently accompanied Cabral on his voyage to the East in 1502, the latter being instructed to follow his advice in all matters. At Cape Verde, on the return voyage, he met and was consulted by Amerigo Vespucci, then setting out to explore the Eastern coast of South America; and the Tuscan explorer, who gave America her name, referred to him in his writings in terms of the highest esteem and admiration.

Joseph Vecinho played a role in the age of the maritime discoveries no less important and barely less prominent than that of his master, Zacuto. He held the rank of physician-in-ordinary to João II of Portugal, and hence enjoyed great influence at the Portuguese Court. His opinion was regularly asked on all questions relating to science. When in 1484 Columbus laid before the Portuguese ruler his plan for exploring the western route to the Indies, it was submitted to a *junta* of five experts, including Joseph Vecinho and a Jewish mathematician named Moses. Vecinho, as we have seen, was also one of the commission which adopted the astrolabe for ordinary nautical use. It was by the means of this instrument that he ascertained the latitude by solar observation on the coast of Guinea, whither he was sent on a scientific mission by the King. On his return he reported the results of his observations at Court on March 11th, 1495. Among those present on this occasion was Christopher Columbus, who did not fail to take careful notes and to record the event in one of his characteristic observations.

The forced conversion of the Jews in Portugal in 1497, one of the most shameful episodes in the history of the Middle Ages, did not affect their scientific interests. Abraham Zacuto went into exile. Joseph Vecinho was compelled to submit to baptism, and, under the name Diego Mendes Vecinho, was prominent in scientific work at the court of King Manoel the Fortunate. None the less, Jewish loyalty remained strong in his descendants, and a century later one finds them settled in Italy as professing Jews, still maintaining, however, their ancestor's scientific bent.

Another victim of the forced conversions was Pedro Nuñez, who, a mere child at the time, subsequently became professor of mathematics at Coimbra and chief cosmographer to the Crown of Portugal. He, too, remained closely attached to Judaism in secret; so much so, that at the beginning of the seventeenth century his grandsons were tried by the Inquisition for judaizing. His *magnum opus* was the Treatise on the Sphere, first published at Lisbon in 1537, and described as "one of the scientific glories of Portugal." This opened the way for Mercator's work and thus for the whole system of modern cartography. The last King of Portugal, Manoel, in his monumental *Early Portuguese Books*, had no hesitation in calling this Marrano scientist, whose Jewish origin he barely suspected, "the most distinguished Portuguese nautical astronomer."

5

The Jews, particularly those of Spain and Portugal, thus provided no small part of the technical equipment of those voyages of exploration which suddenly widened the horizons of Europe at the close of the Middle Ages. But their work as actual explorers was by no means insignificant. It was the Radanite Jewish merchants of the ninth century who, according to Ibn

Khurdadbih, Postmaster-General of the Caliphate of Bagdad, opened up the trade routes between Europe and the Far East, either *via* Egypt and the Dead Sea, or along the Tigris and Euphrates, or overland by the southern route through Northern Africa or the northern across Central Europe (see below, pp. 251 ff.). When Germany was an outpost of barbarism, and all the culture of Europe was concentrated in Moslem Spain, an enterprising Jew, Abraham ibn Jacob, was among the mission which the Caliph of Cordova sent to the northern country, and he brought back with him one of the most informative accounts now extant.

But the greatest medieval Jewish traveller was Benjamin of Tudela, who in 1160 left his native city in Navarre, traversing in the course of the next thirteen years the whole of Southern Europe, Northern Africa, Byzantium, and much of Asia. His *Itinerary*, a classic of Jewish literature, is replete with information concerning not only the various Jewish communities which he visited, but also the social and economic structure of those places through which he passed. For this reason he is still universally consulted and quoted by every writer on twelfth-century history—all the more readily since, by universal consent, he was the first medieval traveller who told the truth. Another adventurous medieval Jewish explorer, whose account is still classical, was Benjamin's contemporary, Petahia of Regensburg.

But there must have been many more, whose identity has not been preserved for posterity. When the great Arabic traveller, Ibn Battuta, arrived in the Turkish city of Majar about 1332, he was amazed to find there a Spanish Jew who had preceded him, making his way overland through Constantinople, Anatolia, and Trans-caucasia, a four months' journey in all. The experiences of later Jewish travellers form an integral part of the history of European exploration. Thus, the venture-some sixteenth-century pioneer, Pedro Texeira of Lis-bon, who explored the overland route between Italy and the Far East with a degree of detail hitherto un-known and wrote an account of his travels which was translated into many languages, was a Marrano. He was by no means the only one of his kind who blazed a trail in regions as yet unexplored.

Even in the heroic period of English exploration, Jews played a significant part. When England first entered into the race in the days of Elizabeth, Jews were little known in the country. Nevertheless, the English pioneers did not scruple to take Jews into their service as interpreters, when they had the good fortune to find them. Thus one accompanied Sir James Lancaster, when he sailed to the Pacific in command of the first fleet of the East India Company in 1601. In the second great period of British exploration, which began in the eighteenth century, the Jews were estab-lished in England and played their part. Israel Lyons the Younger, son of the Instructor in Hebrew at the University of Cambridge, and a well known botanist in his day, accompanied Captain Phipps, subsequently Lord Mulgrave, as principal astronomer in his Arctic Expedition in 1773. Among the other members was a diminutive midshipman named Horatio Nelson, who had on that occasion his classical encounter with a polar bear. It was not long after, that Captain Moses Ximenes, subsequently Sir Maurice Ximenes, led a band of adventurers, partly Jewish, who proposed to establish a colony in West Africa. The party occupied the island of Bulama and raised the British flag, but after several conflicts with the natives they were compelled to withdraw. It was characteristic that one of their first cares after landing had been to organize an educational system for the children.

The next generation provides us with the adventurous figure of Nathaniel Isaacs, born in Canterbury in 1808. In 1822 he left England for St. Helena, where he struck up a great friendship with Lieutenant King, R.N., whom he accompanied on an expedition to the Cape of Good Hope in 1825. They were shipwrecked off the coast of Natal, and before long Isaacs was engrossed in a career of exploration and adventure. For seven years he travelled through the Zulu and Fumos countries, in addition to visiting the Comoro Islands. The party had interviews with Chaka, the great Zulu king, and took the coast lands under their protection. After King's death, Isaacs was made Principal Chief of Natal. His work, *Travels and Adventures in Eastern Africa*, which gives the first reliable account of the topography and ethnology of the country, was republished by the Riebeck Society in a centenary re-issue in 1937.

Another intrepid Jewish explorer of the nineteenth century was Eduard Karl Oscar Theodor Schnitzer. A native of Oppeln, in Silesia, he was baptized in childhood (as were so many other German Jews at that period, in order to assist their careers) and after graduating as doctor of medicine, found the call of the Near East irresistible. In 1875, he joined General Gordon at Khartoum, assuming the name of Emin. When Gordon became Governor General of the Sudan three years later, he appointed Emin Governor of the equatorial provinces. Here he served with considerable distinction for some years. After the fall of Khartoum, he was entirely isolated. Nevertheless, he held out for two more years, and became the center of European interest in Africa in place of his dead leader. Stanley made his way to relieve him. At first he refused to desert his post, but at last was persuaded to accompany his rescuer back to civilization. Inactivity was however impossible for a man of his nature, and he undertook a semi-political voyage of exploration into Central Africa for Germany in 1890. Though disowned and recalled, he persisted. Arabs ultimately brought to the coast the news that Emin Pasha had been assassinated in the autumn of 1892.[1]

Thus we are brought to our own days, when only the Arctic has retained its secret and its glamor. The part played by Jews in contemporary Arctic explora-

[1] It is worthwhile to recall, in this connection, that Professor Palmer, Captain Gill and Lieutenant Charrington, who were murdered treacherously by Arabs while travelling in the Sinai Desert in 1882, were accompanied by a Jew, Bakhor Hassun, whose remains lie with theirs in St. Paul's Cathedral. Another associate of General Gordon was Louis Arthur Lucas, the explorer of Lake Albert Nyanza, whose premature death alone probably prevented him from attaining a very high reputation.

tion has been noteworthy. Greely had a young Jew, Sergeant Edward Israel, with him as astronomer on his Arctic expedition of 1881–4. He was the youngest of the party, yet, even when sick, he refused to accept more than his usual ration of food, with the result that he died before the expedition returned. In 1882, he had rendered especially important services in determining the possibility of an overland route to Hazen Land in Greenland through the Bellows Valley. In reading the burial service, it is said, General Greely remembered the dead man's faith and modified the ritual accordingly.

On General Nobile's ill-fated aerial Arctic expedition of 1928, he was accompanied by Aldo Pontremoli, a nephew of Luigi Luzzatti, the former Italian Prime Minister, who died under circumstances of particular gallantry. By a coincidence, the Russian expedition of relief, but for whose aid the whole party would have perished, was under the direction of Rudolf Samoilo-witsch, who in 1931 conducted a Zeppelin flight over the Pole.

As with the frozen north, so with the parched deserts of Central Asia. From 1899 to 1926, Sir Aurel (Mark) Stein, by his repeated expeditions in Chinese Turkestan, Central Asia, and Western China, not only widened geographical knowledge, but also revealed the treasures and records of a lost civilization. He had only one rival, Sven Hedin, the Swedish explorer of the Gobi Desert and discoverer of the Hedin Mountains. The latter is, as it happens, a descendant of Aaron Isak, the founder of the Jewish community in Sweden.

Other great Jewish explorers of the nineteenth century include Arminius Vambéry (Bamberger), a phenomenal linguist, who was the first European to traverse the heart of unknown Persia, living there for over two years disguised as a native Moslem; Nathaniel Wallich, Asiatic botanist and explorer of Assam; the converts Joseph Wolff and Henry Aaron Stern, who, as missionaries among the Jews, explored Bokhara and Abyssinia respectively; Samuel Sandberg, pioneer traveller in Thibet; Angelo Castelbolognesi, who explored the Sudan; Eduard Foa, who discovered the sources of the Zambesi; Hermann Burchardt, who perished in the Arabian desert in 1909; Siegfried Langer, murdered in the Yemen in 1882; Vladimir Jochelson and L. Sternberg, who explored northern Siberia; Isaac Israel Heyes, who led an expedition to Greenland in 1860, where it joined up with another under the direction of August Sonntag; and many lesser members of enterprises of the same nature in every quarter of the globe.

The same spirit which forced Jews towards new spheres of economic activity urged them to act as pioneers of European enquiry in unexplored regions of the world. Even the Ghetto was unable to quench that spirit of adventure which is to be found in all men alike.

CHAPTER V. *The Jew in Letters*

I

From the beginning of their life in Europe, long before the present national languages and literatures were known, Jews played a prominent part in European cultural life. In Alexandria, when it was the intellectual capital of the Hellenic world, there were Jewish poets, Jewish playwrights, Jewish philosophers, Jewish historians, all writing in Greek and with an eye upon the plaudits of the non-Jewish public. One of the first European Jews known to us by name is Caecilius of Calacte, in Sicily, who flourished in the first century B.C. at Rome. Characteristically enough, he was the representative in his day of the Attic style of oratory, in contradistinction to the verbose Asiatic style which had begun to gain ground. Similarly, he and his Greek friend Dionysius of Halicarnassus were the only appreciative students of Latin literature at a time when it was the fashion to sneer at it in literary circles. The quantity of his work must have been considerable, though not much has survived. However, there can be little doubt that he deserves credit for the famous passage in the classic treatise on *The Sublime*, ascribed to Longinus, which permeated English thought in the

eighteenth century: "Sublimity is the echo of greatness of soul. This is illustrated . . . from the legislator
of the Jews, no ordinary man, . . . who wrote in the
opening words of his Laws: 'God said, Let there be
light, and there was light; let there be land, and there
was land.' "

From the period of this pioneer of twenty centuries
ago the participation of the Jews in the cultural life of
Europe has been almost continuous. For ever since
then, as, indeed, for some time previous, Jews have not
only lived in Europe, but also have spoken and written
European languages. Indeed, the tradition which they
preserved was in some ways purer than that of their
neighbors. A brilliant American scholar, by a detailed
analysis of the various Judaeo-Romance dialects which
were formerly spoken and written by the Jews of
Spain, Portugal, France, Provence, Italy, etc., has
traced these dialects back to a prototype used by the
ancestors of the Jews throughout Europe before the
downfall of the Roman Empire. What the educated
Italian or Frenchman of a generation ago considered
peculiarities of Jewish speech are thus in many cases
relics of an earlier age, before modern Italian or French
was dreamed of, but when the Jews were already
familiar figures throughout the Latin world.

Everywhere, moreover, they translated their litur-
gies and their biblical texts into the language of the
country, which was their own natural native speech.
The importance of these relics for the study of modern
European languages is considerable, and scholars are
becoming more and more appreciative of the fact. The

eleventh-century Franco-Jewish commentator, Solomon ben Isaac of Troyes, or Rashi, who was consulted so much by Christian exegetes of the late Middle Ages, was in the habit of translating difficult words and expressions into the vernacular. These notes, embedded in his various commentaries, are among the oldest specimens of the old French vocabulary. They are eagerly consulted and collected by philologists and a small library has by now been written about them. In 1290, and again, finally, in 1540, the Jews were expelled from Apulia, in South Italy. Many of them ultimately found refuge in Corfu, where an independent Apulian synagogue existed until our own day. With them they brought not only their dialect, but also some of their religious poetry, written in Apulian, though in Hebrew characters. These are among the oldest specimens of Apulian literature now extant.

The Jews were expelled from Spain and Portugal with a refinement of cruelty at the close of the fifteenth century. Their descendants in the Balkans and North Africa still speak the Castilian of their fathers; and students of Spanish dialects and folk-lore find them a happy hunting-ground for·a reconstruction of the life and literature of medieval Spain. Similarly, one might have imagined that Germany would have been proud of the tenacity of her Jewish children who, migrating eastwards at the close of the Middle Ages, preserved in an alien land the German which their fathers had spoken in the Rhineland when the great Cathedral of Speyer was still being built. Even the Arthurian romances and the Tales of the Round

Table, which did not lack Jewish affinities, were familiar to medieval Jews and are extant in old Hebraic
versions, while Sir Bevis of Hampton actually gave his
name to a whole Ghetto cycle.

For the larger part of their literature, to be sure, the
Jews used Hebrew, just as Christians used Latin, and
for the same reasons. It was a semi-sacred tongue; it
was universally read and understood, irrespective of
national and linguistic boundaries; it was of proper
scholastic status. But what they wrote was to a considerable extent European in conception. Hence it
happened that Jewish writers of the period, Moses
Maimonides, Levi of Bagnols, Abraham ibn Ezra,
could be translated into Latin and take their place as
the mental food of the schoolmen. The canonists' legal
opinions were closely paralleled by the rabbinical
Sheëlot uTeshubot. The medieval moralists of the
Rhineland had their counterparts in the *Judengasse*.
Thus, there is little essential difference between the
writings of Berthold of Regensburg and those of his
Jewish contemporary and fellow-townsman Judah,
compiler of the collection of godly anecdotes known
as *The Book of the Pious*. When the German moralists
turned to mysticism, their Jewish neighbors did also,
so that the flights of Master Eckhart (now considered
the incarnation of the "Aryan" spirit, though influenced by the medieval Jewish philosophers and, in
our own day, edited by a Jew) have their parallels in,
for example, those of Eleazar of Worms, author of the
Hebrew ethical classic, the *Rokeach*.

But the most remarkable instance is that classic of

medieval churchmen, the *Fons Vitae*, which was ascribed to the authorship of a Spanish Christian named
Avicebron, and studied with religious reverence by
successive generations of medieval theologians. It was
only in the course of the last century that it was discovered that the author was the synagogal poet, Rabbi
Solomon ibn Gabirol, called "the nightingale of piety."
Nothing could illustrate more forcibly the essential
unity of European culture, whether Gentile or Jewish,
in the Middle Ages.

2

It frequently happened that the parallels converged,
so that we find Jewish writers contributing actively,
even in the age of degradation, to the literary store of
their environment. Thus, in Italy, one of the members
of the poetical school, of whom Dante was the greatest,
was Immanuel of Rome, who, besides being a physician, Hebrew poet, and exegete, was a familiar member
of the circle of the *dolce stil nuovo*. He exchanged
sonnets in Italian with the litterateurs of the time. His
patron was Can Grande della Scala of Verona, to
whom the poet dedicated a *bisbiglio* describing his
busy court. Here he may have met Dante, with whom
he appears to have been on terms of some intimacy,
to judge from the fact that Busone da Gubbio sent him
a sonnet of condolence on the greater poet's death.
The volume of his Italian work which has survived
shows the promise, if not the final fulfilment, of a
genius no less than that displayed in his Hebrew writings. It may be added that Immanuel of Rome is

thought to be the medium through which Dante received (p. 55) his knowledge of the Moslem cosmogony, of which such important influences have been found in his work.

Symptomatic of the Italian outlook of Immanuel of Rome, in whatever language he wrote, was his collection of Hebrew poems, known as the Compositions of Immanuel. In this work, one of the first to introduce to non-Moslem Europe the loosely-woven narrative framework perfected by Boccaccio in his *Decameron*, we find a picture of a completely Italian environment, European literary forms such as the sonnet, a good measure of the licentious spirit of Italian poetry of the time, and, above all, an imitation, or perhaps it is more correct to say a parody, of the *Divine Comedy*.

This work deserves closer examination, for it follows Dante's model from beginning to end. It commences, like the *Inferno*, with an allusion to the age of the author at the time of composition; it finishes, like the *Paradiso*, with a glimpse of the stars. The text is closely modelled on the Italian original—without, indeed, its profundity, its polish or its clarity, for this was only a trifle appended by the author to a miscellaneous collection of poems. The outstanding point of difference lies in the fact that, in *Tophet and Eden*, there is no Purgatory, in conformity with Jewish theological ideas. One other minor feature, however, is noteworthy, for it illustrates strikingly the difference between the Jewish and Christian outlook at the time. Dante places in his Inferno all who did not believe in Jesus and in Christianity, including even those who flourished before the beginning of the Christian Era, and so could neither have known nor believed. In striking contrast to this, Immanuel reserves a place of honor in his Paradise for non-Jews, "the righteous of the nations of the world," and elaborates, subsequently, on his ideal of an eclectic religion, embodying the best in all faiths.[1] This tolerance contrasts strangely with the contemporary Catholic doctrine, which put the proportion of "saved" to the "damned" at one to a thousand, or even one to a hundred thousand.

In other countries, similarly, the Jews participated in literary activity in the vernacular from a very early date. Medieval France knew at least one Jewish *troubadour*, Bonfils de Narbonne. The thirteenth century produced a German Jewish *minnesinger* in Süsskind von Trimberg, who sang of the virtue of woman and the nobility of man, and took high rank among the itinerant poets of his day. In the next century, one Samson Pine collaborated (1336) with Claus Wysse and Philipp Kolin of Strassburg, in adapting into German a French version of the *Parsifal*. In the preface Pine is referred to repeatedly as a Jew and is thanked both for translating the poem into German and finding rhymes for it, the lion's share of the work. Another name that may be mentioned in this connection is that of Johannes Pauli, a converted Jew of the age of Luther, who became a Franciscan friar and was a popular preacher in his day. He is better

[1] Another significant innovation of Immanuel is his placing in the Inferno a certain person "because he was miserly with his knowledge"—a failing for which perhaps only a medieval Jew could condemn a man to punishment in the hereafter!

remembered, however, for his famous collection of jests, *Schimpf und Ernst,* which, first published in 1519, ran through innumerable editions, imitations, and amplifications. Some of the stories were taken over in the *Hundred Merry Tales,* a favorite work of Elizabethan England, used lavishly by Shakespeare himself.

Most marked of all was the participation of the Jews in the literary life of Spain, which had a pronounced effect upon European literature as a whole. Here such activity began at least as early as the thirteenth century, Jews beginning to write in Spanish before it was either fashionable or common. Indeed, modern Spanish is in great measure the creation of the Jewish translators at the court of Alfonso the Wise, who molded the despised Mozarabic dialect into a literary medium of considerable richness and force. Spanish Jewish literature of the Middle Ages would fill many volumes, and a good deal of it is of high quality. Thus the Catalan "Aphorisms" of Judah Bonsenior of Barcelona (fl. 1287–1305), and the "Moral Proverbs" of Rabbi Santob of Carrion, dedicated to Pedro IV of Castile (1357–1360), are considered classics by students of Spanish literature and are read even today.

Spain expelled her Jews in 1492; yet, because of the forced baptisms which had been common for a century before that date, Jewish blood permeated the whole peninsula. Sancho Panza could perhaps (and did) pride himself that his blood was free from any admixture of Jew or Moor, but it is not so certain that his master would have been in the same fortunate

position. It is possible that there was Jewish blood in
the veins of some of the greatest Spaniards of the fifteenth, sixteenth, seventeenth, and eighteenth centuries.
In many cases, it can be proved. The group of poets
at the court of Henry IV of Castile, whose writings
throw so much light upon the social history of the
time, were to a large extent of Jewish birth. Foremost
among them was the impudent Antón de Montoro,
"the ragman of Cordova," who has been called "the
most sympathetic and attractive poet in the entire
Castilian Parnassus of the fifteenth century." He went
out of his way to call attention to his origin in his
audacious satires. Others were Juan de España, Juan
de Valladolid, Rodrigo Cota de Maguaque, and the
rest. Conditions were very much the same in Aragon,
where the revival of vernacular literature under Juan II
was due in considerable measure to the genius of
persons of Jewish blood, and was in part inspired by
the *converso*, Alfonso de Santa Maria. Similarly the
eminent physician, Francisco Lopez de Villalobos, a
classical Spanish stylist, was of Jewish extraction, as
was also Pedro Guttierez de Santa Clara, historian of
the conquest of Peru. And in more recent times, the
famous historical novelist, Camilo Castelo Branco, who
may be described without any exaggeration as the
Portuguese Walter Scott, is descended from a Jewish
family.

Two Marrano contributors to Spanish literature
deserve more detailed consideration because of their
influence on European letters as a whole.

Luis Ponce de Leon was perhaps the greatest lyric

poet that Spain has produced. Going back to the Bible for his inspiration (possibly this is not entirely a coincidence), he introduced a fresh naturalism into Spanish poetry, which lived on in the poets and romancers who came after him. Today, he is remembered for a few odes and hymns which are said to reveal a majestic and serene simplicity not found again till Wordsworth. In his age, however, he was best known as a theologian, and in his lectures was considered to have shown a sympathy for the reform movement. When he was arrested by the Inquisition in March, 1572, it was discovered in the course of his examination that he was of Jewish blood, a great-grandmother having been "reconciled" by the Inquisition in 1512. This added to the seriousness of the charge against him. He remained in prison for over four years. It was only in the autumn of 1576 that he was able to resume his lectures at Salamanca with the classical remark, "As we were saying the other day." [1]

[1] There is some echo of Ponce de Leon in the writings of two other Spanish poets of New Christian descent—Felipe Godinez, reconciled by the Inquisition at Seville in 1624, who wrote plays on biblical subjects, and Juan Pinto Delgado, whom Menendez y Pelayo considered one of the most inspired Spanish poets of the seventeenth century, and who ended his life as a professing Jew. Juan Perez de Montalvan—the friend, confidant, and publisher of Lope de Vega, and the most prominent Spanish playwright between the latter, and Calderon, whom he inspired—was similarly of New Christian extraction. A contemporary of Calderon's, and his rival for the favors of the theatre-going public of Madrid, was the Marrano Antonio Enriquez Gomez, or Enrique Enriquez de Paz, condemned *in absentia* by the Spanish Inquisition in 1660. In the following century, Antonio da Silva was perhaps the foremost Portuguese playwright, one of his comedies being performed

A final illustration may be added. Spain's most important contribution to European literature before *Don Quixote* was *Calisto and Meliboea*, better known as *Celestina*, first printed in 1499. It is a tragi-comedy in prose of two lovers, and was very popular in its day, having been published time after time and translated into many European languages. In the judgment of the great critic, Menendez y Pelayo, the work would have deserved the first place in Spanish literature, had Cervantes not written his masterpiece. Its name became a byword, its passages were universally quoted, and its characters and action long served as model in an age when plagiarism was not yet a vice. In the words of the *Encyclopaedia Britannica* it "caused the new theatre to make a gigantic step onwards. This astonishing novel taught the Spaniards the art of dialogue, and for the first time exhibited persons of all classes of society speaking in harmony with their natural surroundings, thinking and acting in accordance with their condition of life."

Little was known about Fernando de Rojas, the author of this work, until the recent discovery of an Inquisitional record made it clear that he was a *converso*, i.e., a baptized Jew, hampered for that reason in the exercise of his profession, and in addition

---

at Lisbon on the evening of the day when he was burned at the stake.

The name of one more Portuguese man of letters, out of many, may be added to this list—Didaco Pyrrho, of Evora, a foremost neo-Latin poet of the sixteenth century, who ended his days as a Jew at Ragusa under the name of Isaiah Cohen.

married to the daughter of another *converso* who had
been put on trial for judaizing.

The importance of *Celestina* in European literature
was vast. But for our purpose it is enough to point
out its influence on William Shakespeare. Above all,
it had a distinct share in the ancestry of *Romeo and
Juliet*, who were, as a modern critic has put it, "own
children" to Rojas' tragic lovers. Similarly, the "old
bawd" who sustains the comic part foreshadows that
most perfect of Shakespearian characters, Juliet's
nurse.

3

The extent of the interaction of Jewish and other
elements in European culture is illustrated in England
all the more strikingly if we go back to the period
of that astonishing renascence of letters under the
Tudors, when Jews were virtually absent from the
country.[1] Yet English literature of that glorious period was profoundly imbued with the influence of
individual Jews or persons of Jewish blood.

It is, of course, absurd to overlook the Bible in this
connection. Shakespeare did not read and speak, as
does the Englishman of today, an English saturated
with biblical language: he belonged to only the second generation to whom the Bible in English was
readily accessible. But, nevertheless, a recent inquiry

[1] It is possible to go back even further: Geoffrey Chaucer's
Treatise on the Astrolabe, one of the earliest uses of English for
scientific purposes, is based upon a Latin version of the Arabic
treatise, written by the Jewish scholar Mashaala.

has demonstrated the great use which he made of the Scriptures. His biblical knowledge was, moreover, the fruit of deep love and study, developing more and more with the passage of years. He had his favorite books—Genesis, Job, Proverbs, Isaiah, in the Old Testament, as well as Ecclesiasticus in the Apocrypha, and St. Matthew in the New—echoes of which may be discovered in his own magnificent lines. Deprive him of his biblical, i.e., his Semitic, background, and the Shakespeare we know would not be quite the same.

But it is more significant to discover in Shakespeare Hebraic influences much nearer to his own day. Mention has been made above (p. 61) of the eleventh-century Spanish convert Petrus Alphonsi of Toledo, whose *Training School for the Clergy* contains all manner of entertaining fables for homiletic use. These became the common heritage of all Europe, a number being incorporated in the famous medieval collection, *Gesta Romanorum*. Some are printed at the end of Caxton's English *Aesop* of 1483, being thus among the earliest products of the English printing press. More noteworthy still, the collection was the source of many of Chaucer's stories. It was first printed in English by Wynkyn de Worde and republished in 1577. This latter edition was familiar to Shakespeare and greatly used by him. Similarly, the *Hundred Merry Tales*, another Elizabethan classic which Shakespeare read to good purpose, was based in part, as we have seen, on the *Schimpf und Ernst* of Johannes Pauli, a German friar of Jewish birth. Add to this the influence of Fernando de Rojas' *Celestina* and of

Leone Ebreo's *Dialogues of Love* (exerted through the medium of Castiglione's famous treatise on "The Courtier," which taught Europe the ideal of the gentleman) and it will be realized that the "Semitic" influence on Elizabethan literature was far from negligible.

A good deal of Shakespeare's knowledge of things Italian, one of the most characteristic features and the most favored sources of his plays, is derived from John Florio, the translator-in-ordinary to Elizabethan England. The latter's great Italian-English dictionary was probably one of the most influential works of the century. Shakespeare without Florio would certainly have been different. The genius would have been there, and the humor, and the language, but the atmosphere of many of the plays would have been strangely unfamiliar. It is remarkable to find, then, that Florio was of Jewish extraction. His father was Michelangelo Florio, preacher of the Italian Protestant congregation in London and biographer of the ill-fated Lady Jane Grey. In his *Apologia* (Chamogasco, 1557), Michelangelo Florio states: "I was never a Jew nor son of a Jew, but born of a father and mother baptized as papists like yourself; *but if you should say that my progenitors were Hebrews before baptism, this I will not deny.*"

John Florio is best remembered today for his translation of the *Essays* of Michel de Montaigne, which is still classical. The latter was, of course, one of the great figures in sixteenth-century letters. It was he who for the first time made French prose into a literary medium of the highest order, elevated every-day life and personal happenings into a subject-matter for great literature, and invented the essay form, in which the French were afterwards to excel. But what were the elements that went to make up this great Frenchman of letters, Michel Eyquem de Montaigne? His father's name, *Eyquem*, he claimed to be of English origin, deriving perhaps from the village of Ockham. His mother, on the other hand, was Antoinette Louppes or Lopez, and was a member of a Spanish family of Bordeaux. A recent discovery has proved that her progenitors belonged to a New Christian family of Calatayud, that more than one of them had suffered at the hands of the Inquisition and that they were descended from the Jewish clan of Pazagón. It is, possibly, to this admixture of blood that the great essayist owed that slightly sceptical tone which seems to us today the most French of his qualities.

Montaigne's influence in letters was, of course, immense. The new spirit which he introduced into European literature gave an impetus which is not exhausted even today. Permission for an English translation of the *Essays* was issued in London by the Stationers' Company in the very year of their publication in Paris. Shakespeare was acquainted with them, echoing the language sometimes, the thought more frequently.[1] Francis Bacon's elder brother knew the author per-

---

[1] See especially Gonzalo's description of the ideal commonwealth in *The Tempest* II. i. 154 ff., which is nearer a paraphrase than a reminiscence of Florio's version of Montaigne.

sonally, and the indebtedness of Bacon's Essays to Montaigne's may be noted throughout. It is a coincidence only that the classical English translation of Montaigne's Essays was due to John Florio, who was similarly of Jewish extraction, but the two facts, taken in conjunction, illustrate how potent was the influence of Jews on English letters even when religious intolerance excluded them rigidly from the country.

It was with the seventeenth century and the publication of the Authorized Version of the Bible that Hebraic influence in English literature rose to its highest point. It reached its climax in John Milton, who might almost be said to have thought in Hebrew, though he expressed himself in English. This was not entirely dependent, as was probably the case with the majority of his contemporaries, upon acquaintance with the English Bible. He was a competent Hebrew scholar, with a fair knowledge of rabbinical lore, which is manifest in *Paradise Lost*. To what was this due? The authority who has made the most detailed inquiries into the subject speaks only of his university studies at the feet of the erudite Hoseah Meade at Cambridge. But it may be assumed that, during his travels in Italy in 1637–9, he encountered some learned Jews, possibly even in the company of Galileo, who is known not to have been averse to their society. There is evidence, moreover, that the blind poet made the acquaintance of Menasseh ben Israel during the latter's mission to Oliver Cromwell in 1655–7 to secure permission for his coreligionists to resettle in England, and it is by no means improbable that erudite conversations between the two men, who had so much in common, may have ensued.

But Milton was only one out of many. George Herbert and John Donne echoed the Psalmist, Herrick quoted the "Ethics of the Fathers," Bacon cites the biblical commentaries of Don Isaac Abravanel, and even so spontaneous a production as Walton's *Compleat Angler* is filled with Hebraic lore, obtained partly from literary sources and partly through the medium of the learned globe-trotter, Sir Henry Wotton, while he was "lying abroad" for his sovereign. It goes without saying that such influences were not confined to England. The biblical inspiration of many of the dramas of Racine in France, and of Metastasio in Italy, is too obvious to require elaboration; and this spiritual atmosphere is known to have been reinforced, in some instances at least, by contemporary influences and personal association.

4

Direct Jewish participation in English literary and intellectual life began in the generation which followed their re-admission to England. In the group of poets of the mid-eighteenth century (not a very inspired period, it must be admitted) Moses Mendes, a grandson of one of the pioneer settlers, was an interesting figure. His works were produced at Covent Garden and Drury Lane; he wrote dramatic pieces, which were set to music by Boyce and Burney, and poems and songs, which echoed Spenser piously, if without inspiration. He wrote sometimes in collaboration with another poet of Jewish birth—Dr. Isaac Schomberg, who attended Garrick in his last illness, and whose brother Ralph was one of the most prolific and most uniformly unsuccessful writers of the generation.

The last years of the century produced, together with numerous writers of less ability, two, at least, whose role in English letters was far from negligible. Isaac D'Israeli would probably be better remembered today were his reputation not overshadowed by that of his son. His novels are, indeed, as dead as most novels of that period, and his *Commentaries on the Life and Reign of Charles I* have outlived their usefulness. But, on the other hand, his series of literary anecdotes, beginning with *Curiosities of Literature* published in modest anonymity in 1791, and ending with *Amenities of Literature*, completed when he was old and blind, in 1840, still retain their interest after being favorite works with more than one generation. But his literary ability was far excelled by his son's. If Benjamin Disraeli had not attained an abiding place in English history by his qualities as a statesman, he would be known as the most scintillating political novelist that England has ever known.

Just after Isaac D'Israeli began the publication of his gravely mature works, an infant prodigy named Francis Cohen, son of Meyer Cohen, of Kentish Town, aged eight years, translated Homer's *Battle of the Frogs* into French. The resultant work was published in 1797, by his proud father, Meyer Cohen, a stock-broker. Later, Francis Cohen changed his faith and adopted his wife's name Palgrave, under which he became famous. He wrote among other works *The Rise and Progress of the English Commonwealth*, the earliest important study of English constitutional history based upon the records. He may be regarded as perhaps the first English scientific historian.

Sir Francis Palgrave founded a dynasty almost unique in the history of English letters. His eldest son was Francis Turner Palgrave, professor of poetry at Oxford and compiler of that classical anthology, *The Golden Treasury;* the second was William Gifford Palgrave, missionary, oriental traveller and diplomat, author of *A Year's Journey through Central and Eastern Arabia;* the third was Robert Harry Inglis Palgrave, editor of *The Dictionary of Political Economy;* the fourth, Sir Reginald Francis Douce Palgrave, Clerk of the House of Commons from 1886 to 1900, was the editor of *Rules of Procedure of the House of Commons* and author of various works on constitutional practice, as well as a proficient water color artist.

A few other names belonging to this period deserve mention. John Adolphus, member of a well-known Anglo-American family, published among other historical works, a *History of England* from 1760 to 1883, and *Biographical Memoirs of the French Revolution;* his son, John Leycester Adolphus, a well-known critic in his day, was the first to argue methodically in favor of Scott's authorship of the Waverley Novels; and Grace Aguilar, author of many historical writings and novels which still retain their charm.

The second half of the nineteenth century naturally saw, with increase in numbers and growing acclimatization, greater Jewish participation in English literary life. Sir Arthur Wing Pinero summed up the tendencies of the age in his plays, such as *The Second Mrs. Tanqueray* and *Trelawney of the Wells*, and gave English drama a new heart. It was he who with Henry Arthur Jones rescued the English stage from artificiality, thus paving the way for Shaw, Galsworthy, and the other playwrights who were not afraid of ideas in the theatre. A little later was Alfred Sutro, a dramatist, but memorable too for his translation of Maeterlinck's *Life of the Bee*, which he rewrote seven times before venturing upon publication. Israel Zangwill's genius would perhaps have received even wider recognition had he not been so intimately associated with the Children of the Ghetto; yet the new style of genre-fiction which he introduced had a considerable influence on English letters. Max Beerbohm, though best known as a caricaturist, is among the great masters of English prose. The list may be extended almost indefinitely.

Two more figures at least of the first importance in this generation were of Jewish blood. Bret Harte, the first American imaginative writer to speak to England in her own idiom, was a grandson of Bernard Hart, a London Jew who had migrated to the New World; while Sir Henry Newbolt, chronicler and poet of the English navy, was descended from Dr. Samuel Solomon of Liverpool.

In our own day, the list becomes more crowded, and only a few of the many can be mentioned here. It is the considered opinion of many critics that the greatest loss inflicted by the War of 1914–18 on English letters was the death in action of Isaac Rosenberg, a young East End Jew, whose slender volume of surviving verse suffices to place him in the front rank of contemporary poets. Another poet who made his niche at this time was Siegfried Sassoon, who subsequently achieved fame, perhaps immortality, for his pictures of the atmosphere of the Shires. Other living poets include Humbert Wolfe and E. H. W. Meyerstein. Leonard Merrick was one of the most brilliant English short story writers, almost worthy of being ranked with Maupassant. There is only space for mention of W. L. George, Stephen Hudson, Arthur Waley, Louis Golding, Gilbert Frankau, Naomi Jacob, G. B. Stern, and so on.

In another sphere, Philip Guedalla is one of the few contemporary historians who has learned to combine brilliance with research; L. B. Namier has placed the study of English political history of the mid-eighteenth century on a new basis; and Gertrude Millin, besides being a novelist of distinction, may be said to have brought South African historical literature to maturity. In America (where Emma Lazarus, verses by whom are inscribed on the Statue of Liberty, set a great tradition three-quarters of a century ago), the number of prominent contemporary Jewish writers is too long even to list; but Elmer Rice, Fannie Hurst, Ludwig Lewisohn, John Cournos, Gertrude Stein, George and Robert Nathan, Edna Ferber, Michael Gold, Maurice Samuel, Alter Brody, Babbette

Deutsch, Louis Untermeyer, Waldo Frank, deserve at least passing mention.

The contribution of Jews to Shakespearian research, which should be considered the quintessence of English studies, has been particularly high. It was in the 1880's that Sir Sidney Lee began his series of Shakespearian studies, which culminated in his monumental *Life of Shakespeare*—rapturously greeted at the time of its appearance, and still a standard work, having passed through many editions. Yet perhaps Lee's most important contribution to English cultural life was in the capacity of editor (previously assistant editor) of the *Dictionary of National Biography*, to which he contributed over 600 biographies from his own pen, and which might not have been completed but for his systematic persistence. Israel Gollancz approached English studies at first from the philological side and did much work for the Early English Texts Society. His edition of Shakespeare is still a model of its kind and set an example for the popularization of the classics. His most enduring influence, however, was probably as organizer and first secretary of the British Academy, which he raised to a level of dignity and scholarship proper to the Academy of a great empire. The trio of eminent Jewish Shakespearian scholars is completed by Marion Spielmann, art critic and historian, who made an intensive study of the portraiture of William Shakespeare, as a result of which we have a much more accurate idea of the poet's actual appearance and of a number of incidental points connected with his biography and bibliography. In Germany, the most recent of a long line of scholarly interpreters of Shakespeare was Professor Friedrich Gundolf, whose rendering of the English poet in German is one of the most superb achievements in the history of translation. If the sages of Heidelberg are today able to claim Shakespeare as a kindred Nordic spirit, it is partly because he found in Germany so gifted a "Semitic" interpreter.[1]

There is something in the background of the Jew which makes him realize the existence of countries other than his own, and hence provides him with a human world outlook. He seems to have, accordingly, a certain faculty for entering into the spirit of other countries and making contributions to their cultural heritage seldom paralleled by foreigners of other antecedents. To take the field of English history alone, the greatest authority on the laws of the Anglo-Saxons was a German professor, Felix Liebermann, whose writings in this field have not been superseded. In our own generation, the keenest survey of English history in the early part of the nineteenth century is that of Elie Halévy, which has received the compliment of translation into the language in which it might rationally have been expected to be written. There is not quite the same solidity, though far more brilliance, in the studies of André Maurois, which he wrote in order to interpret England to the French, but which have in a way served to interpret the English to themselves. And in the days of bitterness which followed

[1] It may be added that Shakespeare's interpreter to Denmark was the Jew, Georg Brandes.

the War of 1914–18, it was Paul Cohen-Portheim
who, unembittered by years of unnecessary suffering
in an internment camp, set about interpreting the English character to England's erstwhile enemies, and thus
laying the basis for a better understanding.

The most remarkable fact about this group of litterateurs is perhaps its lack of homogeneity. It is remarkable, not so much for its distinction, as for its
comprehensiveness. For the past two centuries Jewish writers of various degrees of eminence have
contributed to English literature in every sphere and
from every angle. It is impossible to trace in them
any common factor; they are as motley, as varied, and
as inchoate as English literature itself. This is amus-
ingly illustrated in the following instances, which
show how far the process of intellectual assimilation
has proceeded. That somewhat absurd composition,
"Home, Sweet Home," is one of the songs in the opera
Clari, the author of which was the American John
Howard Payne, son of one Sarah Isaacs and grandson
of a converted Jew. When it first became known,
perhaps the most popular English song was "The
Death of Nelson"; this was the production of John
Braham, formerly a synagogue choir-boy. "A Life on
the Ocean Wave," "Cheer, Boys, Cheer," and hundreds of less known songs were composed by Henry
Russell, a professing Jew (father both of Sir Landon
Ronald, the musician, and of William Clark Russell,
the writer of sea-stories). It is not suggested for one
moment that these productions are to be numbered
among the masterpieces of modern literature, but they

demonstrate in a remarkable fashion the manner in which the Jew has identified himself with the literary heritage of the country, at its most typical as well as at its best.

5

The German Jewish literary tradition dates back to the Middle Ages, to Süsskind von Trimberg, Samson Pine, and Johannes Pauli. How far this literature might have developed but for the virulent persecution which raged at the close of the Middle Ages, it is impossible to say. The improvement in German Jewish conditions in the middle of the eighteenth century witnessed, however, a revival, associated with the name of Moses Mendelssohn. He was a more important figure in German than in Jewish literary life, though the fact is often overlooked; for it was by his contributions to German letters generally that he first achieved a reputation in intellectual circles, subsequently to be echoed in his own community.

His first important independent work, *Letters on Sentiment* (1755), virtually founded modern German philosophic-aesthetic criticism. His *Phaedon*, a charming adaptation of the Platonic dialogue on immortality, was the most widely read book of its time in Germany, no less for its subject-matter than for its clear style, unusual hitherto in philosophical discussion. It was reprinted time after time, translated into almost every European language, and did more than any other work of the age to enhance the reputation of the German philosophical genius abroad. There was one possible exception, Lessing's famous *Laokoon*, inspired largely by Mendelssohn's writings and by his correspondence with Nicolai. This work diffused the Mendelssohnian point of view in a yet wider circle. Moreover, Mendelssohn's writings were the first to arouse German interest in their native philosophers, in particular Leibniz; and in the formation of the Romantic tradition which dominated Europe for the following generation, his influence was profound. It is something more than a literary curiosity that Samuel Taylor Coleridge, whose best friend at Highgate was the Jewish writer Hyman Hurwitz, was a devoted student of Mendelssohn's philosophical works and that his copies of *Jerusalem* and *Morgenstunden*, preserved in the British Museum, are enriched with manuscript annotations.

Mendelssohn's intellectual interests were inherited by his brilliant daughters and their associates, whose *salons* were the centers of intellectual life in Berlin over some decades. Dorothea's second husband was Friedrich von Schlegel. Her novel *Florentine* (1801) was one of the finest specimens of romantic fiction of the generation, and it was she who introduced Mme. de Stael and Victor Hugo to the German-reading public. Her friend, Rachel Levin, who married Karl August Varnhagen, was another leader of Berlin intellectual life. "The little woman with the great soul," Goethe called her. . . . "She was the first to understand and recognize me." Rachel's brother was Ludwig Robert, poet and dramatist, whose *Die Macht der Verhältnisse* was the first play by a Jew to be presented on the German stage. But the most remarkable and most beautiful of the group was Henrietta Herz, who knew a dozen languages—English so well that she taught it in the household of the Duchess of Courland—and was a brilliant conversationalist.

When the intellectual life of Germany was beginning to stir, the houses of this group of cultured Jewish forerunners of the feminist movement, whose sense of Jewish loyalty, incidentally, was non-existent, formed the principal center. They knew everybody and had met everybody; they were the first to discern the genius in promising young men of letters and to give them their initial encouragement. In their houses, Fichte, Schiller, Niebuhr, Humboldt, Schlegel, and Schleiermacher could meet illustrious foreigners like Mme. de Stael, the Prince de Ligne, and Mirabeau. It was in this melting-pot, presided over by Jewish hostesses, that German literature of the early nineteenth century was molded and invigorated.

The tradition, it must be admitted, was a ponderous one. From this, it was saved by Heinrich Heine—"a German Parisian, a Jewish German, a hated political exile who yearns for a dear, old, homely Germany, a sceptical sufferer with a Christian patience, a romantic poet expressing in classic form the modern spirit, a Jew and poor," as Israel Zangwill characterized him. He and his fellow-Jew, Ludwig Börne, that brilliant stylist and mordant critic, were associated in founding the liberal party, *Young Germany*. More enduring, perhaps, or so it seemed until a few years ago, was their creation of a new standard for German journalism, which they saved from the overwhelming portentousness of the eighteenth century and imbued with a new spirit and technique. This amazing couple, indeed, invented the *feuilleton*, without which the press of Central Europe would now be unthinkable.[1]

Heine's own countrymen never forgave him for his French sympathies. Yet he was, in spite of all, one of the foremost European poets of his age, and one of the greatest German poets of all time. Though his native country has done its best to obliterate his memory, half a dozen at least of his lyrics remain among the most popular in the German language. His *Lorelei* and his *Grenadiers* can hardly be driven out of the recollection of the German child even by anti-Semitic reaction.

At one time Berthold Auerbach rivalled Heine, in popularity at least, and seemed likely to play the same rôle in fiction which the former had done in poetry. Time has brought a truer perspective, yet Auerbach remains one of the great names in German literature of the middle nineteenth century. But there was one profound difference between the two men. Heine's taste, his wit, and his verve, were French, or in any case, non-Teutonic. Auerbach, on the other hand, represented the quintessence of German sentimentality and *Gemütlichkeit*. As was the case in art, a certain objective externality was necessary for the aesthetic appreciation of the slow-moving folk-life of the countryside, and just as Liebermann enshrined the life of the German people in his canvases, so Auerbach

---

[1] The art was brought to perfection by another Jew, Daniel Spitzer, of Vienna.

achieved fame through his warmly intimate pictures of the life of the peasantry of the Black Forest, the heart of unspoiled Germany. Though in his student days he had suffered imprisonment for his democratic views, he later became a staunch advocate of German Nationalism and distinguished himself for his patriotic effusions during the Franco-Prussian War. The fact that he had done so little for his own people did not save him from attack when the anti-Semitic movement raised its poisonous head. This in the end drove him to his death.[1]

Imaginative literature could hardly be said to flourish in the late nineteenth-century Germany after the death of Heine. It is significant, nevertheless, that the most gifted of the German novelists of the time, Paul Heyse, who received the Nobel Prize for literature in 1910 was a half-Jew. He typified the heavy Augustan tradition, today barely readable, though at the time considered the height of good taste. On the other hand, the naturalistic and expressionistic schools, which have revived German literature in our own day and given it a European significance which it never previously enjoyed, provide a disproportionate number of Jewish names. Among these are Jacob Wassermann, Franz Kafka, Stefan Zweig, Arnold

[1] Auerbach is best remembered outside Germany for his novel, *On the Heights*.

Mention may be made in this connection also of Emil Franzos and Georg Hermann, well-known novelists in their day, who, though they devoted their talents in part to the Jewish scene, were much appreciated by the general world of letters. The latter in particular was an imaginative writer of the first rank.

Zweig, Lion Feuchtwanger, Emil Ludwig, Ernst Tol-
ler, Richard Beer-Hoffman, Alfred Neumann, Franz
Werfel, Max Brod, and very many others of less note.
Ernst Lissauer, lyricist and dramatist, became famous
with his patriotic song, "Hassgesang gegen England"
(it is not quite correct to translate it "The hymn of
hate"). And one of the great losses suffered by
German letters in the war of 1914–18 was the death of
the promising poet, Walter Heymann, who fell in
action.

Special attention may be directed to Ludwig Fulda.
His first story appeared in 1884, when he was 22
years of age, and for a generation he remained one of
the most popular as well as the most prolific German
writers. His books were published in edition after
edition, while his play, *Die Zwillingsschwester*, first
produced in 1901, was played throughout Germany
for years. As a playwright, he is noteworthy for his
social dramas, in which, in advance of his age, he used
the theatre as a medium for directing public attention
to problems of the moment.

An even more important place in contemporary
letters is that of the Viennese Jew, Arthur Schnitzler,
one of the foremost dramatists of our generation. His
plays are familiar in the repertoire of many countries.
Apart from this, his influence has been a particularly
potent one in modern German literature, for to him
is partly due the credit for making that naturally
ponderous language more human and the subject-
matter for imaginative treatment more real. Moreover,
it was he who introduced for the first time the medico-

scientific approach which is associated with the term psychoanalysis.

In the field of history, no German Jew has risen to the eminence of Ranke, Mommsen, or Gregorovius, but many have attained a considerable reputation. Thus Robert Davidsohn, the German banker-critic turned historian, whose researches have placed the early history of Florence on an entirely new basis, was a Jew, as was also Ludo Hartmann, historian of Italy in the Middle Ages. A Jew, by birth, was Heinrich Friedjung, the greatest, perhaps, of Austrian historians, whose writings range from *A Life of the Emperor Charles V* to *A History of the Struggle for Supremacy in Germany* (1859–1866), still the best historical introduction to the "Austrian Question." Martin Philippson, son of one of the religious paladins of German Jewry, was forced to leave Germany owing to anti-Semitism, and Brussels, where he then settled, owing to anti-Teutonism. The greater part, however, of his considerable historical output was devoted to strictly non-Jewish subjects. One should mention also the great classical historian Ludwig Friedländer and the medievalists Harry Bresslau and Philipp Jaffé, foremost among the six Jews who collaborated in the *Monumenta Germaniae Historica*.

In connection with historical study, a further point may be accentuated. It is to a German of Jewish stock that Clio owes the popularization of the materialistic interpretation of history, which looks primarily to economic forces and factors for the explanation of historic phenomena. It is not necessary to follow this

school in its wilder extravagances or to its political de-
ductions to realize the solid substratum of truth on
which it rests. There can be no doubt, moreover, as to
the profound influence which it has exercised on contemporary historiography, or the manner in which it
has infused past movements and causes and leaders
with the breath of life.

As is the case with Shakespeare studies in England,
German literary criticism and research may be assessed
by the study of Goethe. All his most scholarly biog-
raphers and interpreters, as it happens, have been Jews.
The pioneer of Goethe studies in Germany was Theodor Creizenach; later experts include Morris, Geiger,
Meyer, Bielschowski, Simmel, Priower, and Gundolf.
For many years, the Goethe Archive in Weimar was
under the direction of Julius Wahle, co-editor of the
standard "Sophien Ausgabe" of the poet's works.
Similarly, it was Eduard von Simson, an outstanding
figure in German politics and law, who founded the
Goethe Gesellschaft.

A final illustration may be presented. When in 1876
the German Ministry of Education decided to elimi-
nate foreign terms and expressions from the German
language, one of the commission assembled for that
purpose was the Jewish lexicographer, Daniel Sanders,
whose researches on his native language have never
been surpassed either in quality or in bulk. Logic
should force present-day purists to believe that the
tongue formed as a literary vehicle by Luther's Bible
translation, made malleable by Mendelssohn, human
by Heine, and purified with the aid of Sanders, is no

longer a proper vehicle for expressing the thoughts of "Nordic" man.

6

The Jew had been a part of European intellectual life for a generation or more, as is apparent from the foregoing pages, when the impact of modernism began. In view of the impression which is widely held, it is necessary to emphasize the fact that the part played by Jews in the origins of this movement was negligible. Of the degenerate leaders of the *fin du siècle,* one only was a Jew, the poor, demented Otto Weininger, who committed suicide at the age of 25. None of the other fathers of modernism were Jewish. On the other hand, the sternest opponent of the modernistic school was Max Nordau, who thundered against these unhealthy tendencies in his *Degeneration,* and whose Jewish allegiance, for he was one of the founders of modern Zionism, was positive.

In France, indeed, the Jewish element in letters tended to the side of convention, or rather conventional unconventionality, typified by Alexander Dumas the younger, if one assumes the truth of the report that he was partially Jewish. There was no truer boulevardier than Philippe Auguste d'Ennery, dramatizer of *Michael Strogoff* and part-author of *The Two Orphans* and some hundreds of other plays. His name was seldom absent from the Parisian playbills for nearly half a century. His *Ambigu* alone was performed 1,000 times. Catulle Mendès, novelist, poet, and dramatist, was one of the most faithful portrayers of

Parisian life under the Third Republic. Georges de Porto-Riche, after a succession of failures, opened a new era in the history of the French stage by his *La Chance de Françoise*, presented at the Théâtre Libre in 1888. He was henceforth ranked as the leader of a school. Tristan Bernard rivalled this success and enriched the French vocabulary with a few immortal characters and phrases; his son, Jacques Bernard, is among the leading dramatists of the younger school in France. There was no suspicion of Jewish coloring in any of these authors; though Henri Bernstein, one of their rivals for the favors of the theater-going Parisians in the early years of the twentieth century, turned his attention to Jewish problems in a couple of his plays, perhaps with more enthusiasm than understanding. Similarly, Baron Henri de Rothschild, aside from his achievements in medicine and philanthropy, made himself something of a reputation as a dramatist under the pen name of André Pascal.

A potent influence was that of Gustave Kahn, one of the leaders of the symbolist school, who introduced into French literature the *vers libre*, "strophes of psychical rather than syllabic unity, variable in number and duration in accordance with musical necessity." Though this new versification has not achieved the sweeping triumph that was at one time expected, it revivified the faltering tradition which was still dominating French poetry. For that reason alone, quite apart from his far-reaching work as editor and critic, Kahn deserves to be remembered as one of the important figures in Parisian letters at the close of the nineteenth century. The *vers libre* was perfected by André Spire, another figure of considerable importance in contemporary French literature. It is noteworthy that both these writers, unlike most of their contemporaries, show particular interest in Jewish subjects and affairs. Spire's enthusiasm had been first aroused at the time of the Dreyfus affair, when he was serving in a cavalry regiment. Among essayists, Julien Benda, the philosopher, and André Suarès, the poet, deserve at least cursory mention.

The literary significance of Marcel Proust, whose mother was Jewish, is particularly great. In his hands, the novel assumed a new form. Introspective analysis began to be used as a medium in fiction for interpreting human emotions. Whether there is anything Jewish in his uncanny faculty is still a matter for inquiry; but it may not be a mere coincidence that Italo Svevo, called by his admirers the Italian Proust, was of Jewish birth. His name was originally Ettore Schmitz. Of Jewish origin, too, is André Maurois, who, in conjunction with Emil Ludwig in Germany, has created a new school of biography, displacing the former ungainly monuments of departed heroes.[1]

---

[1] The names of writers whose appeal is essentially Jewish have been intentionally omitted from this survey, no mention having been made even of the great Hebrew poets, Jehudah haLevi in the Middle Ages and Chaim Nachman Bialik in our own day, or of the latter's contemporary, the philosopher-essayist Ahad Ha-am. Yet it should be realized that a man like Sholem Asch (to cite one outstanding instance), though writing in Yiddish and of a Jewish environment, has become a great force in modern letters generally.

7

In other countries, too, Jews have made their contribution. Thus Denmark, with its comparatively small Jewish community, produced in the past generation Georg Brandes, Professor of Aesthetics at the University of Copenhagen, and one of the outstanding literary critics of his age. He did more perhaps than any other man to enhance the reputation of Danish intellectual life abroad. His brother, Eduard was one of the most successful Danish playwrights of the late nineteenth century, while another brother, Ernst, was a prominent economist. Slightly before their day was Meir Aaron Goldschmidt, who, prevented from qualifying as a physician because of the prevailing anti-Jewish prejudice, became a stormy petrel in journalism and a successful novelist. To him and Georg Brandes is due the opening of Danish intellectual life to modern ideas. Both retained their interest in Judaism, the latter to a marked extent. Henrik Hertz, on the other hand, one of the most prolific and widely translated Danish poets of the nineteenth century was baptized in middle life. Henri Nathansen is another modern Danish-Jewish playwright of international reputation.

Sweden produced Ludwig Oscar Josephson, dramatist, critic, and theatrical producer, pioneer of the New Drama and one of the staunchest supporters of Ibsen and Strindberg; Sophie Elkan, well-known as an historical novelist; and the poet and critic, Oskar Ivar Levertin, the foremost Swedish romanticist.

Holland contributes Herman Heijermans, outstanding modern Dutch novelist, dramatist, and leader of the naturalistic school; Isaak Costa, a famous poet; Israel Querido, who vindicated his origin by turning to the Bible for inspiration; and many others.

Hungary's great names include Franz Molnar, Ludwig Biro, Ludwig Hatvány, Melchior Lengyel, and Andreas Latzko, the Hungarian Barbusse (himself, incidentally, said to be of Jewish extraction).

In Czechoslovakia there are Ottokar Fischer and Frantisek Langer; in Poland, Julian Tuwim and Antoni Slonimski; in Russia, Isaac Babel, the novelist, and Boris Pasternak the lyricist. Fet-Tschenschin, perhaps the greatest Russian lyricist, was of Jewish descent, as were also Nadson and Chosadevitch. The greatest poet that anti-Semitic Roumania has as yet produced is the Jew, Ronetti Roman, whose play *New Lamps for Old* is one of the very few specimens of Roumanian literature known abroad.

Italy, in particular, with its handful of some 40,000 Jews, certainly provides a disproportionate number of names. From poets of a century and a half ago, such as Salamone Fiorentino, whom his admirers compared to Petrarch, to those of today like the half-Jew Umberto Saba; from historians like Samuele Romanin, who laid the foundations of Venetian historiography, to classical prose-writers like Giuseppe Revere; from popular romancers like Guido da Verona to more profound imaginative novelists like Italo Svevo; from playwrights like Sabbatino Lopez to critics like Eugenio Camerini; from Alessandro d' Ancona, the literary historian, who introduced the historic method into Italy, to Graziadio Isaia Ascoli, the foremost Italian philologist of all time, both leaders of that group of thinkers to whom the renewal of Italian culture in the nineteenth century was due. The Jewish interest in philology has indeed been particularly marked. It owes its origin to the Jewish savants of the Middle Ages, who because of the intimate relations of Hebrew and Arabic made their grammatical studies the beginning of comparative philology. Great scholars such as Sanders in Germany or the brothers Darmesteter in France demonstrate the universal interest in the subject in our own day. Nor should one forget that remarkable genius, Lazar Geiger, whose bust stood until recently in the entrance hall of the Frankfort Public Library. His researches on the origin of language were of sensational importance and led him to the same conclusions as Darwin, that evolution reigns in all nature. It is said that he died from grief when he learned that the English scientist had anticipated his discovery.

Nothing indicates more clearly than these names, and the innumerable others which could be mentioned, the complete fusion of the Jewish element in the intellectual life-blood of the Western World. The antecedents of these writers and scholars may have helped in some instances to widen their horizons, but did nothing to narrow their sympathies or to qualify the fidelity with which they mirrored the tone, the atmosphere, and the fashions of their environment.

APPENDIX: *Journalism and the Jew*

THE dictum, "Let me write a people's ballads: I care not who makes their laws," needs revision in the light of conditions of the present day, when the written word and the power of the press have attained an influence unknown in any former age. The implications of this should not of course be exaggerated, for recent experience in England and America has shown that on great public issues the popular suffrage has sometimes gone in a diametrically opposite direction to the general consensus and advice of the popular newspapers. In this connection, the same picture presents itself as in so many other branches of activity, intellectual and economic.

In the first impetus of their emancipation the Jews flocked to journalism and played a considerable part in that profession. But there was never any distinctively Jewish quality in their contribution; and the new conceptions and ideas which they introduced became common property before long.

The rapidity with which the Jews grasped the potentialities of the new instrument is attested by the fact that in the seventeenth century two Jewish newspapers were established in Amsterdam, one in Spanish and one in Yiddish. The former, at least, was probably intended for a wider circle. Yet for Jews to engage in general journalism was as yet impossible. It is true that Oliver Goldsmith writes of a Jewish journalist in 1771, in his *Haunch of Venison*. But this instance, if not jocular, was isolated, and from certain points of view the earliest English journalist in the modern sense was Lewis Goldsmith, a violent pamphleteer of the Napoleonic era.

It was in German journalism that the influence of Jews in the early nineteenth century was most pronounced. In particular, the contributions of Marx to the *Rheinische Zeitung*, and the brilliant feuilletons contributed from Paris by Heine and Börne, to the *Augsburger Zeitung* in particular, aroused the German periodical press from its traditional pompous lethargy and set a fresh example for European journalism as a whole. In Austria, L. A. Frankl and particularly Ignaz Kuranda, in his audacious *Grenzboten*, performed a somewhat similar function, though with more explosive results. It is significant that, once this semi-subterranean periodical had achieved its end and a constitution had been granted, Kuranda founded the *Ostdeutsche Post*, which was of conservative tendencies and even overemphasized the Pan-German standpoint. This in turn disappeared before the once famous *Neue Freie Presse*, in its day one of the world's most important journals, which was founded and managed by a group of Jews. It was due to his brilliant feuilletons in the columns of this periodical that the founder of political Zionism, Theodor Herzl, owed his original reputation.

The same period saw the establishment in 1872 by Rudolf Mosse and Georg Davidsohn, its first editor, of the *Berliner Tageblatt*, which speedily became known as one of the world's great newspapers. But the leading German journal was the *Frankfurter Zeitung*, which was begun by Leopold Sonnemann. Other great figures in pre-war journalism in Germany included men like Maximilian Harden, the greatest opponent of William II's megalomaniac absolutism, and a little later Theodor Wolff, editor during a long and critical period of the *Berliner Tageblatt*. A rôle of real importance was played, too, by men like David Kalisch, who founded in 1848 the famous German humorous weekly, *Kladderadatsch*, and Moritz Gottlieb Saphir, the best known humorist in continental Europe, who laughed Metternich out of the Dual Empire. Kalisch's principal collaborator was Rudolf Loewenstein, the famous poet, whose verses were found prior to 1933 in every first grade reader in German schools.

In England, the most notable Jewish figure in the newspaper world in the nineteenth century was J. M. Levy, who founded not merely the *Daily Telegraph*, but, as a result, popular journalism as a whole in England. Contemporaneously, there were a few outstanding figures such as Blowitz, the great foreign correspondent of *The Times*. The latter's attitude was one of the many indications that Jewish sympathies have on the whole been markedly absent in the more prominent Jewish journalists. Blowitz was so "objective" that he maintained a somewhat shameful detachment even during the progress of the Dreyfus Case. In this, however, he was outdone by Arthur Meyer, editor of *Le Gaulois*, which became under his direction the mouthpiece of the Clerical, Monarchist, and anti-Semitic parties in France. So much for "Jewish solidarity."

The nineteenth century witnessed the rise of various Jewish newspaper administrators of genius—men like Adolph S. Ochs, who made the *New York Times* one of the most powerful stabilizing forces in American public life; Joseph Pulitzer, a half-Jew, who developed the *St. Louis Post Dispatch* and the *New York World* into great liberalizing institutions, and founded the School of Journalism at Columbia University; and Leopold Ullstein, founder of what was in its day one of the most important German publishing houses. One of the rare features common to these enterprises was that in so few cases has control continued in the same family. Thus, no member of the Levy (Lawson) family is now associated with the London *Daily Telegraph*, while the Ullstein Press was "coordinated" by the Nazi government. In fact, Jewish influence in contemporary journalism has not been particularly great. In Germany, before the Nazi revolution, it was fashionable to describe all papers of the Left (i.e., Democratic and Socialist) as "Jewish." Really, no more than ten out of the eighty-five more prominent German papers had a Jewish editor-in-chief, while there were fewer than twenty Jews out of some 400 on the editorial staffs of the entire German Socialist Press. In England the influence is even less. Today not a single important English daily paper is controlled by a Jew; only one has a Jew as chairman of its board of directors, and not one has a Jewish editor-in-chief.

In the development of the news service, which is all-important for modern journalism, Jewish enterprise had a vital share. All three of the pioneers in the establishment of European news-agencies were Jews—Reuter, Wolff, and Havas. The greatest of these three was indubitably the first. Havas operated at the outset chiefly in France, and Wolff in Germany. But Reuter boldly made London his base, assuming British nationality. The pre-eminence which was established by his enterprise has never been challenged. It is characteristic of what has happened in so many other enterprises that the Jewish element in all three of these organizations has now entirely disappeared. The Wolff agency, which played so important a rôle in Germany during the war of 1914–18, was the last to retain some sort of Jewish direction, but it has now come under Nazi control.

In the realm of publishing, Jewish participation has been more important than extensive. It is sufficient to mention that greatest of German publishing houses, the firm of Fischer, whose intellectual guidance was largely responsible for the revitalization of German literature at the close of the last century. Bernard Shaw is one only of the foreign authors whose introduction to the German public was entirely due to them. To suggest any "racial" bias in such activities becomes all the more preposterous when one recalls the strange irony that even Nietzsche, the major prophet of National Socialism, was discovered and supported by Jews.

CHAPTER VI. *Art, Music, Stage*

I

IT was long believed that until modern times the Jewish share in the visual arts was negligible owing to the rigorous interpretation of the Ten Commandments. A most sensational recent archaeological discovery has made it necessary to revise this view. At Dura Europos, formerly a frontier city on the borders of the Roman and Persian Empires, there have been discovered the remains of a third-century synagogue, in a remarkable state of preservation. The walls still stand to a height in some places of nearly twenty feet. They are adorned with frescos of considerable vitality, representing biblical scenes, the visions of the Prophets, the Temple at Jerusalem, and so on. Contrary to all preconceived ideas, no qualms whatsoever are entertained at representing the human figure, notwithstanding the religious nature of the building. The Egyptian disaster in the Red Sea or the dedication of Aaron leaves nothing to fantasy; while a portrait of a priest, probably intended to represent the Prophet Jeremiah, closely resembles the early representations of Jesus of Nazareth. These frescos, in fact, are distinctly related to those

146

discovered in the Christian catacombs and the mosaics in the earliest Roman churches.

In view of these discoveries, some scholars go so far as to suggest that the ideas previously held with regard to the origins of Christian art must be revised. It was formerly thought that it had its roots in pagan Egypt; now it appears probable that the Church simply carried on the tradition which already existed in the Synagogue. But European painting depends, in the last instance, on ecclesiastical and early Christian origins; hence, if this new theory is correct, the tradition of Giotto and of Cimabue goes back ultimately to a Jewish prototype.[1]

Whether or no this is the case, the Jewish inspiration of much European art cannot be denied. Three-quarters at least of European paintings before 1500, and a very high proportion after that date, deal with biblical, i.e., Hebraic, characters and scenes. It is difficult to conceive Italian art of the Renaissance without such familiar episodes as the creation, the lives of the patriarchs, the triumph of Judith, and so on; while, though the fact was not conveyed in pictorial art until the last century, the central subject of all, Jesus and the Madonna, was essentially Jewish.

It was Dutch painting which first made a definite breach in the ecclesiastical tradition in art. Yet this by no means signified a revolt against the Hebraic subject matter. Rembrandt, for example, turned again

---

[1] It may be added, in connection with this, that a professional Jewish animal-painter named Eudoxios lived at Rome in the imperial period.

and again to the Bible for inspiration, though he was more attracted by its dramatic than its spiritual values. Moreover, his realistic sense led him to the Jewish quarter of Amsterdam in order to obtain local color, with the result that the scope of his work extended from the Hebrews of old to the Jews of his own day, who were depicted with a characteristic intermingling of realism and romanticism. For many years, Rembrandt lived among Jews, painted Jews, and worked frequently under Jewish auspices. It is interesting to recall in this connection that he illustrated a book for Menasseh ben Israel, the founder of the modern Jewish settlement in England. In view of all this, it has often been suggested, though without any documentary evidence, that he was himself of Jewish blood.[1]

For the paradoxical reason that art was so specifically Hebraic in character, the Jews could participate in it to only a very limited degree in the great age of European painting. It occupied itself largely with New Testament scenes; it was destined to a large extent for ecclesiastical decoration—or, rather, venera-

[1] Other Dutch and Flemish artists who are suspected to be of Jewish extraction include the fifteenth century master-engraver, Lucas Jacobsz, known as Van Leyden, son of the painter S. H. Jacobszoon; the family of engravers and artists of the seventeenth century, the De Jodes; and the Ruisdaels—Izaak Jacob, Jacob Salomons, and Salomon. Evidence based on names is, however, a little tenuous, particularly in the seventeenth century, when the Puritan tradition became so strong. It is believed with a greater degree of probability that the great Spanish painter Bartolomé Bermejo of Cordova was of Marrano extraction, as was also perhaps Cosimo Tura, a distinguished fifteenth-century artist of the School of Ferrara.

tion. Hence a very large proportion of the training, the activity, and the livelihood of the artist were cut off from the Jew. He compensated himself by interpreting with increasing rigor the biblical prohibition which forbids making graven images or any likeness. Finally, social prejudice prevented the Jew from entering the profession which of all handicrafts assumes the most intimate and friendly association between patron and worker.

2

Hence, from the close of the classical age down to the period of the disintegration of the Ghetto, Jewish artists working for the Gentile world, though not absolutely unknown (a few instances have been given above, pp. 65–6), were few and far between. However, as soon as art lost its ecclesiastical bias and social prejudices decreased, they began to play a more active rôle. They began with a branch of art in which social connections and religious allegiance were unimportant.

As a natural outcome of their commercial interest in precious stones, they mastered the art of gem and seal cutting, which developed into engraving and medal-making. In Germany in the seventeenth and eighteenth centuries these professions were very commonly followed by Jews. Many of the petty courts had a Jewish seal engraver in their employment, and some of the best medalists of the period were Jews. It is enough for our purpose to mention Jacob Abraham, who held an official appointment in the Court of

Prussia in the second half of the eighteenth century, and his son, Abraham Abrahamson, both prolific workers.

From gems and seals, the transition to miniature-painting was easy. This art was exemplified in the eighteenth century by Raphael Bachi in Paris, the Pinhas and Treu families in Germany, and at the beginning of the nineteenth century by David Alexander Fiorino, one of the best miniaturists of his day, in Dresden.

Thus, by gradual degrees the Jew began to acclimatize himself in the artistic world. By the close of the eighteenth century a couple of figures of first importance were of Jewish origin. Anton Rafael Mengs, court painter at Madrid, a much-read writer on the theory of art and the first person to recognize the genius of Goya, was the son of a converted Danish-Jewish enamel worker named Ishmael Mengs. The younger Mengs' reputation in his day was enormous, probably exceeding his merits. He had, moreover, a lasting influence in the history of painting as the founder of the neo-classical school, which received its greatest development in that superb painter, David. The latter's name makes one believe that he, too, was of Jewish extraction. So, according to the latest researches, was John Zoffany, one of the original members of the Royal Academy in London and a master of the conversation-piece; he was, it appears, born at Frankfort of Bohemian Jewish parentage, and certainly lodged in the house of a Jew when he first came to London.

This brings us to England, which exemplifies most strikingly the rôle of the Jew in painting—always in essence a child of his environment and of his age.

The first great English artist who professed Judaism was the famous miniaturist of the Stuart period, Abraham Cooper, who however was apparently a convert from Christianity. Later on, the features which characterized English painting were on the whole faithfully imitated, the English Jew showing himself as conservative as his Gentile neighbors. If Solomon Alexander Hart, professor and librarian of the Royal Academy, was a noteworthy exponent of what may be termed the pontifical school in British painting, that wayward genius, Simeon Solomon, was not the least remarkable member of the pre-Raphaelite group. Another distinguished exponent of the classical tradition in England both as portraitist and as painter of figure compositions was Solomon Joseph Solomon.

In view of the early Jewish association with the art of miniature-painting, it is interesting to note that it is a Jew, Alfred Praga, who was responsible for the revival of the art in England. In our day, Sir William Rothenstein and Philip Laszló, both of Jewish birth, represented the conservative tradition, in contrast to the younger artists, Mark Gertler, David Bomberg, Bernard Meninsky, Jacob Kramer, and so on, who have shared with their non-Jewish comrades in the exciting struggles of the modern movement.[1]

[1] The names of two famous caricaturists must be accorded a place: Max Beerbohm and Henry Ospovat (famous also as book-illustrator), each of whom built up a remarkable reputation.

3

It was characteristic that, while in England Jewish artists were typical members of the placid British school, on the Continent they were caught up in the feverish new tide which had its origin in France. During the course of the nineteenth century Paris became the artistic center of the whole world, and under the inspiration of Manet and Monet, Millet and Renoir a new tradition in art began. It is not generally realized that one of the founders of the New School was a Jew, Camille Pissarro, who had a profound influence on the earlier development of Cézanne. The peculiar atmosphere of the streets and boulevards of Paris have had no more faithful chronicler than in his "luminous vibration," though he brought to his work as well something of the atmosphere of his West Indian birthplace. His landscapes are among the most solidly constructed achievements of the Impressionist movement. But more important was his warm humanity. It is to this common factor that one seems forced back when one considers the Jewish contribution in every sphere.[1]

[1] Before this period, France produced at least one outstanding Jewish artist, Rosa Bonheur, the famous animal painter, whose father, Raymond Bonheur, had also enjoyed a high reputation. Her work was remarkable for the firm handling of the subject, coupled with extraordinary accuracy. She was the first woman to receive the Cross of the Legion of Honour (1894).

Camille Pissarro's son, Lucien Pissarro, settled in England, where he made a name not only as artist but also as founder of the Eragny Press, whose beautiful productions are famous wherever fine printing is appreciated. Another great Jewish typographical artist is the American, Joseph Ishill.

With the twentieth century the stream of Jews who went to study and work in Paris grew greater and greater, producing painters of the calibre of Chagall, Pascin, Soutine, Szyk, Kisling, and above all, Modigliani, the Botticelli of the twentieth century, who before his untimely death had attained great fame.

It was in the generation following Manet, that the characteristic Jewish function of acting as intellectual intermediary began to be felt, for it was to a large extent by Jews that the spirit of the impressionists was carried beyond France, to initiate a new tradition in painting throughout Europe. Thus, Serafino de Tivoli, who had studied in Paris, brought the new conceptions back to Italy, where he founded what was irreverently called the school of the "macchiaiuoli." Josef Israels took it to Holland, becoming the most significant figure in Dutch art since the seventeenth century and certainly the nearest in spirit to Rembrandt van Rijn. It was typical that this Jew was the first person of his age to enter into the spirit of the people, to go to the fisherman, the peasant, and the artisan for inspiration without any sense of patronage, amusement, or charity. A similar democratization was achieved in Russia by Isaac Levitan, of whom the anti-Semitic *Novoye Vremya* wrote: "This full-blooded Jew knew, as no other man, how to make us realize and love our plain and homely country scenes."

In this, Israels and Levitan were at one in spirit with their great contemporary, Max Liebermann, who on the authority of the *Encyclopaedia Britannica* is one of the two first-rate figures in German painting. There had been eminent German-Jewish painters of the conventional school in the generation which had preceded him—Veit and Oppenheim and Possart and the Bendemanns, father and son. It was Liebermann, however, who by bringing the Impressionist school to his country, disturbed the complacent traditionalism shared by these Jewish painters. Germany was for a long while reluctant to recognize him, and it was only when his fame had re-echoed back from abroad that his supremacy was at last realized. Following the example of Israels and their common master, Millet, he devoted himself to depicting the life of the poor, finding his best subjects in orphanages, asylums, peasants, and villages. He democratized, as it were, the subject matter of German painting. "His pictures hold the fragrance of the soil and the breezes of the heavens," states the *Britannica*. But his influence was exercised not only through his painting. It was he who in 1900 organized the first Berlin Sezession, a landmark in the history of German art. In 1919 he was elected President of the Berlin Academy of Fine Arts, serving until the Nazi Revolution, and distinguishing himself by a receptiveness to new ideas and new currents most unusual for one in such a position.

Liebermann was almost unique among academicians in his realization that in art the revolutionary of yesterday is the conservative of today. The absence of any stylistic coherence among Jewish artists may be realized from the fact that Jews were so prominent among the German expressionists and their successors, whose rise in the first decades of the twentieth century marked the decline of his influence. The most distinguished Jewish artist after Liebermann, in the pre-war period, was probably Lesser Ury, a genius in color, while Yankel Adler subsequently made his name known among the radicals. But there was nothing in the artistic temperament of the Jew which inclined him to revolutionary idealism; and, when the *Neue Sachlichkeit* sounded the call for the back-to-nature movement, one of its leaders was Josef Bato.

Sculpture was for centuries the most ecclesiastical branch of art, and this is perhaps the reason for the Jew's late entrance into it. In the romantic period, Mark Matveyevitch Antokolski was easily the most eminent Russian sculptor, gaining the first prize in the international competition of 1878. As the Russian art-critic, Stassov, wrote: "He is the greatest sculptor of our age. He represents in his personality something altogether different from what all the rest of our sculptors stand for—both ancient and modern."

The next generation produced Enrico Glicenstein, N. Aronson, Arrigo Minerbi and others of equal reputation. Today, the magnificent virility of men like Jacques Lipchitz, Osip Zadkin, and Jacob Epstein and of women like Chana Orloff is leavened by the classical purity of Arnold Zadikow, while Benno Elkan leads a return to the Renaissance ideal in wedding a sculptor's imagination to sober utilitarianism.

4

What that prodigious melting-pot of genius, which is known as the United States, may produce in the future in the realm of art, no man can yet foretell. But the emergence during the present generation of an almost unending series of talented young men and women, combining the untrammeled American spirit with the Jew's passionate feeling, points to the possibility that there may come into existence before long with their aid a great American artistic tradition, comparable to anything that the Old World ever knew. It is more than a coincidence that a Jew, Alfred Stieglitz, to whom his disciples have dedicated a remarkable volume of essays, is regarded as the father of modern art in America. He is the man who inspired young Americans, led them towards new goals, and showed them that to make their contribution they should not slavishly follow Old World models but interpret their own American environment and mentality.

Among the great American Jewish artists of today, it is possible only to mention a few outstanding names, resisting the temptation to particularize, for they constitute a remarkable roll. Among the important painters are Maurice Stern and Max Weber, both honored by the Museum of Modern Art by retrospective exhibitions and monographs, Leon Kroll, Abraham Baylinson, the Soyer brothers, Benjamin Kopman, William Mayerowitz, Theresa Bernstein, Abraham Walkowitz, reckoned with Weber among the fathers of modernism in the United States, and Louis Lozowick, who has done much to interpret the school to the outside world. Etchers include William Auerbach-Levy and Abbo Ostrowsky.

In the plastic arts, leadership was established in the last century by Sir Moses Jacob Ezekiel, perhaps the most distinguished American-born sculptor of that day. His lead was followed by Jo Davidson, of world reputation, who designed for the French government a heroic group to commemorate the first victory of the Marne. William Zorach undoubtedly excels him in fire and passion, while among the younger generation there are outstanding names like Louis Slobodkin, one of the great hopes of the future. The wood-carver, Hayim Gross, and the stone-carver, Nadelman, well known in Europe, deserve at least passing mention, while Oscar Bach and Samuel Yellin, whose intense Jewish sentiment atones for the former's lack of it, are distinguished as practical artists in wrought iron. Their achievements almost bear comparison with the productions of the classical period. In America, industrial design has entered into its own. The most important influence in modern industrial arts in the country is Florence Levy, founder of the Art Center, with its multifarious activities; she is ably seconded by designers like Henry Dreyfuss and Paul Frankl.[1]

5

In architecture the Jew had little opportunity to demonstrate his talent until comparatively recent years. The Herodian Temple in Jerusalem was reckoned among the wonders of the ancient world; but there

[1] The outstanding Mexican artist, Diego Rivera, also claims Jewish affiliations, but it is not easy to decide whether he should be included in this list.

was no possibility of emulating this achievement, even on a reduced scale, in the Diaspora. The medieval synagogue was, of necessity, modest and unpretentious. It is remarkable how faithfully it reflected the fashions of the environment. The earliest German synagogues are perfect specimens of the Romanesque style, as that of Worms, constructed in the eleventh century and deliberately destroyed by anti-Semites with the aid of minnewerfers in the twentieth; or of the Gothic, as the Alt-Neu Schul of Prague. Those of Spain, e.g., at Toledo, Segovia, or Cordova, reproduce the flowing Arabesques of the neighboring mosques. Italy, at Venice or Padua or Ferrara, brings in the baroque influence, while the wooden synagogues of Russia and Poland are thought to reproduce the style and fashions of the ancient pagan temples, of which no other trace survives.

In only one respect was the medieval Jew responsible for an important architectural innovation. His precarious existence made it desirable for his dwelling place to be as strong as possible, and his widespread connections suggested the means. Accordingly, it appears that he was the pioneer of domestic architecture in stone in Northern Europe. It seems more than a coincidence that all over England ancient houses of especial solidity are even now associated with the names of the Jewish owners of seven centuries ago. In what was formerly the Lincoln Jewry, above all, some admirable specimens survive, said to be the oldest dwelling-houses in Europe, with the exception of Spain, which are still inhabited.

The nineteenth century at last opened the doors of architecture to the Jews, and they were not slow to take advantage of this opportunity. English Jewry provided at least one important figure, George Basevi, whose works include that perfect specimen of the neo-classical style the Fitzwilliam Museum at Cambridge. In Germany, in the middle of the century, the most prominent name in this sphere is that of Georg Hitzig, president of the Academy of Art, who designed the Bourse (1859–64) and the Reichsbank (1869–77). Many of the local branches of this institution, in the full fortress-like floridity of the close of the last century, were erected by E. Jacobsthal, while in Austria, a new tradition in theatrical architecture was started by Oscar Strnad. Hyper-patriotic admirers of the neo-Gothic style in Germany date the revival from 1905, when Alfred Messel completed the Wertheim Building in Berlin, and, according to the reactionary *Freiheits-kampf*, "a new epoch opened for German architecture." Today, there is one Jewish figure of international significance in architecture, Erich Mendelssohn, who, ruthlessly sweeping away traditional forms, took cognizance of the sun and air. His style symbolizes and sustains the modern concept of the sun as a therapeutic agent, while his interplay of horizontal and vertical lines has stimulated the evolution of the American skyscraper from a utilitarian curiosity to an unprecedented architectural form of rare beauty.[1]

[1] Another name associated with the development of the skyscraper is that of L. J. Horowitz, head of the company which erected the Woolworth Building. In the previous generation,

In America, there are two outstanding names, Eli Jacques Kahn, who is regarded as second among contemporaries to Frank Lloyd Wright, and Albert Kahn, designer of the Ford Motor Plant, who possesses (in the words of the University of Michigan, in conferring an honorary degree upon him) "creative imagination attested by imposing structures that combine utility with dignity and beauty."

In artistic criticism and history the part played by Jews has been of the utmost importance. One of the greatest living students of Italian art of the Renaissance is Bernhard Berenson, an American critic of Lithuanian birth, while there was no greater authority on medieval Italian sculpture than I. B. Supino. Germany has, of course, provided a larger number of workers in this field including Marc Rosenberg, the outstanding expert on goldsmith's work, Adolph Goldschmidt, authority on medieval sculpture and manuscript illumination, and Max J. Friedländer, author of a monumental work on Dutch painting. Some of England's most eminent art critics and historians, too, have been Jews. Sir Charles Walston, Slade Professor at Cambridge, to cite one, wrote extensively on the aesthetics of art; in addition he was a great archaeologist. The name of Salomon Reinach is famous, not only in

---

Dankmar Adler, who designed the Chicago Stock Exchange, was a notable figure in American architecture and was head of the firm which erected the first steel construction skyscrapers in the country. Among contemporaries who deserve mention is the Swiss Julien Flegenheimer (1880–1938), architect of the Palace of the League of Nations at Geneva.

France, as author of what is perhaps still the best introduction to the history of art—*Apollo*.

6

Music, like painting, is a particularly faithful index of assimilation, and Jewish religious and folk-music have on the whole reflected with the utmost fidelity the atmosphere of the Jew's environment. Northern Jewry generally imitates in home and synagogue the German musical tradition of the Middle Ages and after; southern, that of Spain. The melodies common to both elements, which might, therefore, be presumed to be of ancient Palestinian origin, are conspicuous by their rarity. Thus, it is probable that the tradition of Temple cantillation may today be traced in the oldest music of the Catholic Church rather than in that of the Synagogue. Indeed, it may be argued that this primitive Jewish influence on Christian plain-song was the origin of the polyphonic, and is thus in a sense fundamental to Western music in general. On the other hand, in a later age, synagogue music has occasionally been drawn upon by gentile composers. Benedetto Marcello found the settings for many psalms in the Ghetto at Venice, while the historic tune to the English hymn, "The God of Abraham Praise," was carried away from the Great Synagogue in London one Friday evening in 1772 by the Wesleyan minister, Thomas Oliver, after hearing Leoni chant the doxology, *Yigdal*. But the tide has generally flowed in the other direction. Students of medieval Spanish music, for example, are now beginning to devote increasing

attention to the folk-music of the Jews in the Levant,
who still possess a vast store of uncontaminated folk-
songs and ballads of the age of Columbus.

Jewish musicians, whose performances were enjoyed
by non-Jewish audiences, were indeed to be encountered throughout the Middle Ages. As with their
neighbors, it was only with the Renaissance that individual composers began to emerge. The first known
to us by name was one Joseph ("Giuseppe Ebreo"),
who flourished at the court of Lorenzo de' Medici,
where he collaborated with the Jewish writer,
Guglielmo da Pesaro, on the art of dancing. At the
court of Mantua there were also a number of singers,
instrumentalists, and composers. Some of their work,
which was mainly of secular interest, was published.
Among them may be mentioned David Civita, whose
Premitie Armoniche appeared at Venice in 1616;
Allegro Porto, who dedicated three volumes of compositions to the Emperor Ferdinand; and Salamone de'
Rossi, who divided his attention impartially between
compositions intended for synagogal and profane use.
In Venice the Jews had in the Ghetto their own musical academy, which exchanged courtesies and compositions with similar bodies in the city.

The development of the Catholic reaction destroyed
this promising beginning. With the Jews restricted to
their Ghettos and forbidden ordinary intercourse
with their fellow-citizens, and with Church compositions, the easiest, if not the only, avenue to recognition,
the tradition languished. Hence it was only in lands of
greater freedom that the Jewish musical ability found

its outlet, and a modest one at that, until the great revival of the nineteenth century.

It was Germany which led Europe in music, and it was natural that German Jews showed greater prominence than their coreligionists across the Rhine or the North Sea. Here Felix Mendelssohn-Bartholdy, the baptized grandson of the great Jewish philosopher, exercised an influence so potent that it can hardly be believed that he died before attaining his fortieth year. England knows him as a composer, almost the last real genius of the melody which was once music. His *Midsummer Night's Dream* all but enhanced the charm of Shakespeare; more than normal obtuseness was necessary to have his masterpieces banned in Nazi Germany, on the ground that the composer was "non-Aryan." His sacred oratorios, a branch of music to which he gave a new lease of life, meant more abroad than they did in his own country, and his *Elijah*, in particular, has not only preserved its classic popularity but has had almost too powerful an influence on composers of English church music.

In the words of Sir Hubert Parry, one of England's greatest musical scholars, "he was one of the few composers to whom in his best moments all the resources of art were equally available. His choral writing was, on the whole, the most practical and the most fluent that has been seen since Handel and Bach, and for mastery of choral effect he had no real superior in his time. His harmony is full of variety and sufficiently forcible, and his facility in melody quite unlimited."

But, even had he not composed a note, Mendelssohn

would still be an important figure in musical history. In 1827–8, in the face of considerable opposition, he began propaganda on behalf of the music of Bach, which finally resulted in the formation of a Bach Society and the publication of his Masses and Cantatas; it was to this that the Renaissance of Bach, long forgotten among his countrymen, is to be traced. Mendelssohn's transference to Leipzig in 1835 as conductor of the Gewandhaus Orchestra made Leipzig the musical center of Germany, as Germany was of Europe. He founded, too, the Leipzig Conservatoire. Upon the staff of this famous institution were a number of eminent Jewish instrumentalists, many of whom were at the same time composers of note. They included Ignaz Moscheles, founder of a new school of piano-forte-playing, whose long life enabled him to link the pianistic tradition of an earlier day with modern times; Joseph Joachim, "one of the loftiest names in the history of the violin" and the interpreter *par excellence* of the classical tradition. His "Hungarian Concerto" and "Hebrew Melodies," for viola and piano, testify to the range and catholicity of his musical sympathies. Ferdinand David combined the qualities of the classics with the technical skill and brilliance of the moderns, and it is because of him that Leipzig long remained the center of violin playing in Europe. "Leipzig is a Jewish metropolis," grumbled Wagner in 1869.

Contemporary with Mendelssohn was a group of other Jewish composers, almost on the same plane. The "Cyclopaean" Giacomo Meyerbeer, son of a Berlin banker, became famous in the one sphere all but un-

touched by his great contemporary, namely, opera.
He anticipated or instructed Wagner in his genius for
matching the pageantry of scene with that of tone,
and a more immediate influence is sometimes discernible. His works still hold the stage, on the Continent
especially, while his style, setting, and orchestration
have had a subtle effect on many subsequent composers. The travelling fellowships which Meyerbeer
established by his will were then something novel in
musical annals and have not been without their permanent influence. His work shows distinct affinity to
that of Fromenthal Elie Halévy, one of the great
figures in French music along with Thomas, Gounod,
Bizet, or Saint-Saëns. The last two mentioned are both
said to have been of Jewish extraction. In Paris at least,
where a street is named after him, his works are still
regularly played and enthusiastically received. His
name, alone of the more eminent Jewish composers of
the nineteenth century, is associated with a work on a
Jewish theme, though it has no Jewish characteristics
in its music—his masterpiece, *La Juive*, still a favorite.

Jacques Offenbach linked Germany with France.
He was the son of a synagogue cantor at Cologne, but
he passed his most active years in Paris, where during
the Second Empire he was one of the outstanding figures in the musical world. He was the father of the
Opéra Comique. The artistry of his hundred or more
compositions makes them of living interest to the present day, and among them there is one at least which is
assured of immortality, *The Tales of Hoffman*.

More solid was the operatic work of Karl Goldmark, especially remarkable for the rich splendor of the orchestration. Gustav Mahler was a composer in the grand manner, whose works mainly of Catholic and German folk-music evoked great devotion and are marked by a spiritual power of moving impressiveness. In England, though no names of equal calibre have as yet emerged, Sir Frederic Cowen, conductor as well as composer, was a prolific creator of songs, instrumental music, and choral work of abiding value.

The nineteenth century produced a number of other Jewish composers, perhaps less universally known than those mentioned above but of considerable reputation nevertheless—Salomon Jadassohn, Ignaz Brüll, and Moritz Moszkowski in Germany and Austria; John Barnett, Julius Benedict and Isidore de Lara in England; Camille Erlanger and Paul Dukas in France; Federigo Consolo and Alberto Franchetti in Italy.[1]

In the modern school of music, Jews, at last afforded ampler opportunities, are among the leaders. It is enough to mention Arnold Schönberg, "the first musician since Debussy to have carried forward the form of opera," whose innovations have profoundly affected a large body of disciples, although he is now an exile from his native Germany; Darius Milhaud, the leading member of the Modern French School, remarkable in that his revolutionary music often ex-

---

[1] According to some authorities the names of Sullivan, Leoncavallo, Costa, and even Beethoven (!), but the likelihood is slender, should be added to this list, as having been of Jewish extraction. Maurice Ravel, though bearing a distinctively French-Jewish name and attracted by Jewish themes, is stated authoritatively not to be a Jew.

presses religious emotion; Mario Castelnuovo-Tedesco, one of the most gifted of the younger Italian composers of our time; the brothers Krein, prominent in the contemporary Russian musical world; and those Jews who have contributed to modern American folk-music, such as Gershwin, Copland, and Gruenberg. Ernest Bloch, Swiss by birth, is considered one of the outstanding composers of the day. As Director of the San Francisco School of Music, he had a great influence on the younger American composers. He is one of the few modern Jewish musicians who has devoted his talent to Jewish themes. Far, however, from diluting the pure source of European music with an extraneous element, he has endeavored to put a Jewish content into modern European musical forms, as for instance in his recent titanic experiments in synagogal composition.

7

In music, unlike any other branch of art, interpretation is all-important, and, since the first half of the nineteenth century, Jews have figured in disproportionate numbers among the instrumentalists in every land. Indeed, the concert hall of today would be inconceivable without the Jewish *virtuosi* who constitute no mean proportion of its major attractions. The violin has had a special attraction for Jews—particularly, by some freak of environment, for those of Russian birth; witness the names of Joachim, David, Elman, Heifetz, Kreisler, Zimbalist, Achron, Auer, Seidel, Menuhin, Szigeti, Hubermann, and Pollitzer (Elgar's master).

Pianists include Anton Rubinstein, one of the greatest the world has ever known and at the same time a composer of merit,[1] and his brother, Nicholas, founder of the Russian Musical Society. Nearer our own day, there are Myra Hess, Ossip Gabrilowitch, Moritz Moszkowski, Moriz Rosenthal, Harold Samuel, Moiseiwitsch, Consolo, Horowitz, Solomon, Hambourg, Schnabel, Arthur Rubinstein, and so on. Among 'cellists, the names of Feuermann, Piatigorsky, and Bernhard Cossman are pre-eminent.

Great singers have not been quite so common, yet they include Giuditta Pasta, for whom Bellini wrote "La Norma," and Pauline Lucca, the first "Africana," as well as Julius Lieban, Joseph Schwarz, Alexander Kipnis, Hermann Jadlowker, and Richard Tauber.

Among the Jewish conductors may be mentioned Walter Damrosch and his family, whose services for the upbuilding of the great musical tradition of the United States have been so conspicuous. Hermann Levi was one of the most notable Wagnerian conductors and producers, the first conductor of *Parsifal*, and for many years the only one to whom Richard Wagner entrusted it. Nearer to our own day and equally famous are Bruno Walter, Otto Klemperer, Ferdinand Hiller, Léo Blech, and the Frenchman, Pierre Monteux, who, it is said was engaged to replace Bruno Walter at a concert in 1933 under the impression that he was "Aryan." [2]

[1] It was on his advice that Paderewski turned to the piano.

[2] Another great name is that of Sir George Henschel, singer, composer, founder of the London Symphony Orchestra, and first conductor of the Boston Symphony Orchestra.

Critics and theoreticians include Heinrich Porges, Wagner's greatest champion, and Eduard Hanslick, his greatest opponent; Guido Adler, leader of the "Vienna School"; Max Friedländer, the great authority on German folk-music; Oscar Bie, historian of the dance and the opera; and Egon Wellesz, one of Schönberg's foremost followers in Austria and a distinguished student of Byzantine and Oriental music.

As patrons of music, moreover, the rôle of Jews has been all important. They have been among the most sedulous frequenters of concerts, the most discerning appreciators of talent, the most receptive students of new ideas, currents, and methods. "How can I be anti-Semitic when I know that without our Jewish friends all our opera-houses and concert-halls would be more than half empty?" asked Richard Strauss. This would have been, and is still true, not only of Central Europe, but also of London, Paris, and New York. Nor is the phenomenon a new one. In eighteenth-century England, when Handel was sedulously neglected by the nobility and aristocracy, he found encouragement and support from the London Jews, who thus had their part in identifying with England one of the most potent influences on English music. Rossini's life was rendered possible through the friendship and unflagging support of James de Rothschild in Paris. Perhaps it is for this reason that his works are at present banned in Germany, for he had no traceable Jewish blood.

Even Richard Wagner, notwithstanding the anti-Semitic extravagances which he expressed in his *Judaism in Music*, found that the Jews were not only among his finest interpreters, but also his most practical supporters. Jewish subscriptions poured in for the foundation of the Bayreuth Theatre, while it was the Jewish pianist, Karl Taussig, who devised the plan to raise 300,000 thalers for its construction. Attempts have been made to trace Semitic influences in the glitter and elaboration of Wagner's music. Rather is it to be found in the essentially Teutonic themes which he developed for his story, for the action both of *Tannhäuser* and *The Flying Dutchman*, which he himself ascribed later to some unspecified and untraceable collection of legends, were dependent upon the genius of Heinrich Heine. "In Heine's truly dramatic treatment of the redemption of this Ahasuerus of the Sea," Wagner had written in his *Autobiographical Sketch* of 1843, before his anti-Jewish prejudice had developed, "I found all I wanted to make of the Saga an opera subject. *I came to an understanding in the matter with Heine himself.*" [1]

That there is anything Semitic in the compositions of Mozart has never been suggested, though it is a fact that a handful of Jews were among the first persons to encourage him during his visit to England as an infant prodigy in 1764. However, no small part of the enjoyment of those who listen to his operas, particularly *Don Juan* and *The Marriage of Figaro*, comes from the extraordinary ability of his librettist, Emanuel Conegliano of Ceneda in Italy, better known under his bap-

---

[1] It may be added that there is strong ground for suspecting that Wagner himself, for all his anti-Semitism, was half-Jewish, his father being named Geyer.

tized name of Lorenzo da Ponte. He rivalled Casanova
in his amorous adventures and autobiographical audac-
ity, contributed considerably to the success of the most
famous of Mozart's operas, brought the first Italian
opera company to America, and brought to a close an
eventful life at New York at a venerable old age in
1838. The librettos of most of Richard Strauss' operas,
including his *Rosenkavalier*, were written by that
stylistic genius and Liberal reformer, the half-Jew,
Hugo von Hoffmannsthal.[1]

8

One of the most important strands in the complex history of the theatre is, of course, biblical. The medieval
Miracle Play, presenting to the people in dramatized
form the familiar episodes of scriptural history, was
generally based upon the Old Testament or Apocrypha when it was not upon the Passion or the Nativity
of Jesus. The stories of Joseph and his brethren, of
Susannah, of the deluge, of the sacrifice of Isaac, were
favorites, and it was from these simple representations
that the modern stage emerged.[2]

[1] Beethoven used the words of a Jewish poet, Jeiteles, for his
famous song, *An die entfernte Geliebte;* while Brahms, Schumann,
and Hugo Wolf similarly composed some of their best songs
to the words of Heine and other Jewish poets. Conversely, Schu-
bert set the 92nd Psalm to music for the Vienna Synagogue.

[2] Hebraic echoes are to be discerned even in some of the morality
plays. Thus the famous *Everyman* has its parallel in a familiar
passage in the collection of Rabbinic teachings known as
The Ethics of the Fathers: "When a man departs from this world,
there accompany him neither silver nor gold nor precious stones
nor pearls, but only learning and good works." The thought is

This universal European practice was paralleled by the Jews in their Ghettos. It was perhaps symbolic that while among their neighbors these dramatic representations were associated especially with the seasons of greatest solemnity, among the Jews they took place at carnival-time, at the feast of *Purim*. It was inevitable that the story of Esther and Mordecai, commemorated at that season, was a specially favored subject. However, there were others, the sale of Joseph, David and Goliath, and so on. Precisely when this tradition started is uncertain.[1] Traces of it may be discerned in the dark ages in the East; in the late Middle Ages it developed, and at the period of the Renaissance, the performances of the Jews were famous, and attracted numerous Gentile spectators. Thus we are informed by the industrious Marino Sanuto how, at Venice in 1531 "there was performed by the Jews in their Ghetto a very fine comedy; but no Christian was permitted to be present, by order of the Council of Ten." Ultimately, it seems that a permanent theatre was instituted in the Venetian Ghetto, where plays, composed by writers not unknown to the outside world, were presented.

---

natural enough, but it is significant that in the English version (in which, incidentally, God is referred to as *Adonai*) "knowledge," corresponding to *Torah*, accompanies "good deeds," a typically Hebraic conception. The more elaborate version of this contained in the *Chapters of Rabbi Eleazar* is even closer in spirit to the Morality Play, introducing the dramatic form.

[1] Jewish actors had, of course, been known even in classical times. Josephus mentions one, Alityros, who was a favorite with the Emperor Nero.

This practice certainly had some influence on the Italian theatre and indirectly on that of modern Europe in general. Jewish interest in the drama appears to have been particularly strong at Mantua, where the actors were famous for their histrionic ability. Accordingly, during the sixteenth century, whenever it was desired to give a dramatic performance at the court of the Gonzagas, in honor of some visiting Prince or Grandee, the obligation and, incidentally, the expense, generally devolved upon the Jews. We are informed that on Friday the performances had to commence in the morning, so that they would end before the Sabbath, while on Jewish feast days they either had to be postponed or deprived of their most attractive features. Thus, at the formative period of European drama, when the influence of Italy was felt throughout Europe, and Italy looked with interest to Mantua, the Jewish community of that city was closely associated with, if not responsible for, the dramatic performances at court.

The Jews of Mantua did not provide the actors only. Leone de' Sommi Portaleone, by profession a scribe, by predilection a Hebrew poet, was a prolific writer of Italian prose and verse. He composed in addition several plays of the insipid pastoral character then fashionable—of course, of a specifically non-Jewish nature. He was impresario and producer at the Ducal Court; and the poet Manfredi entrusted him with the production of at least one of his plays. But above all he is remembered as author of a volume, *Dialogues on the Dramatic Art*, composed in 1556, the first work of that nature ever written in a European tongue. It is a body of sane theory and pioneer understanding of stage practice, in some respects in advance of its age. The work was not published in full until recent years. Nevertheless, the author had many opportunities to put his theories in practice, and some at least became commonplaces of the Italian, and ultimately the European, theater.[1]

Considering this long Jewish tradition in the theater, it is not surprising that Jewish writers of today have furnished so high a proportion of dramatists. In the English-speaking countries, we have had Pinero, Sutro, Zangwill, Merrick, Benn Levy, Belasco, and among the disturbing figures of the younger generation in America, Elmer Rice, S. N. Behrman, Clifford Odets, George Kaufman, and Lilian Hellman; in France, Bernstein, d'Ennery, Porto-Riche, and the two Bernards, father and son; in Denmark, Henrik Hertz; in Sweden, Josephson; in Holland, Heijermans; in Italy, Sabbatino Lopez; in Hungary, Franz Molnar, Melchior Lengyel; in Germany, Schnitzler, Fulda, Hoffmannsthal, Beer-Hoffman, L'Arronge; in Russia, Semjon Juschkewitch and Ossip Dymow . . . their name is legion. In our own day, the Palestine Arts Theater, *Habimah*, has elevated the drama into a spiritual experience. And it is remarkable that the one Nobel artist-prizeman is a Jew, Leo Bakst, the scenic artist whose presentation of *Scheherazade* in 1910

---

[1] It is noteworthy that the greatest authority on the history of the medieval stage, Gustave Cohen, of Paris, is a Jew, as was also Alessandro d'Ancona, the great historian of the Italian theater.

brought him international fame and whose designs for Russian ballet had so profound an influence on the modern stage.[1] But neither the eye of prejudice nor of enthusiasm can possibly find any common factor in all these strangely diverse types, at one only in fidelity to their age and environment.

9

Jewish actors of genius, to whom Europe and America have owed no small part of their dramatic enjoyment in the course of the past century and more, are too numerous to list, and include some of the greatest names of all. If Rachel, the queen of tragedy, a Jewess, had an equal, it was the half-Jewess, Sarah Bernhardt. Less widely known than either of these, but hardly less talented, was Esther de Boer, for half a century queen of the Dutch stage. Their spiritual heiress today is Elizabeth Bergner, an exile from Germany. Nazimova, too, is a Jewess. Ada Isaacs Menken is hardly to be mentioned in the same breath as these, yet Swinburne could write of her: "Lo! this is she that was the world's delight."

If Jewish actors have not quite attained the overwhelming place of Jewish actresses, they have nevertheless provided some of the great names in the history of the theater. When Sheridan's *Duenna* was produced at Covent Garden in 1775, the part of Isaac was taken by "Mr. Leoni" (Myer Lyon) on whose ac-

---

[1] Of scenic artists in other parts of the world, the contemporary Americans, Lee Simonson, Mordecai Gorelik, and Jo Mielziner, are outstanding.

count performances were suspended on Friday nights.[1]
In the Edwardian Era, the English stage was almost
dominated by Sir Beerbohm Tree. Holland has never
had an actor to equal Louis Bouwmeester, one of the
most remarkable figures of the European theater of
his day. Two Hungarian Jews, Ludwig Barnay and
von Sonnenthal, played a leading role in the theatrical
history of Germany and Austria respectively. On the
German and Austrian stages Jews have been prominent for more than a century, and in the last generation especially they were among the foremost actors.
It is sufficient to mention Emanuel Reicher, Rudolf
Schildkraut, Fritz Kortner, and Max Pallenberg.

As theatrical *entrepreneurs*, too, Jews have been
prominent, though they showed a tendency, which to
some professionals may have seemed distressing, to
proceed from the parallel and normally non-conver-
gent functions of management to more intimate participation.

In New York, Italian opera was first introduced by
Lorenzo da Ponte, Mozart's Jewish librettist. Oscar
Hammerstein, besides managing many theaters, presented a galaxy of new stars to the operatic world at
the Manhattan Opera House, which he built. David
Belasco dominated the American theater for many
years, as producer as well as actor, and playwright.

In Germany Otto Brahm who was founder of the
Freie Bühne and whose activity at the Deutsches
Theater left an indelible mark on German stage his-

[1] The report that Edmund Kean was a Jew has no foundation
in fact; the same applies to the American Edwin Booth.

tory, and Leopold Jessner, who was formerly director of the Berlin Staats Theater and who introduced expressionism to the stage, are among the foremost figures. They would be even better known were it not for the activity of Max Reinhardt, whose rationalistic productions have completely revolutionized the theater in our day and who, with Brahm, was responsible for the intimate atmosphere which led to the evolution of the fashionable "little theaters." In fact, the modern German theater, which came to mean so much in the cultural life of the period after the war of 1914–18, is all but a Jewish creation. To quote a recent work, "the Jew has been foremost in raising the activity of the stage-director from a perfunctory job to an art characterized by imagination, style, and creative approach." [1]

In the new art of motion pictures, where there were no established traditions or prejudices to hamper their progress, the Jews entered whole-heartedly. They found it a newcomer, relegated to back-streets and uncomfortable halls and occupying itself in cheap extravagances. It was largely under Jewish auspices that it developed to a great industry, not challenging but supplementing the theater; the center of a new art which brought a new standard of comfort as well as of achievement to the reach of the poorest pocket. There was a period when the subject-matter, reflect-

[1] Myerson and Goldberg's *The German Jew, His Share in Modern Culture*, an admirable work to which I owe more in the compilation of certain portions of this book than I can adequately acknowledge.

ing post-war moral standards, tended to be sordid and
sex-centered. If Jews were associated with this,
they were associated no less with the subsequent regeneration, which in recent years has made such remarkable progress. No man, for instance, did more
to enhance the dignity of the motion pictures industry
than Irving Thalberg, whose death in 1936 was
mourned by critics all over the world as a major disaster.

10

Much has been said, from the days of Wagner onwards, of the contamination of the pure source of
European inspiration by the "alien" element introduced by the Jew. An examination of the facts shows
that this suggestion is untrue. In music, in art, in literature, as, indeed, in science and in medicine, the Jew
has brought to bear a keen critical faculty, highly
developed through centuries of intensive culture and
an innate respect for intellect and intellectual achievement. This is coupled with great receptivity, a reluc-
tance to accept tradition *per se*, and perhaps a critical
aloofness, natural in those whose identity has for centuries been maintained as that of a small minority in
a hostile world. Thus there is inherent perhaps in the
Jew a mental attitude which qualifies him peculiarly
to brush away the cobwebs of conventions, though
rendering him no less receptive to prevailing tendencies.

The Jew, therefore, is very often found in the van-
guard of a new movement. But, on the other hand, he is

less frequently responsible for the first revolutionary step. He generally works through the medium most favored at the time; with the romantics he is romantic; with the impressionists, impressionistic; and with the moderns, ultra-modern. There may conceivably be something Jewish in the essence—a feeling that spirit is more important than form, some mystical abstraction which defies analysis. In certain instances, there is a tendency to seek relief from everyday drabness in a riot of color. There is generally a warm feeling for humanity. This, however, is all that can be conceded. The style is that of the moment; the subject is the environment, or what is demanded by convention. Thus Israels, Auerbach, Levitan, were the interpreters in paint or in prose of the Dutch, German, Russian countryside. Only, coming as they did from the obscurity of the Ghetto, they were perhaps able to see more than those whose fathers had been familiar with the tints and folds and figures of centuries past.

If there is any other common factor about the Jews' contributions to art, music, and letters, it is due to the simple fact that, forming as they do a single sociological group, brought up in a similar environment, they tend to reflect something of that group's outlook. There are signs that a new art may perhaps develop in Palestine. But it is an art rooted in the Western milieu, using a Western technique. If anything specifically Jewish may evolve, it is still to make itself known.

CHAPTER VII. *The Jew in European Thought*

I

IT is commonly assumed, perhaps too hastily, that the Hebrews of the biblical period were not interested in philosophy. A courageous attempt has recently been made to correct this impression. The Old Testament gives evidence of a native Hebrew philosophy, Platonic in type but not in origin, which is especially noticeable in the Book of Ecclesiastes. In particular, the well-known "wisdom" passages of the 4th and 8th chapters of Proverbs are held to be the "remains of generations, and indeed centuries, of keen and devoted thinking on the problems raised by the phenomena of life." [1]

That this is in the main true is clear. The Old Testament is obviously the product of profound and exhaustive meditation on divine purpose and human destiny. But a distinction should be drawn between philosophy as a technical discipline and thought in the wider sense which includes feeling. The Book of Job is classical expression of the rebellion of the human heart against the apparent tyranny of the ways of the

[1] Macdonald, *The Hebrew Philosophical Genius* (Princeton, 1936), p. 49.

universe, but its protest is not made in the technical forms of the syllogism, and its ending is as illogical as it is magnificent. In the same way the Hebrew Bible as a whole offers a view of life which is both consistent and rational, but it would not seem to have been "thought out" in terms of logical analysis and is not, therefore, in the strict sense of the term philosophy.

Yet men live by feeling and not by logical analysis, and the influence of the Hebrew Bible on European philosophy is greater than that of any philosopher or philosophical system. The reason is simple. The Hebrew Bible laid down for the European peoples, largely through the channel of Christianity, certain leading principles concerning the ultimate origin and nature of the world. These principles thus became the data of philosophical speculation, setting forth the problem even if they were not accepted as that problem's solution. Hebraic theism gave Europe its vision of supreme reality and is thus at the base of the European intellectual outlook. We may rebel against it, but our very negations affirm it. It is there, inescapable, an integral part of our minds.

It may be thought that with the Old Testament the Jews' work was finished, to be gathered up and merged into the New Testament and Christianity. Yet it is an interesting and typical fact that the theology of Christian theism itself was built up, after the completion of both Old and New Testaments, with help derived from Jewish thinkers. The work of the Jew Philo, the first who offered a synthesis between "revealed" and "philosophical" religion, passed into the structure of patristic Christianity; while in the great age of the schoolmen, when Christianity boldly undertook to embrace the whole intellectual world, the way was traced by the Jew Maimonides.

The last named is so important as to merit more than passing mention, but before turning to him, we should enquire what were the elements in the old Hebraic outlook which offered something fresh to the world. The answer is an old one, although none the less true. Hebraism has always meant what it means today and will mean tomorrow, monotheism and its attendant ideas. That well-known passage of Longinus which has been referred to above (p. 103), quotes the verse of Genesis: "God said let there be light, and there was light." This verse is typical of the Old Testament, of Genesis, of Isaiah, of Job. It expresses the idea that behind the manifoldness and the discord and the contradictions of the world in which we live there is one supreme source to which the whole owes its being. And this source is active, creative. "God said, 'Let there be light,' and *there was light*"; by His "word" the "heavens were *made*."

The God of the Old Testament is thus not a mere hypothesis to account for the wheels of the world going round. But neither is He a mere cosmological force. Among the "work of His hands" are human beings, and He is interested in them *because* they are the work of His hands. The Creator is the Father, not in the physical sense of the old Greek mythologies, but in the moral sense that He *cares*, that He approves and disapproves, that He punishes and forgives, loving those who live as He would wish, hating those who live as He would not wish. We have all heard of the dark side of this picture, especially in these days when the word "puritan" has become a term of reproach. Yet Cromwell's *Ironsides* were men of whom any people might be proud, and men who recognized by the biblical names they gave themselves what spirit it was that made them what they were. The Hebrew genius is ethical, and it is its ethical quality which has affected men's lives, both in the daily grind and in those outbursts of enthusiastic return to religious faith heralded by Luther, Milton, Wesley, and in our day, Karl Barth. What has mattered in history is not so much the Jewish revelation of the unity of God as the Jewish intuition of that God's moral nature.

But men's lives rest not only on what the great Hebraic Christian moral teacher and philosopher Immanuel Kant called the "categorical imperative," the austere command "Thou shalt" or "Thou shalt not" by which we do the right because we must. Men need a vision which gives meaning to moral striving. This can take the form of one of two ideals in which present inequalities are redressed, the one that of a perfected social order, the other that of a perfected individual life-cycle. Both these ideals took shape in the Hebraic tradition, the former receiving more stress in Judaism, the latter in Christianity. Although obviously compatible with one another they have appealed separately to different persons and different ages, and both have stimulated reflection, the one on the practical problem of social justice, the other on the religious problem of immortality. If one adds the institution of the Sabbath, so derided by the classical writers, which is nothing other than the voluntary limitation of the hours of labor which raises man above the beasts and asserts man's moral dignity as a human being, we have a trio of Hebraic ideals directly derived from the Old Testament which yet have a role to play in our civilization.

2

Mention was made of two Jewish philosophers, Philo and Maimonides, whose work is woven into the texture of Christian theology. But the outlook of the medieval schoolmen was not merely theological in the narrow sense. All knowledge was their province. This medieval world of knowledge is, almost as if by deliberate intention, an object lesson in the inextricability of the heterogeneous strands which go to make up any culture worthy of the name. The ultimate base of scholasticism religiously is Hebraic. But philosophically and scientifically it is Greek. The Greek came through Syriac and Arabic and often Hebrew before it assumed its Latin dress. The fathers of the Church were content to draw on them all without discrimination; and Greek, Arab, and Jew jostle one another on their pages in complete promiscuity.

In fashioning this surprisingly unified world of knowledge, the Jews played a large and important part in the field of philosophy as well as in those of medicine, mathematics, and astronomy (see pp. 195 f., 222 ff.). Among the best known was the physician

Isaac Israeli (Isaac Judaeus) of Kairouan, whose surviving works include a logical treatise *On Definitions* and an exposition of Aristotelian physics called *On the Elements.* The former is a treatment of various philosophical terms, derived ultimately from Aristotle, which were taken over subsequently by the schoolmen and became the basis of medieval Christian philosophical terminology. More important as an original thinker was Avicebron (Ibn Gabirol), the synagogal poet living under Moslem rule in Spain in the eleventh century, whose *Fons Vitae,* the first philosophical treatise compiled in that country, was accepted for centuries as the production of a Christian thinker and approved or disapproved as one of the typical expressions, of Neo-Platonic metaphysics (see pp. 61, 107). The anti-Semitic William of Auvergne, not suspecting his real identity, termed him "unique, and most notable of all philosophers." It was this remarkable treatise which introduced Neo-Platonic thought among the Arabic-speaking thinkers of the Iberian peninsula, and popularized it ultimately among the Christian schoolmen. Thus when the reaction against Aristotelianism and its exponents began, thinkers like Duns Scotus (following in this the great Franciscan, Alexander of Hales) leaned heavily upon Gabirol, though it is doubtful whether they would have done so had his Judaism been known. One of the principal points of difference between the two schools was that the latter adopted Gabirol's theory of the existence of a material substratum to spiritual beings, and declared the essence of the Divine nature to be in will rather than in intellect. The special ferment of thirteenth-century scholasticism may hence be traced in large measure to the influence of Gabirol's thought.

Greatest of all was Moses Maimonides ("Rabbi Moysis," as he was known to generations of schoolmen) whose epoch-making work, the *Guide for the Perplexed* (1190), was translated into Latin shortly after its composition and was followed by Thomas Aquinas on almost all the great issues common to Judaism and Christianity. The later history of this remarkable book is illuminating. The early Latin version was reissued in the sixteenth century (Paris, 1520), and superseded by the new one of the Christian Hebraist Buxtorf in the seventeenth (Basel, 1629), this in turn to give way to the French version of Munk (Paris, 1856–66). In the interim it had inspired Spinoza, not necessarily always to agreement; stimulated the social and political inquiries of men like Bodin, Selden, and Grotius; presided over the birth of modern anthropology in Spencer's *Laws of the Hebrews* (1685); and had been made the subject of a series of penetrating comments and summaries by Leibniz. It is now a standard repository for students of the conceptions forming that common medieval world-view, which in many respects still provides some of the permanent elements in Western civilization.

3

At the time when these philosophers, translators, and scientists were helping to erect the structure of medieval rationalism, a mystical revolution was brewing which became hardly less significant, although doubt may be felt as to its real value. Gathering up elements the origins of which are lost in the remotest antiquity, the Zohar, the book of "Splendor," flashed on the Jewish world in the beginning of the fourteenth century, and Christian Hebraists soon discovered that this "secret doctrine" of the Hebrews contained hints of the mysteries of Christianity. It is difficult to exaggerate the influence exerted by these writings. The obscurity of the Zohar and its kindred literature is only equalled by the insight of their occasional inspiration. They show remarkable affinities with the compositions of Raimon Lull and other contemporary Spanish mystics, whose influence reverberated through Europe. They entered deep through men like Reuchlin and Pico della Mirandola into the harmonizing temperament of the Renaissance. A by-product is said to be a metaphysical theory of space which commended itself to various philosophers, from the Italian Patrizzi to the Englishman John Locke—to the latter as the result of a conversation with no less a person than Isaac Newton. Since the conception would seem to have reached Newton through the Cambridge Neo-Platonist Henry More, we have here another suggestion of the tangled origin of modern ideas. But be that as it may, it is important to note that no account of the Renaissance would be complete without an inquiry into the so-called "Cabbala" of the Jews, and there is little doubt that its influence is to be found within such broad boundaries as the humanist martyr

Giordano Bruno in Italy and the creator of the biblical epic, John Milton, in England.

Not that the stream of mysticism ever was, or ever is, unmixed. Both in its sources and its later history the Cabbala was always infected with some philosophical elements, and the interesting result is offered by one of the now forgotten but once famous books of the sixteenth century, the *Dialoghi di Amore* of Judah Abravanel (Leone Ebreo), son of the last Jewish scholar-statesman of Spain, Don Isaac Abravanel. Composed originally, in all probability, in Hebrew, and published originally in Italian, this work ran through edition after edition in many of the languages of Europe. It exerted a great influence on Castiglione's *Il Cortegiano*, which provided the seventeenth and eighteenth centuries with its new ideal of aristocracy, in which the old knight merged into the modern gentleman. Translated into English, this book was widely read in Shakespeare's England. The conception of "Platonic love" is one of the heritages of the *Dialoghi di Amore* to the modern world.

4

It is with the seventeenth century that the greatest Jewish philosopher, one of the outstanding names in modern thought, emerged. Though the Synagogue of Amsterdam cast him out, nervous lest his impiety should endanger its newly won religious liberty, Spinoza was Jewish in feeling and in background.

Volumes have been written about the Jewishness of Spinoza, which has been denied as vigorously as it has been affirmed. But all would agree that his peculiar flavor owes at least something to his origin. By "origin" is not meant some mysterious and indefinable quality of the blood which made Spinoza what is called a monist; but only that the cultural tradition from which Spinoza sprang and in which he spent his early and impressionable years, a tradition rooted as it was in an austere monotheism, was such as to suggest a monistic key to the riddles of existence. Monism is, of course, not monotheism, and the religion of the Synagogue which Spinoza left is not the five books of the *Ethics* which Spinoza bequeathed as a new Pentateuch to mankind. But if the Synagogue taught anything it was the unity of God, and Spinoza's philosophy is a hymn to the unity of God's work or nature. The characteristic dogmas of Judaism and Spinozism are thus closely akin. Whatever Spinoza derived from other sources is subordinated to this ultimate vision, and the unitary character of the resulting system, crushing in its simplicity, is only another sign of its primary inspiration.

The extent and profundity of Spinoza's influence on modern thought is a matter on which two opinions cannot be held. He is one of the great thinkers of the world. It is common to mention him with Plato, and like Plato he has survived even his admirers. Indeed, he is most like Plato in that he is a fruitful source of ideas even for those who profess themselves his opponents. Personal intercourse with Leibniz at the very close of his life gave the determining influence to the latter's thought, which was destined to dominate the eighteenth century. No book on Spinoza fails to tell of his position in the history of the formation of the German mind in its days of true greatness, the days of Lessing and Herder and Goethe. And no student of Hegel can avoid seeing the debt that dominating and fruitful personality owes to Spinoza. But it is absurd to lengthen the string of names. Spinoza is Spinoza, and there is nothing to it but that.

5

As one looks at the present-day scene, one may observe an outpouring of talent among Jews, which is clearly prodigious. This is as true in philosophy as in any other sphere of human activity. It is not so much the power to see new things; it is also, and that is of even greater importance, the power to see old things in a new way. We may note this gift in some—it is pointless to catalogue all—recent Jewish thinkers who have displayed it most obviously.

Bergson, it has been said, has rediscovered time, and it is as the rediscoverer of time that he will probably be remembered. And so Einstein, among his many other fruitful ideas, rediscovered space and Freud rediscovered dreams. Each of these men started, as it were, anew. They looked on old problems with new eyes. They brought to the tired discussions of centuries the freshness of approach of a child. And their results, too, are elementary; elementary in the profound sense that they reach deep, offering a foundation for a whole world-view. These Jews and innumerable lesser ones are among the master-builders of the modern intellectual world, and it is not for us to "claim" or "reject" them as "Jewish" or "un-Jewish"; they are men. If the fruitful doctrines of creative evolution and dialectical materialism are due to Jews; if the Jew, Hermann Cohen, founded a new and fertile school of Kantian criticism, or the Jew Meyerson indicated new paths in the interpretation of science; or the Jew, Durkheim, stimulated new ideas in the study of human society; or the Jew, Worms, established the International Sociological Institute; or the Jew, Husserl, initiated a new movement in logic and metaphysics; these are contributions freely given to civilization as a whole and in civilized times as freely received. Who cares and who should care, when considering Lévy-Bruhl's work on the mind of the primitive, or Léon's life of Fichte, or Cassirer's history of the theory of knowledge, or Brunschvicg's edition of Pascal, or Samuel Alexander's massive defence of the realistic attitude in metaphysics which begins with space-time and ends in Deity—who cares and who should care that these men are Jews and as such have given of their best to the world? The list could be extended tenfold. It is not only that the Jew is in every movement, old and new. It is that he is there as an integral part of the movement, a powerful leader, a faithful comrade, a courageous follower.

As an instance of the part taken by Jews in the humbler, but possibly in the last analysis more important, work of secondary interpretation rather than primary discovery, one may note the part played in France by the centers of publication and discussion which Jewish savants put to the service of the community. There, the traditions of Renaissance humanism survive undisturbed, and the study of philosophy has always been a part of the official system of national education. But it would be difficult to overestimate the assistance given to the maintenance of philosophical thinking by such reviews as the *Revue Philosophique* directed for many years by Lévy-Bruhl, or the *Revue de Métaphysique et de Morale* founded and edited until his death by Xavier Léon. To the latter is due, too, the Société française de Philosophie, whose Bulletin is now in its thirty-fifth year, and the initiation of the series of international Congresses of Philosophy. With the fate of the *Kant-Studien* and its exiled editor before one's eyes, it is good to end on this note of modest and prolonged public service.

CHAPTER VIII. *Scientific Progress*

I

THE question is often asked, why the Romans, with their high powers of organization and their remarkable technical ability, as shown in their buildings, their baths, and especially their roads, never made any greater progress than they did in engineering science. One answer out of the many is particularly cogent. The reason lay above all in their cumbrous and elementary system of numbering. If a simple figure, such as 478, has to be represented by a long and complicated row of letters, cccclxxviii, it is obvious that arithmetical calculations are difficult, the study of higher mathematics closed, and many scientific and engineering developments, dependent upon mathematical calculations, enormously hampered. It was only when the Western World was introduced to the more convenient so-called "Arabic" system of numbers, and with it higher mathematics, that the path to the material civilization of today was opened. One may affirm then that the introduction of the Arabic numerals to Europe with the use of the zero and decimal system was one of the landmarks in the history of Western civili-

193

zation. It is hardly too much to say that our mathematical system is the key to the material pre-eminence achieved by this culture in the past four centuries.

The so-called Arabic numerals are not, in fact, Arabic. They originated in India, where they were familiar twenty centuries ago; thence they were carried westward by the Arabs, from whom in turn they were taken over by medieval Europe. Recent inquirers have suggested that the introduction of Arabic numerals was due to the "Radanite" Jewish traders of the Dark Ages, who penetrated as far as India and must necessarily have spread abroad a knowledge of the number systems used in recording prices and market computation. There is extant, however, a more circumstantial account, preserved in the writings of the medieval Jewish philosopher and exegete, Abraham ibn Ezra, who visited London in 1158 and whose character inspired Robert Browning's famous poem. He writes:

"In olden times there was neither science nor religion among the sons of Ishmael . . . till the great king, by name Es-Saffah [750–5] arose, who heard that there were many sciences to be found in India. . . . And there came men saying that there was in India a very mighty book on the secrets of government, in the form of a fable . . . and the name of the book was *Kalilah and Dimnah*.[1] . . . Thereupon he sent for

[1] For this famous work, see above, p. 56. This Jewish translation of *Kalilah and Dimnah* was afterwards superseded by the classical version of the Persian Ibn El Mukaffa.

a Jew who knew both languages and ordered him to translate this book. . . . And when he [i.e., the King] saw that the contents of the book were extraordinary —as, indeed, they are—he desired to know the science of the Indians, and he sent accordingly the Jew to Arin, whence he brought back one who knew the Indian numerals, besides many other astronomical writings."

A Jew was thus responsible, if this account is to be believed, for the transmission of the Hindu numerals from India to the Arabic-speaking world. How did they make the next, and more vital, transition—from the Islamic world to the Christian?

In this process, too, Jewish agency is to be traced. One of the most active of the band of translators of Jewish birth who worked at Toledo in the period after the capture of that city by the Christians was, as we have seen, Johannes Hispalensis, or John of Seville, whose Arabic name, Ibn Daud, was corrupted by the schoolmen into Avendeath. The most important composition introduced to the Christian world by his means was a work of the Persian, Muhammad al-Kwarizmi [1] (fl. c. 830) on practical Indian arithmetic. In this the so-called Arabic numerical notation is used for the first time in Latin literature—a milestone in the history of Western culture. So fundamental was al-Kwarizmi's work that for centuries what we now call mathematics was known after him as "Algorism." Though it was not till the sixteenth cen-

[1] The town of Kwarizm is the modern Khiva.

tury that the new method had completely permeated
Europe, it may be said that the whole of modern
mathematics, and with it a great part of modern science
and philosophy, dates back to this translation from
the Arabic by a Jewish scholar of a system first introduced to the Arabic world by a Jew.

Even before this period, mathematics had come under the influence of a very ancient Hebrew composition, *The Treatise of Measures*, ascribed to a Rabbi
Nehemiah. This remarkable work, a handbook for
surveying and dividing landed inheritances, was probably composed about A.D. 150. It has many an original
approach to mathematical problems and exercised considerable influence on Arabic—and, hence, medieval—
science generally.

At approximately the same time, Indian mathematics, or a little later, Indian geometry also was introduced to the Latin world. The medium was in this
case a work by a famous and devoted Jewish scholar
and religious philosopher, Abraham bar Hiyya of
Barcelona, or Savasorda (d. 1136), whose *Treatise on
Geometry* was translated from the Hebrew into Latin
during his lifetime by Plato of Tivoli, under the title
Liber Embadorum. This work, together with that of
al-Kwarizmi of which we have been speaking above,
was used by Leonardo da Pisa as the foundation for
his textbooks on Indian arithmetic, geometry, and
trigonometry, on which the whole of medieval mathematical studies were based. It is upon them, ultimately,
that the technical progress and the material civilization
of the present day depend.

2

In the blundering progress of scientific and technical achievement in the Middle Ages, the Jews of Europe did not fail to play their part. Throughout the period one finds mention of them, now translating a fundamental scientific work, now introducing a new process from one country to another, now referred to as authorities, now making their original contributions.

An impressive list of Jewish inventors and scientists of the Middle Ages could be compiled. Many of them have been mentioned above, in connection with the evolution of various nautical instruments and tables. But their interests were not by any means confined to this. The fourteenth-century philosopher, Levi ben Gershom, inventor of the so-called "Jacob's Staff," is distinguished in the history of science also as discoverer of the *Camera Obscura*, of which he gave a detailed description, many generations before Alberti and Della Porta, in a mathematical work soon translated into Latin. His interest was, of course, dependent on the fact that the device could be used for astronomical observation. The importance of this becomes apparent when one realizes that on this simple idea depends the whole of photography and cinematography as we know them today.[1] Levi ben Abraham, an obscure Provençal scholar of the thirteenth century, whose mathematical writings are just beginning to receive the attention which they deserve, is mem-

[1] It may be added at this point that in a later age the use of sensitized paper for photography was the invention of the younger Herschel.

orable for having recognized heat as a form of motion, four centuries before Robert Boyle.

Here and there throughout the course of the Middle Ages and the Renaissance other Jewish inventors and scientists make their appearance. According to some authorities, Typsiles, who re-invented gunpowder in Augsburg in 1353, was not a Byzantine but a Jew. In anti-Semitic Venice of the fifteenth century, a certain Jew named Solomon enjoyed a high reputation as a hydraulic engineer, and, for this reason, was granted special privileges. At the court of Ferrara, Abraham Colorni distinguished himself as a military engineer, and devised a primitive quick-firing gun as well as a taximeter and an instrument for measuring distances by means of reflectors. A Jewish engineer was employed to build a bridge in Brazil in 1640. Jewish mining engineers were found in Germany, Italy, even England, where in the reign of Elizabeth a certain Joachim Gauns of Prague directed smelting-works.

Many other instances may be adduced, serving to indicate that, in the gradual, anonymous, development of technical progress before the nineteenth century, Jews collaborated with other sections of the European population. It is not perhaps without significance that one of the earliest chemical utensils, the *Bain Marie*, or "water-bath" of our modern chemical laboratories, is legendarily associated with the name of its hypothetical discoverer, a Jewess named Maria.

This same intellectual alertness was given a fresh outlet after the breakdown of the Ghetto. In the course of the nineteenth century, the energy and inventiveness which had previously been confined to talmudical studies, or to the difficult task of earning a living through menial occupations, began to be turned to science in its wider sense. Jews now not only earned distinction, but produced a few scholars who were the unchallenged leaders in their particular branches of research. The institution of the Nobel Prizes provides some sort of index. Jews who were given that coveted award down to 1934 numbered at least seventeen, in addition to whom there were at least four half-Jews. Of the seven American prizewinners two were Jews, and while the Jews do not exceed 1 per cent of the general population of the Western World, they contributed 9 per cent, or, with the half-Jews 12 per cent, of the Nobel Prizewinners. Numerically they exceeded all but the French and Germans, several of whom, on the other hand, were Jews. In fact, of the thirty-eight Germans who have been awarded Nobel Prizes, nine were Jews and one partly Jewish, while the antecedents of two more are doubtful. Proportionately, Jews were exceeded only by Scandinavians, but it must be recalled that the Nobel Prizes are a Scandinavian foundation. As will be shown elsewhere, a majority of the Jewish Nobel Prizemen received the award—characteristically, it may perhaps be added—for services to medicine. Proportionately, the next highest number were awarded for services to the cause of peace. There has been one award for scenic art and one for literature. The remainder were singled out for their services to one branch or the other of scientific inquiry in the more restricted sense.

3

The characteristic feature of our modern civilization is a technical progress, which has had a widespread influence upon the amenities of life in all countries and in every class of the community. This, in the last resort, is dependent to a very large extent upon physical and mathematical advances, with the result that those who have led in these fields may be reckoned among the benefactors of the modern world. It is, perhaps, in instinctive appreciation of this fact that Albert Einstein, the full implications of whose theory of relativity can be appreciated only by very few, has received in our day an unexampled degree of public recognition. But, among the workers in the same field whose names are indubitably in the first rank are several more of Jewish birth or descent: Niels Bohr, Danish on his father's side and Jewish on his mother's, the greatest theoretical physicist of his time; James Franck, youngest of all Nobel Prizemen, who received the award in 1926 for his experimental confirmation of the quantum theory; his associate, Gustav Hertz, given the prize in physics for research in the theories of atoms; Albert Abraham Michelson, the American whose experiments broke down the theory of a stationary ether which had previously prevailed, through which all motion took place and the transmission of light and electricity was conditioned; and the great mathematical physicist, Max Born, formerly editor of the *Physikalischen Zeitschrift*.

The mathematical propensity of the Jews, traceable

perhaps to the rigidly logical character of their training, continued the notable medieval tradition to which reference has already been made. Ozanam, the greatest French mathematician of the seventeenth century, is generally reported to have been of Jewish extraction.

The nineteenth century produced a remarkable galaxy in this field. It is believed that even Lobatschewski, one of the discoverers of absolute geometry, was the son of Jewish parents who had been converted to the Greek Catholic faith. The great pioneers of the last century include, too, K. G. J. Jacobi, of dynamic as well as pure mathematical fame, co-inventor of elliptic functions; the two Cantors—Georg, the romantic among mathmeticians, and Moritz, the historian of mathematics; Luigi Cremona, reformer of Italian mathematical instruction, whose name is associated with the theory of geometrical transformations; the brilliant Gotthold Eisenstein, who might have excelled them all but for his premature death before he completed his thirtieth year; and many others of renown.

In the following generation in Germany were Edmund Landau, formulator of the analytic theory of numbers, and Paul Ehrenfest, originator of the theory of adiabatic invariants; in France, Jaques Hadamard, who proved the prime number theorem, and Georges-Henri Halphen, prizeman of the Berlin Academy; in Italy, Guido Castelnuovo, founder of the study of surfaces. Emmy Noether, their contemporary, was not only one of the outstanding algebraists of the day, but in addition unquestionably the most eminent woman mathematician of all time. Perhaps the greatest, how-

ever, of modern Jewish mathematicians is Hermann
Minkowski, who apart from his outstanding work on
the geometry of numbers, gave a great impetus to the
mathematical basis of relativity, following upon the
conception of a four-dimensional time continuum;
while Tullio Levi-Civita, one of the most distinguished
figures in Italian Academic life today, developed the
absolute calculus, which was the mathematical instrument necessary for the fashioning of Einstein's ideas.

It was in conjunction with Michelson, Minkowski,
and Levi-Civita, that Einstein's remarkable thesis of
relativity was developed. If it is possible to say that
there is something Jewish in the tenacity which can
persist in a long sequence of thankless research, in the
flash of genius which can evolve a new explanation of
the data so laboriously collected, and in the courage
to maintain an unpopular theory in the teeth of opposition and contempt, then the theory of relativity
is, as the adverse critics of its author maintain, essentially Jewish. But scientific research knows nothing
of racial and religious distinctions, and in point of fact
this, like every other conquest of knowledge, is a
human achievement, built up on human experiments
and human theories, in which a Jewish strand can no
more be set apart than any other.

England, for some reason, has not produced the
same long sequence of distinguished Jewish students
in this field as Germany. There are, however, a handful of the highest eminence. Thus the greatest English
pure mathematician of the nineteenth century, with
the possible exception only of his collaborator, Cayley,

was James Joseph Sylvester, Savilian Professor of Geometry in the University of Oxford. He was the foremost worker in developing, and perhaps author of, the doctrine of invariants in algebra, and he enriched the science of number with important work on partitions. In addition (a surprising diversion for a mathematician), he was the author of a considerable body of verse of high quality, as well as translations from foreign languages and a theory of versification. It was an English Jew, too, Benjamin Gompertz, who laid down the principles as to the decline of resistance to death which are the foundation of all actuarial tables in use.

4

Chemistry, too, furnishes a few names of first importance, whose investigations are felt in every branch of our daily life. It was in 1859 that Adolf Frank began to study systematically the plant-consumption of potash, which had been noticed by the great chemist Liebig. In 1861, as the results of his researches, he set up his first factory, thus founding the great potash industry which was exclusively German until recent years. In addition, he developed all the commercial by-products—bromide, ammonia, and the various chlorides—which themselves became the nuclei of great industries. Frank's collaborator, Nicodem Caro, one of the most prolific workers in German chemistry, joined with him in perfecting a method for obtaining nitrogen from the air, a discovery of great practical significance. Fritz Haber carried these discoveries a step further, when he devised his method for producing ammonia from the nitrogen in the air and hydrogen, thereby making available unlimited supplies of natural fertilizer. For this discovery, he was given the Nobel Prize in 1919. It was because of his discoveries that Germany was able to withstand a world in arms between 1914 and 1918. Nevertheless, he died in voluntary exile, and it was in England that his services to science were formally commemorated. Another great German-Jewish chemist whose work is closely linked with that of this group was Victor Meyer, a brilliant worker in stereo-chemistry. His apparatus for the determination of vapor-densities is widely used and his brilliant work in elucidating the constitution of molecules is of great importance. In 1882, he discovered in impure benzine the sulphur-containing compound thiophene, and thereby did a good deal to further the production of cheap industrial chemicals, now so necessary.

The dyeing industry provides a typical demonstration of the interaction of science and industry. Not only does it give employment to tens of thousands, but in addition its modern development has had a marked effect upon the life and the aesthetic outlook of the ordinary man and woman. In the Middle Ages, as will be demonstrated (p. 260), Jews were prominent in this calling, until the Italian cities secured the monopoly. Later, in the nineteenth century, with the evolution of aniline dyes, Germany took the lead. Two of the most important names in this field are Jewish. Heinrich Caro, director of a great industrial concern in Baden, discovered aniline red, induline, Manchester brown, eosine, and Victoria blue, and was the co-discoverer of phosgene dye-stuffs. The dyeing industry was revolutionized by his work, and important technical advances in the field of medicine were facilitated by rendering possible the coloring of various tissues. Later on, the researches of Richard Willstäter, one of the greatest living chemists, were in large measure responsible for the superior position of the German dye industry in our own day. In the field of biochemistry, too, his work has been of paramount importance in determining the chemical structure of the colors of flowers and of the haematin of the blood. Yet he was forced to vacate his chair at Munich through anti-Semitic agitation, a fate shared by many other contemporary German scholars, who have been spoken of in these pages.[1]

In England, work along similar lines was done by the eminent naturalist and chemist, Raphael Meldola, who discovered many important compounds and coal-tar dyes, some of which proved to be of great commercial importance. He was, in addition, one of the greatest recognized authorities on photo-chemistry. A biologist of considerable distinction, and a valued friend of Charles Darwin, his intellectual interests may perhaps be ascribed to the fact that he was descended

[1] The only name to be mentioned by the side of these two is that of the Nobel Prizewinner and founder of the great Baeyer Manufacturing Co., Adolf von Baeyer, who discovered eosin (much used in medicine), artificial indigo, and many other aniline dyes; he was a half-Jew, his mother belonging to the Hitzig family (p. 159).

from a long line of rabbis. Ludwig Mond, a German, who settled in England in 1862, revolutionized the chemical industry of the country by his process for the recovery of sulphur from alkali waste. Subsequently, he perfected the Solvay process for the recovery of ammonia soda, and by his discovery of nickel carbonyl devised a process for the extraction of nickel from its ores.

In the new branches of science, such as colloid chemistry, Jewish investigators have played a noteworthy part. Jacques Loeb left Germany at the close of the last century for the United States, where he was a pioneer worker on colloid science as well as (below, p. 241) a leader in physiological research. More recently, Herbert Freundlich, perhaps the foremost authority on colloids today, was forced by reason of his partly Jewish origin to leave Germany to the benefit of the University of London. In the same sphere, one must mention Jerome Alexander in America, Emil Hatschek in England, I. Traube, P. Rona, and a host of younger workers. And among contemporaries two more names cannot be neglected: Kasimir Fajans, formerly director of the Physical Chemical Institute at Munich and one of the best known physical chemists of our day, and Friedrich Adolph Paneth, formerly of the University of Berlin, famous for his fruitful work on radio-activity.

5

The most dramatic technical triumph of modern times is the astonishing improvement in communications. Until the close of the Napoleonic Era, these had hardly surpassed the standard attained by the Romans eighteen centuries before. Since that date, distances have been annihilated by successive inventions. The reactions on economic organization, on social life, on intellectual outlook, have been immeasurable.

The first stage, the Steam Age, was in the main the result of the activity of English and American inventors. Jews did not play a part of any importance,[1] except that some of the wealthier among them, quick to realize the implications of the new inventions, took an active share in making possible their practical application—the Rothschilds in Austria, the Péreires in France, the Josephs in Canada, de Hirsch in Turkey, and so on.

The Railway Age was, however, challenged by two new inventions. At the close of the nineteenth century, the automobile made its appearance, and at the beginning of the twentieth, air communications began to develop. By this time the Jews had emerged from the Ghettos, to which they had hitherto been compulsorily confined. Their collaboration was therefore possible, and it was considerable.

It is said that the earliest electrically driven automobile was made and driven in the streets of Darmstadt, Germany, in 1854, by a Jew named M.

[1] This is not to be interpreted too rigidly. Joseph Simon of Lancaster, Pennsylvania, was closely associated with the genesis of the steamboat; it was in their joint workshop that his partner, William Henry, made his first unfortunate experiment in 1763, and under their tutelage that Robert Fulton, who constructed the first effective steamboat in 1807, developed his abilities.

Davidsohn. For the moment, however, this means of traction was premature, and subsequent development was based upon an oil-driven engine. A short while before petroleum was first refined and utilized in America, in 1854, the discovery was anticipated by a Galician Jew, Abraham Schreiner, who thus paved the way for the modern system of transportation. His amateurish efforts robbed his discovery of real significance and he died in penury, but his invention links up with the work of another Jew, Siegfried Marcus, inventor of the automobile. It was in 1864 that the latter built his first horseless carriage and in 1875 the second, which was the first benzine-driven vehicle to function. This earliest motor-car, now in the possession of the Vienna Automobile Club, he drove about the streets of Vienna amid general astonishment. His automobile patents were registered in Germany in 1882; it was not until four years later, in 1886, that the first Daimler motor-car was built. In honor of his invention a tablet was affixed by the Town Council of Mecklenburg outside the house in which he was born. No doubt it has been removed in the course of the past few years, when men's ancestry has come to attract more attention than their achievements.

Aviation, too, owes a distinct debt to Jews. One of its pioneers was a certain German Jew named David Schwarz, so far forgotten even by his co-religionists that he does not figure in the columns of most Jewish works of reference. It was in 1890 that he first devised a rigid airship with a gas-container made of metal. He presented his scheme to the Austrian War Ministry, which rejected it on financial grounds. Not discouraged, in 1892 he went to Russia, where the first rigid airship was constructed under his direction at St. Petersburg. Unfortunately, the container was made of inferior metal, and the experiment was only a qualified success. However, the German government became interested and invited him to Germany to make a trial flight. The excitement was too much for him, and when he was handed the official telegram, he collapsed and died in the street. His widow, however, carried on the work, and a new airship was constructed under her supervision. At the trial, a certain Count Zeppelin was present, and was so impressed that he purchased the patents from Frau Schwarz, so that the successful dirigible which finally resulted bears his name alone. But Jewish collaboration did not end, for Karl Arnstein was chief construction engineer in the Zeppelin works, and in 1924 piloted the first Zeppelin across the Atlantic to America.[1]

[1] Other important inventions in connection with flying which are due to Jews are those of Emile Berliner who devoted his later years to devices for stabilizing aeroplanes; and of Theodor von Karman, author of the theory of the "vortex strut," who occupies a premier position among mathematicians in aviation. Lazare Jean Weiller (p. 212) has contributed to various appliances used in flying, and Hunefeld was one of the first to cross the Atlantic by aeroplane, west to east. Mention should be made also of the services rendered to aviation by Henri Deutsch de la Meurthe by his writings (especially Le pétrole et ses applications), the prizes which he instituted, and his foundation of the Aerotechnical Institute of St. Cyr.

There is nothing but the name to support the belief that Otto Lilienthal, who advanced the idea of a heavier-than-air flying machine, was a Jew.

6

Let us now consider another aspect, with which modern technical progress is intimately bound up, the advance in the harnessing and utilization of electricity, with its many varied outlets—power, lighting, communications, telegraph, the radio, and so on. Joseph Popper (Lynkaeus), a pioneer also in the theory of flight, is said to have been the first person to suggest the possibilities of transmitting electrical power, in a paper submitted to the Imperial Academy of Sciences at Vienna in 1862. Other names in this field, however, enjoy a less vulnerable distinction.

Foremost among the physicists of the nineteenth century was Heinrich Hertz, a half Jew, who, bringing optics and electro-dynamics under one doctrinal discipline, made an important advance towards the unification of modern physics. His *Principles of Mechanics* is still considered after many years the fundamental work in this branch of study. The great discovery with which his name is associated is the transmission of electro-magnetic waves through space, the basis of the wireless system suggested first by Clerk Maxwell and subsequently applied to commercial purposes by Marconi, and of the radio which has assumed such importance in every household during the past two decades. Hertz died, before reaching the age of forty, in 1894, when he is believed to have been on the point of anticipating Röntgen in the invention of the X-ray.[1]

[1] It is a little absurd to try to evaluate the paternal and maternal contribution to genius. But it is not without its significance that

In this connection mention may be made of Leo Graetz, son of the famous historian of the Jews, the first person to investigate the dispersal of electrical waves, whose name is thus intimately associated with the whole range of modern science.

So much for the theoretical side. On the mechanical there is fully as much to be said. It was a Jew of German birth, Philip Reis, who was responsible for the genesis of that everyday necessity of modern life, the telephone. The son of very poor parents and almost self-educated, he began to be interested in the possibilities of controlling sound-devices before he was twenty years of age. At first he copied the structure of the ear, making an electrified ear-drum, which was improved upon until it could be shown at a meeting of the Frankfort Physical Society and again, in 1864, before a conference of physicists in Giessen. Alas for the theory that Jews have unlimited money for all purposes! Reis had neither the means nor the health to develop his invention, his "telephone," commercially; and it was left to Graham Bell to elaborate the device in conjunction with Edison, and to place it on the market. Nevertheless, the standard works of reference record Reis' name as the first inventor of the telephone, and a monument to his memory was erected by physicists in 1878.

The microphone, on the other hand, was the invention of Emile Berliner, a German-Jewish scientist who

---

Hertz' cousin on the side of his Jewish father was the Nobel Prizeman, Gustav Hertz; this seems to indicate that, in this instance, the Hebraic factor was decisive.

lived in America, whose work is hence associated with the telephonic and gramophonic devices now in general use. Indeed, the claim has been made with a considerable degree of justification that he was the true inventor of the gramophone, though the commercial triumph of Edison has obscured his claim to recognition. What has been said above does not of course belittle in the slightest degree the discoveries of the latter, the greatest inventor, perhaps, of all time. But it is worthy of note that the two devices with which his name is particularly associated owed a great deal to Jews, but for whom their perfection would certainly have been retarded, and might have been impossible. Similarly, Lord Kelvin's system for multiple telegraphy, elaborated in 1858, was based upon a discovery of that astonishingly versatile Russian-Jewish genius, Hayim Selig Slonimski, who two years previous had produced an electro-chemical device for sending four telegrams at once. Later on, the copper alloys which made possible long-distance telephoning were first used in Europe by Lazare Jean Weiller. And it was Robert von Lieben who invented the radio amplifier which made possible the development of modern radio, as well as of the sound film, an achievement which earned for him, until they discovered his Jewish origin, the enthusiastic plaudits of the anti-Semitic press in Germany.

7

Minor mechanical devices and processes of Jewish origin which are in daily use are numerous. The sewing-machine, which made possible the immense reduction in the price of clothing, was developed to a high degree of efficiency by Isaac Singer. Nahum Salamon's invention of the spider-wheel made the modern safety-bicycle possible.

Ernst Fleischel devised the capillary thermometer, and the Luxemburger, Gabriel Lippmann, was discoverer of the capillary electrometer and of color photography, the latter gaining for him the Nobel Prize. The Italian, Samson Valobra, invented the safety-match; Abraham Stern made the first calculating machine; L. B. Phillips, an able etcher of the last generation, invented the keyless watch, which is now used almost universally.

Aaron Hirsch introduced various improved metallurgical processes; Moritz Hermann Jacobi, a prominent German architect of his day, was the inventor of galvanoplasty, with all its manifold subsidiaries, including electrotyping; Joseph d'Aguilar Samuda, the most eminent nautical engineer of early Victorian times, was a pioneer in the use of iron for the construction of steamships. Joseph B. Strauss of Cincinnati, was one of America's greatest bridge-builders, his outstanding achievement being the great Golden Gate Bridge at San Francisco, the longest span bridge in the world. The great humanitarian, Lewis Gompertz, devised the expanding chuck, still widely used in industry, from which a more practically-minded person might have made a fortune. This was only one of his thirty-eight inventions, designed, for the most part, to make the lives of dumb animals more bearable.

8

Jewish interest in natural history and allied branches
of science goes back to a remote period. When in the
tenth century a copy of Dioscorides' work on botany
reached Cordova, it was the Jewish physician, Hasdai
ibn Shaprut, who translated it into Arabic with the
aid of a Byzantine monk. It was thus that the work
of the great Greek scientist became available to the
Spanish schools and ultimately to medieval Europe.
This was typical of the part Jews played in spreading
medieval science.

Mention is made elsewhere (pp. 230–31) in another
connection of the vastly important medical work of
the Marrano physician, Garcia d'Orta, founder of tropical medicine. But his famous *Colloquies*, first published
at Goa in 1563, marked an epoch, too, in the history of
botany; for it contains the earliest scientific description
of a large number of plants and is the first work that
treats a flora different from that of the classical writers,
Dioscorides, Theophrastus, and so on. D'Orta's botanical work was further developed by another Marrano scholar and traveller, Christoval Acosta, whose
Treatise on the Drugs and Medicines of India (Burgos,
1578), is still much more than a bibliographical curiosity (see p. 232).

One of the earliest Jewish natural scientists who attained a European reputation in modern times was
Marcus Eliezer Bloch (1723–1799) who, unable to
read German until he was nineteen years of age, nevertheless had such a desire for knowledge that within

eight years he was able to take his medical degree at
the University of Frankfort-on-Oder. His passion,
however, was the study of fish. His collection of
specimens, acquired by the Prussian government, was
until recently to be seen in the Zoological Museum in
Berlin. In 1781, he began to publish his superbly illustrated *Allgemeine Naturgeschichte der Fische* in
twelve volumes, which was completed in fifteen years.
This work, considered to have laid the foundations of
the science of ichthyology, for many years remained
the standard work on the subject and even today may
be consulted with profit.

While Bloch was at work in Germany, the wayward Emanuel Mendes da Costa was active in England, where he was considered the greatest living
authority on fossils and conchology. The twelve
volumes of his correspondence with contemporary
savants, which is preserved in the British Museum, is a
remarkable monument of eighteenth-century encyclo-
paedic scholarship. The name of Moses Harris, the
great English entomologist of the same period, would
seem to indicate a Jewish origin. There is no doubt as
to Nathaniel Wallich, the eminent Anglo-Indian
botanist, whose best work was accomplished in the
first half of the following century and who was father
of the marine biologist, George Charles Wallich, one
of the founders of deep-sea exploration.

This tradition was carried on by such eminent German botanists as Ferdinand Cohn, whose researches
led to his epoch-making discoveries in the field of
bacteriology; Julius von Sachs, associated especially

with the development of plant physiology and micro-
chemical processes; Nathaniel Pringsheim and Eduard
Strassburger—all figures of the utmost importance in
the history of the study of organic life. In England, the
second Lord Rothschild ranked among the foremost
natural historians of our day, his writings and his collections enjoying a world-wide reputation.

9

In the study of the stars, the Jews in modern Europe
were indubitably among the pioneers. The beginnings
do not redound altogether perhaps to their credit according to modern standards. In the Middle Ages they
believed for the most part, in common with their
neighbors, that the actions of man were influenced by
the planets and could be predicted by their study.
This fact marks a regrettable recession from earlier
beliefs, when, as Josephus and Tacitus agree, the Jews
were distinguished by their refusal to pay attention
to celestial indications. There were, of course, exceptions, and no more authoritative voice was raised
during the whole course of the Middle Ages against
the pseudo-science than that of Maimonides, in an astonishingly rationalistic communication sent to the
rabbis of Marseilles. But even his views did not command universal acceptance, and before his day and
after Jews were regarded as pre-eminent in this field.
This was the case especially in Spain, where both Moslem and Christian courts frequently had a Jewish as-
trologer in their employ.

Yet astrology, however far-fetched its conclusions,

was dependent upon a careful and accurate observation of the motion of the heavenly bodies. Hence, just as alchemy and the search for the philosopher's stone did a good deal to advance chemistry, so, but to an even greater degree, astrology was the basis of the modern science of astronomy. Above all, the instruments upon which astronomical study is based are a heritage from the medieval observers. The Alfonsine Tables drawn up by two Toledo Jewish savants (*supra*, p. 82) form the basic document of all scientific astronomy. The astronomical works of Abraham ibn Ezra were popular in various European languages, and were much used centuries after the author's death.

Mention has been made above of the improved astronomical instruments which are due to Levi ben Gershom of Bagnols and of the tables drawn up by Abraham Zacuto of Salamanca, which were of incalculable importance for the maritime discoveries at the close of the Middle Ages. These instances may be multiplied.[1] The names of no less than 252 Jewish astronomers who flourished, mainly in Europe, before the year 1500 have been enumerated—a remarkable number, rivalled by very few European peoples during that period.[2]

Interest did not end with the Middle Ages. It is

[1] It may be added that the earliest literary reference to a sun-clock occurs in II Kings 20: 9–11, in connection with the illness of King Hezekiah of Judah.

[2] One interesting figure was the convert Pierre de Notre-Dame, physician to King René of Anjou, and grandfather of the famous Nostradamus.

known that Galileo was on friendly terms with the
Marrano poet, Immanuel Boccaro Frances, and that
both Kepler and Tycho Brahe knew the Hebrew
chronicler, David Ganz of Prague, who prepared for
the latter a German translation of the Alfonsine tables
from the Hebrew.

It is probable, too, that Sir William Herschel, the
greatest of astronomers, was of Jewish birth, for the
name is typically Jewish, and he came over to England from Germany as a musician in a Hanoverian
band. Benjamin Gompertz, who has been mentioned
above, began the construction of tables for the mean
places of fixed stars, but was anticipated by Bessel.

Moderns include Hermann Goldschmidt, who between 1852 and 1861 discovered fourteen hitherto unknown asteroids between Mars and Jupiter; Wilhelm
Beer, brother of the composer Meyerbeer; Maurice
Loewy, one of the greatest observational astronomers
of the nineteenth century, who devised the two-part
telescope now in common use; Sir Arthur Schuster,
the famous physicist, who headed the eclipse expedition to Siam in 1875; Max Wolf of Heidelberg, who
introduced the method of photography into astronomy; Karl Schwartzchild, most eminent of all, who
was responsible for the equations for the atmosphere
of the sun and the stability of the rotary masses;
Rudolf Wolf, the great historian of the science; and
in our own day Schlesinger, Weiner, Bethé, Freundlich, and very many others. One of the newly-dis-
covered planets, even, is named after a Jew—
"Mauritius," which embodies the name of Moritz Op-

penheim, devoted German patron of the sciences.[1] In astronomy, moreover, more almost than in other branches of study, the work of the cloistered observer, known to only a limited circle of inquirers, is essential to any advance of knowledge. It is by these modest workers as well as by the giants that the cultural contribution must be judged.[2]

[1] That Von Seeliger was a Jew is widely stated, but not certain.

[2] Arnold Zweig, in his *Insulted and Exiled*, calls attention to one remarkable dynasty of German-Jewish scientists and scholars, that of Pringsheim. The founder achieved fame as a railway pioneer in the middle of the last century. One son was Nathaniel (already mentioned above, p. 216), an originator of the modern science of vegetable physiology (it was he who first discovered sexuality among the lowest forms of plant-life) and founder of the German Botanical Society. One of his brothers, Alfred, was Professor of Mathematics at Munich. In the next generation came Ernest Pringsheim, the eminent physicist; Klaus Pringsheim, the musician, now in Tokyo; and a daughter who married Thomas Mann and bore children who have already achieved a reputation in the literary and artistic world.

CHAPTER IX. *Medicine*

I

THE earliest and what is perhaps still the noblest
panegyric of the healing art appears in the apocryphal
Book of Ecclesiastes, compiled by a Jerusalem notable,
Joshua ben Sirach in the second century B.C.: "Honor
a physician with the honor due unto him for the uses
which ye may have of him: for the Lord hath created
him. For of the Most High cometh healing, and he
shall receive honor of the king. The skill of the
physician shall lift up his head, in the sight of great
men he shall be in admiration. . . . Then give place
to the physician, for the Lord hath created him; let
him not go from thee, for thou hast need of him. There
is a time when in their hands is good success."

These glowing words make it probable that even at
this early date a flourishing school of medicine was to
be found among the Jews. There is no trace of this in
the Bible; but that work contains some remarkable illustrations of medical intuition. In the words of the
great medical historian, Karl Sudhoff: "Two of the
greatest hygienic thoughts of mankind owe their
origin to 'Semitism' . . . the weekly day of rest and

the direct prophylaxis of disease. The first will be immediately evident to all, even though it has not yet been clearly recognized and proclaimed as a hygienic manifestation of prime importance. . . . Had Judaism given nothing more to mankind than the establishment of a weekly day of rest, we should still be forced to proclaim her one of the greatest benefactors of humanity. . . . It is a most interesting fact that, despite its theory of natural causation, Greek medicine was blind to the fact of contagion or direct transmission of disease. But in the Old Testament we have a methodic inspection of a leper by the priest who, according to the diagnosis, isolated the patient temporarily or permanently, and admitted him again to free intercourse only after indubitable convalescence or cure. . . ." [1]

It is not surprising, under the circumstances, that throughout the ages the Jew has shown a remarkable predilection for the healing art, and that in all epochs his skill has been recognized. In the Middle Ages half of the best-known Jewish scholars, philosophers, and litterateurs—men like Moses Maimonides, Jehuda ha-Levi, Immanuel of Rome, and so on—were physicians by profession, a striking illustration of the respect in which that calling was generally held. The great bibliographer, Moritz Steinschneider, who devoted much of his life to a study of Jewish contributions to medieval science, was able to enumerate no less than

[1] The idea of direct prophylaxis was first applied in Europe only in the fifteenth century, when, subsequent to the ravages of the Black Death, the public officials of Marseilles and Venice first organized a system of sanitary control for incoming vessels.

2,168 Jewish physicians, who flourished between the Dark Ages and the eighteenth century and who were of sufficient eminence to be recorded; yet his list is manifestly incomplete, and for some periods could easily be doubled. The record, deeply impressive for the Middle Ages, becomes in modern times of almost overwhelming importance.

The Talmud preserves some scattered notions of ancient Jewish therapeutics. The earliest extant specifically medical document of Jewish authorship is, however, the well-known compilation of "Asaf Judaeus" who, according to the most recent researches, flourished in Syria or Mesopotamia in or about the seventh century. His famous medical treatise, the earliest experiment in this genre of literature which has survived in Hebrew, sums up the scientific outlook which prevailed at the period. In one important point he strikes out for himself, for he is the first medical writer who seems to have had any inkling of the hereditary character of certain maladies. Noteworthy, too, is Asaf's treatise on the medicine of the poor, comprising remedies which required no outlay, for "he made his pupils take an oath that they would accept no fee for this work, but would attend the poor and needy free of charge for the sake of charity."

2

After Asaf, the earliest of the great Jewish physicians in the classical tradition was Isaac Israeli of Kairouan, known to the European scholars as Isaac Judaeus. He was described by a Moslem contemporary as a man of the highest character who, though much occupied about Court, was indifferent to wealth and personal advancement. During the Middle Ages he was one of the best-known of his profession, and his views on fevers in particular had the utmost influence. Like many another Jewish physician he was also a philosopher, and as such, too, exercised great influence. To Israeli belongs the credit of having introduced scientific medicine into Northern Africa, and his writings later exercised no small influence on medieval Western medicine. His great composition, translated into Latin by Constantine the African under the title *De Gradibus Simplicium*, was one of the few early standard works on pharmacology, a main source and basis of most of the subsequent medieval treatises on the same subject, and therefore of singular importance in the history of medicine.

One of the great thinkers who came under Israeli's influence was Avicenna, "the Aristotle of the East," who possessed powers of codification hardly surpassed even by his Greek prototype. His writings impressed medieval thought in every department, but his *Canon* especially was the most widely read of all medical compositions of the Middle Ages, and was used as a textbook in European universities until the middle of the seventeenth century. Avicenna is said to have been of Jewish origin.[1] There is, indeed, nothing improbable in this, for near Bokhara, where he was born, the Jews had been settled from time immemorial. But, whether it is so or no, it is a fact that a large propor-

[1] See A. Soubiran, *Avicenne, Prince des Medicins*, Paris, 1935.

tion of Avicenna's writings reached Europe through the medium of the Jewish scholars and translators who worked in Spain, Italy, and Provence, and whose activity (as has been indicated above) was so important an influence in the earlier stages of the Renaissance. The material on which they worked was partly Avicenna's own (thus his treatise *On the Soul* was translated by the Jew, John of Seville, in collaboration with the Archdeacon Dominicus Gundissalinus), partly that of the series of scholars who carried on and developed his tradition.

Foremost among these and among the physicians of Moslem Spain was Avenzoar (d. 1162), friend of the great Averroes. He, though a Moslem, was, so at least it is said, of Jewish descent, and may thus be included among the great Jewish physicians of history. His most important work was his *Taysir*, or Aid to Health, one of the most widely-read medical works of the entire epoch. At an early date it was translated into Hebrew, the language of the author's forbears. From Hebrew it was translated into Latin in 1280 by a Paduan physician, working in collaboration with a converted Jew, Jacob of Capua, thus reaching the European world. It was at Padua, too, that the Jew Bonacosa translated into Latin the *Colliget*, or General Rules of Health, of Averroes, which was long used as a medical textbook and frequently published even after the invention of printing.

Similarly, the most popular of all medieval books of remedies, which goes by the name of *Mesue*, itself based in part on Jewish sources, was translated into

Hebrew, and thence into Latin. This version was printed no less than thirty times between the invention of printing and 1581, and its influence is still traced in modern pharmacopoeia. So is that of the drug-list associated with the name of *Serapion Junior*, a joint production, based on Hebrew and Arabic sources, of the Christian, Simon Cordo of Genoa, and the Jew, Abraham ben Shemtob of Tortosa.

A foremost figure in this band of translator-scientists was the enigmatic character of the eleventh century known as Constantine the African (above, pp. 61, 223), who was the ultimate source of much European medicine. The works which he translated and thus introduced to Europe were largely of Jewish origin. His main sources, in fact, are the works of Isaac Israeli and the latter's pupil, also a Jew, Ahmed ibn al Djezzar. That he was materially assisted in his work by Jews is certain. Indeed, there is some ground for believing that he was himself of Jewish birth.

The most important name of the Middle Ages in Jewish life was that of Moses Maimonides. His overwhelming importance as philosopher and codifier obscures the fact that he was by profession a physician, and that his achievements in the field of medicine were such as to have secured him in any case a high place in the annals of science. The volume of his written work in this field was considerable; much of it was translated into other languages, and continued to be published and re-published long after the invention of printing. Of his *Treatise on Poisons and Antidotes*, a work which was cited in the thirteenth and fourteenth centuries by writers like Henri de Mondeville and Gui de Chauliac, a modern authority states: "The book is written in so scientific and independent a spirit, with such practical advice, that one often feels in reading it that it is a modern work." [1] More popular still was Maimonides' *Aphorisms*, the Latin translation of which appeared in no less than five editions for the use of European physicians between 1489 and 1579 and was praised by the great Mercurialis as being not inferior to the similar work of Hippocrates. As late as the close of the eighteenth century, six centuries, that is, after its original composition, it was still being quoted.

Maimonides' medical writings are in some respects astonishingly modern in tone. Modern writers stress his common sense, his rationalism, and his treatment of disease on scientific principles, rather than upon guesswork, mysticism, and superstition. Even the exception which he makes to this rule shows him to have been far ahead of his time; he sanctioned faith treatment in cases of dangerous illness on psychological grounds, *for the sake of the patient's peace of mind!* He believed in the strong curative power of nature herself and the importance of proper diet. In an ultra-modern fashion he stressed the superiority of prevention over cure, suggesting that the physician should be consulted regularly in order to keep the patient in good physical condition, instead of waiting till sickness came. He insists on the reciprocity between the mental and bodily

[1] *Bulletin of the History of Medicine* (Johns Hopkins University, Baltimore), iii (1935) 571.

state, emphasizing the corollary that the physician should have regard for the former no less than for the latter.

In other details, too, Maimonides was surprisingly up-to-date. He advocated something in the nature of eugenics, while insisting at the same time that for the benefit of the offspring there must be complete psychological harmony between husband and wife during sexual union. He commended exercise and sport, though only in moderation. He insisted on the importance of bodily cleanliness and on the beneficial effects of fresh air and sunshine. The house, he advised, should be properly ventilated, and plenty of natural light should be allowed to enter it, for "the sun is the best disinfectant."

In all this, as modern authorities agree, Maimonides shows himself surprisingly in advance of his age. In many respects he was the most modern medieval physician. The progress of medical science between the thirteenth century and the seventeenth owed much to his teaching; it would have been better had his theories been drawn upon even more.

3

Though the greatest names in medieval Jewish medicine are bound up with Spain and the Moslem world, it was by no means without its influence elsewhere. The foundation of the famous medical schools of Salerno and of Montpellier, through which the Arabic medicine was first transmitted to Christendom, is traditionally associated with the work of Jews. The report is of such antiquity, and of such insistence, that it cannot be neglected entirely, notwithstanding the absence of documentary evidence. For it is in complete harmony with what we know of contemporary conditions. From the Dark Ages onwards Jewish physicians had figured prominently all over Europe in the service of kings and princes. One of the earliest Italian physicians whose record has survived was the Jew, Sabbetai Donnolo, born at Oria in 913. His extant works justify us in considering him one of the most important figures in the scientific life of Latin Europe in his age. Incidentally, he provides the earliest medieval description of a magnifying- and burning-glass.

Such was the reputation of the medieval Jewish practitioners that in the thirteenth century the Count of Flanders sent to England to summon the scholar and physician, Master Elias of London, to cross the narrow seas to attend upon him. Later on, after the Jews had been expelled from England, Jewish physicians were sometimes summoned from abroad when the occasion demanded. Thus, in 1410 the ailing Henry IV sent to Italy for a Jewish expert, Dr. Elias Sabot (i.e., ben Sabbetai) of Bologna. In the previous year Richard Whittington, of nursery-tale fame, sent to France to fetch the Jew, Master Samson de Mirabeau, to come to England to the sick-bed of his wife, the Lady Alice. In other parts of Europe similar conditions prevailed. It was seldom that one or another of the Spanish courts did not have a Jewish physician in its employ. The kings of France, no less than the Holy Roman emperors and the Doges of Venice, often con-

sulted Jewish medical advisers, and at the curia of the
Pope in Rome there was a long succession of Jewish
practitioners considered in their day among the most
eminent in Europe. One of these, at the close of the fifteenth century, conducted the first recorded experiment in blood transfusion.

With the Counter Reformation, a determined effort
was made to drive the Jewish physicians out of practice. The medieval regulations, which forbade them to
attend Christian patients under the pretext that they
might obtain too strong a hold over their minds, were
renewed, and for the first time consistently put into
effect. Henceforth in Catholic Europe it was only at
times of emergency that the Jewish physician found
his activity unhampered. This happened in 1630, during the plague of Venice, when Dr. Valensin extended
his activities from the Ghetto itself to the neighboring
districts, which had been deserted by the Gentile practitioners, or during the War of Candia in the middle of
the century, when Elkanah Circoletto attended the
Venetian wounded without accepting any fee. Yet in
the Catholic world as a whole, the old tradition of the
Jewish physician, which had been the rule in the
Middle Ages throughout Europe, was now at an end.

For some generations, accordingly, we must look
for the manifestation of Jewish genius in this direction,
not among professing Jews, but in the first instance
among the Marranos or crypto-Jews of Spain and
Portugal. These had been compelled to embrace Christianity at the time of the persecutions of the fourteenth
and fifteenth centuries, culminating in the Edict of

Expulsion from the larger country in 1492 and from the smaller in 1497. They still continued to cherish their ancestral faith in their hearts, and the enforced outward change of religion could not affect their natural proclivities for the healing art. Hence, a remarkably large proportion of the eminent Spanish and Portuguese practitioners from the sixteenth century onwards are known to have been of Jewish extraction, and in many cases gave concrete expression to their religious allegiance, either by flight to a land of greater tolerance or at an auto da fé. It is obvious, however, that not all of them proved their Jewish sympathies, and that many remain unidentified. Were the list complete, it is doubtful whether many eminent Portuguese or Spanish physicians of the period would not be included.

The Pope of Rome and the Queen of England, the Doge of Venice and the Stadtholder of the Netherlands, the Kings of France, Spain, Portugal, and Denmark, the Czar of Russia and the Sultan of Turkey, all had at one time or another Jewish medical attendants of Marrano birth, who had attained the very highest standing in their profession. It would take too long even to enumerate them all here, but a few who have left a lasting trace in the history of medicine will be mentioned.

"Among the Portuguese worthies who have established for their country a claim to permanent remembrance in connection with the history of India and the Farther East, the name of Garcia d'Orta stands in first rank," wrote Sir Clements Markham. His services to medicine and to science were immense. D'Orta was, in fact, the most important figure in materia medica and pharmacognosy from Dioscorides in the first century of the Christian Era to his own time. He was one of the first great philosophic naturalists to be classed with such men as John Hunter and Alexander von Humboldt, who observed men in their relation to nature. His writings, particularly his *Colloqios dos simples e drogas medicināes* (1563), the first scientific work published in Portuguese and the greatest scientific monument of the Portuguese Renaissance, give the earliest description by a European of tropical diseases, and the accounts which he furnishes of medicinal plants are still unsurpassed. Asiatic cholera was an undescribed, if not unknown, disease to European medicine before his time; the account given of it by him brought it to the attention of the Western World in so complete and circumstantial a form to make it a classic of clinical description.

Historians of medicine, both in Portugal and outside, had written rhapsodically about the medical importance of Garcia d'Orta, without having any idea as to his origin. A brilliant piece of research by a Portuguese scholar, Augusto da Silva Carvalho, has, however, recently established the fact that this great figure in the history of medicine was a Jew in everything but name. His forbears had been victims of the forced conversion in Portugal in 1497; some of his closest relatives were persecuted by the Inquisition as secret *judaizers;* one of his sisters was burned alive, and only his timely death saved the great physician himself from arrest and trial on the same charge. His bones were, in fact, dug up and burned.

D'Orta's work was the basis of that of Cristoval Acosta, known as "The African," a distinguished Portuguese surgeon, physician, botanist, and traveller of Marrano extraction, who spent some years in India practicing medicine and subsequently undertook many long journeys in tropical countries for the purpose of studying natural history. His famous *Tractado delos drogas*, first published at Burgos in 1578, based partly on material supplied by his illustrious predecessor, is still regarded as an authoritative work on materia medica and drugs.

Amatus Lusitanus is another of the great names in European medicine of the sixteenth century. His books are referred to even today for the immense number of case-histories which they contain. He was born at Castel-Branco in Portugal in 1511 as Juan Rodrigo. The name Amatus, which he subsequently assumed, was a translation of Habib, the original Hebrew name of the family. He was graduated at Salamanca, emigrated to Italy, where he was in attendance on the Pope, and lectured at Ferrara, and ultimately sought refuge from the rigors of the Inquisition in Salonica, where he died in 1568. Among his pupils was Giovanni Battista Canano, who during one of his lectures received the first impetus for his discovery of the importance of the valves in connection with the circulation of the blood. His published works were numerous, but most important were the famous *Centuriae*, which, issued from 1551 onwards, had passed through a dozen editions, in five countries, by the beginning of the following century. Even today, the collection is regarded as a medical classic and one of the most valuable sources of medical practice of the sixteenth century.[1]

Rodrigo de Castro, a native of Lisbon, sought religious freedom in Northern Europe, settling ultimately in Hamburg. Here he distinguished himself by his self-sacrificing devotion in the plague of 1594 and for his outstanding services to the city in subsequent years. He achieved contemporary recognition, being summoned to attend the King of Denmark, the Archbishop of Bremen, the Count of Holstein, and other persons of eminence in the region. But he is best remembered for his *De universa mulierum morborum medicina* (1603), which is generally regarded as having laid the foundations of gynecology as we know it today. Castro is also one of the fathers of medical jurisprudence, having written one of the first books on this subject.

In England the names of two Marrano physicians of special eminence stand out among the many. Jacob de Castro (1704–1789) was one of the enlightened group who endeavored to introduce vaccination against small-pox into England, advocating it in a succession of pamphlets, in English and Latin, from 1721 onwards—half a century, that is, before Jenner's

[1] Amatus Lusitanus was not related to Zacutus Lusitanus of Amsterdam, another important Jewish figure in medical history of the period, who was a descendant of the astronomer Abraham Zacuto. It has, however, been conjectured that he was related to Elijah Montalto, yet another very prolific Jewish medical writer, physician to Catherine de' Medici, Queen of France.

activity commenced. He is frequently confused with his more ostentatious namesake, Jacob de Castro Sarmento (1691–1762), author of a large number of medical works, who is memorable for having popularized the use of quinine in Portugal to stem the ravages of malaria in that country. Ribeiro Sanchez, another Marrano physician, who lived for a while in England in the eighteenth century, introduced the Russian vapor-bath into Western Europe, but he is remembered even more as a pioneer of educational and prison reform. On the other hand, the Dutchman, Hermanus Boerhaave, leader of the world of medicine in the eighteenth century, was so much under the influence of Spinoza that the latter, though no physician, has been spoken of as "father of Boerhaave's medicine."

4

With the eighteenth century the regulations against Jewish physicians fell into fairly general desuetude. Jews were allowed to study at one or two universities and medical schools, and their natural ability reasserted itself.

Perhaps it is not altogether a coincidence that the rebirth of medical studies dates from this period, for it is no exaggeration to say that the world is indebted to Jewish workers for a considerable proportion of modern medicine. It may be added that a remarkably large number of the eminent Jewish physicians of the nineteenth and twentieth centuries were Germans, just as a particularly large number of the eminent German physicians were Jews. German Jewry has, in fact, provided the world with a disproportionately large quota of its relief from suffering. To say that Jews dominated German medicine is irrelevant. Jews did their share, and more, in the activities which were carried on in Germany, and assisted in bringing them to their high level. To resent this participation, or to submit the proportions involved to microscopic examination, is absurd.

It may be remarked, incidentally, that to judge from present indications, the Jewish members of the younger medical school in the United States seem likely to perpetuate in the future this tradition of outstanding service to stricken humanity.

It is not intended to give here a detailed analysis of the Jewish contribution to modern medicine—indeed, it is impossible to disentangle the various strands in a complicated science—but simply to indicate some of the most remarkable contributions for which Jews have been immediately responsible.

Modern therapeutics are to a large extent dependent on the comparatively new science of bacteriology. In Classical times and throughout the Middle Ages the doctrine of spontaneous generation was held; that is, the idea that under certain circumstances living organisms and life could come into existence from inanimate nature without any outside agency. This conception was destroyed by Ferdinand Cohn (*supra*, pp. 215–16), a botanist, whose researches had far-reaching implications on medical science. His studies of the development of bacteria and investigations into their life history disposed once and for all of the theory which had previously prevailed. He is thus the father of bacteriology, and without his preliminary investigations, the great discoveries of his pupil, Robert Koch, who found the organism of tuberculosis, and even those of Pasteur, who finally disproved spontaneous generation, would have been impossible. The latter's researches into hydrophobia, it may be added, were paralleled and almost forestalled in England by the distinguished pathologist, Julius Dreschfeld.

The great Frenchman's life work, too, was carried on by a part-Jew—a Russian, this time, Elie Metschnikoff, who was his real successor in France, a zoologist and embryologist of world reputation, a leader in the gallant campaign against infectious diseases, and author of the theory of phagocytosis. Of nearly equal importance was the deeply-religious Waldemar Haffkine, who, after working under Pasteur in Paris, discovered the method of inoculation against cholera. In 1893, at the invitation of the Indian government, he went to India in order to conduct a campaign against bubonic plague. At the risk of his life, Haffkine continued his investigations and at last discovered a method of inoculation which reduced the mortality rate by over eighty per cent. In recognition of his work, the bacteriological laboratory at Bombay has been renamed the Haffkine Institute. When one realizes the terrible ravages of the bubonic plague, not only in Asia but also in Europe, ever since the dawn of history it will be realized how Haffkine's researches benefited the world. It was this specific malady which led to the Great Plague of London in 1665. Later, the serum against typhus was invented at the Pasteur Institute by another Jew, Alex Besredka.

One of the best known names in modern medicine is of course that of Paul Ehrlich, father of chemico-therapy and the greatest biochemical philosopher of all time. His most notable discoveries testify at the same time to the fact that his genius consisted in an infinite capacity for taking pains. With Karl Weigert, also a Jew, he introduced the idea that every cell and tissue of the human body had a specific chemical composition, which reacts differently to coloring matter and may hence be analyzed by the use of dye-stuffs. This theory, worked out in painstaking detail, is the basis of the modern science of haematology and is fundamental to modern therapeutics.

Better known to the general world is Ehrlich's salvarsan, generally referred to as 606 because it was the 606th substance that he tried as a cure for syphilis. This preparation, which has saved the lives and careers not only of many men and women, but even of children yet unborn, won its author the Nobel Prize in 1908 and entitles him to be ranked among the great benefactors of mankind. "As a therapeutic achievement," declared Emil von Behring, "the production of salvarsan and neo-salvarsan has never been surpassed." In England alone, it is said, the lives of 5,000 babies are saved each year through Ehrlich's researches, and through his discoveries there is a reasonable hope that the disease will become extinct in that country.

It is remarkable that in this particular sphere a

majority perhaps of the other discoveries of foremost importance have been made by Jews. Ehrlich was himself greatly helped by Alfred Bertheim, who had previously worked on the arsenical preparation, atoxyl. A further great name was that of August von Wassermann, who in 1906 discovered the famous Wassermann Test for syphilis, which was used until it was superseded by a new method elaborated in 1927 by an American Jew, Reuben L. Kahn—in each case, of course, based on the work of earlier observers. Kahn, too, was the first person to demonstrate the immunizing powers of the skin. Albert Neisser, an outstanding bacteriologist and clinician, discovered the organism of gonorrhea. Indeed, the only name of first rank in the history of this branch of medical research which is not Jewish is that of Schaudinn, the Austrian who discovered the organism of syphilis.

Hardly less important than Ehrlich, though not so well known, was Jacob Henle, the greatest German microscopic anatomist of his day and one of the greatest anatomists of all time. With an early thesis of his begins modern knowledge of epithelial tissues. His *General Anatomy* of 1841 almost revolutionized medical science. It was Henle who first accurately described the cellular structure of the skin and of the tissues lining the intestines and other parts of the body. He first investigated the minute anatomy of the kidney, and his researches on the ligaments, the muscles, the viscera, and the vascular nervous system were without number and were of epoch-making importance.

The most eminent of the great Virchow's disciples,

without a doubt, was Julius Cohnheim, Professor of
Pathology at Kiel, who in the course of his short life
(he was only 45 years old at the time of his death) did
work of immeasurable importance in the field of pathology. In opposition to his master's views, he established the fact that the essential feature in inflammation
of any part of the body is the passage of white blood-
cells through the walls of the vessels, the migration
of these corpuscles being the origin of pus. This discovery initiated a revolution in pathology. Cohnheim
was, moreover, one of the founders of experimental
pathology in the modern sense by his transmission of
tuberculosis to the cornea of the eye. As a teacher,
too, Cohnheim's position was of the utmost importance. Among his pupils were Ehrlich, as well as the
great American physicians, Welch and Councilman.

In the comparatively new science of endocrinology,
the study of internal glands, one of the greatest names
of all is that of Moritz Schiff, a German Jew who
taught in Switzerland and in Italy. His investigations
covered the whole field of the nervous system as well
as of the glands. He has been described as the "great
anticipator" of many subsequent discoveries. Above
all, he is famous for his researches into the function of
the thyroid gland, and the gland treatment which has
recently become so conspicuous is to be traced back
to his researches. Similarly, the brilliant if unconven-
tional anatomist, Benedikt Stilling was the first person
in Germany and one of the first in the world to conduct operations on the ovary. More recently, superb
work in the same field has been conducted by Bernard

Zondek, one of a most able group of brothers, and co-discoverer of the remarkable Zondek-Ascheim test for pregnancy.

The researches of Robert Frank in the field of sex hormones have opened up new avenues which may be of incalculable benefit to mankind. Again, both the founders and most prominent workers in the field of otology, the study of the diseases of the ear, were the Austrian Jews, Politzer and Bárány, of whom the latter was awarded a Nobel Prize while a prisoner of war in Russia in 1914.

Several Jews, in addition to those mentioned above, have received the Nobel Prize for their researches in medicine and allied sciences. One of the best known is Otto Warburg, who was given the award for his great work on the metabolism of cancer, which has afforded fresh hope for many sufferers. Another great worker in this field, director of the Institute for Cancer Research at Berlin, was George Klemperer. Yet another Jewish Nobel Prizeman is Otto Meyerhoff, who devoted his life to the study of the dynamics of living phenomena and to the chemistry of the muscles.

Otto Loewi, who was awarded the prize in 1936, attained international reputation through his researches on the chemical nature of the transmission of nervous currents and on the structure of the heart; his work is now regarded as fundamental, and is being actively developed in many countries. Oskar Minkowski, the eminent endocrinologist, laid the foundation for the treatment of diabetes by his famous experiment of removing the pancreas and producing the disease artificially, thus making possible the discovery of the universally-employed curative agent, insulin.

Some other names may be mentioned at random. Ehrlich's collaborator, Karl Weigert, was responsible for a famous explanation of inflammation as an over-eager attempt of nature to replace damaged tissue. This is the basis of all protein therapy, now so widely employed. Cellular formation in live tissues was discovered by Saloman Stricker, who introduced the use of wax and gum cells for microscopic work. Gottlieb Gluge made special studies on the subject of inflammation, introduced the current treatment for rheumatic fever, and conducted important investigations on influenza. The micrococci of pneumonia were discovered by the lung specialist, Albert Frankel. Jacques Loeb, head of the department of experimental biology in the Rockefeller Institute, New York, endeavoring to interpret physiology in terms of physics and chemistry, conducted experiments in artificial fertilization, which seem likely to have far-reaching consequences on our understanding of the generation of life; while his brother, Leo Loeb, has made fundamental studies in endocrinology and cancer. Harry Goldblatt of Cleveland, has made a fundamental contribution to the nature of high blood pressure, while Max B. Lurie of Philadelphia, has done searching investigations in the character of natural and acquired resistance to tuberculosis. Valy Menken of Harvard, has made profound studies on the physical and chemical nature of inflammation.

Dittel invented the operation for calculus; Hollander was the pioneer of modern scientific dentistry; Georges Fernand Widal discovered the absolute diagnostic blood test for typhoid fever, known by his name, which is now regarded as indispensable and is universally used. Theodor Rosenheim was the founder of esophagoscopy. James Israel, a specialist in diseases of the kidney, was one of the greatest German physicians and surgeons of his day. Gustav Magnus, just a century ago, was responsible for the epochmaking discovery that all tissues "breathe," that is to say, they absorb oxygen and give out carbon dioxide. Ludwig Traube, to whom a monument was erected in the court of the Charité, conducted what was in its day one of the most celebrated clinics in Europe. With Henle, he was the founder of experimental pathology, and his studies on digitalis, fever, and diseases of the lungs, heart, and kidneys brought him a great reputation.

Simon Flexner, at present Director of the Rockefeller Institute for Medical Research, has discovered the germ of dysentery and developed a serum to cure meningitis. The studies on the compatibility of types of blood conducted by the Nobel Prizewinner, Karl Landsteiner, have made scientific transfusion practicable. His researches on the chemical nature of antigens and anti-bodies have vindicated the once-discarded "side chain" theory of Ehrlich, and afford the greatest promise for the ultimate control of infectious diseases and possibly also of cancer.

Schenk was founder of modern medical embryology. Alexander Marmorek, the Zionist leader, was a gallant fighter in the struggle against tuberculosis. Ludwig Kaspar is father of criminal medicine, a notable advance in humanitarianism as well as therapeutics; Hugo Kronecker laid the foundations of the scientific study of the physiology of the heart; Sir Felix Semon was the most eminent throat specialist of his period —a reputation later held by Heinrich Neumann of Vienna, one of the band of highly talented Jews who made that city, previous to 1938, the capital of the world's medical science.

Modern medicine depends to a considerable extent on operative treatment, possible only through the vast improvement in the system of anaesthetics. In the development of this, too, Jews have been prominent. The introduction of chloral and the scientific manufacture of hypnotic drugs, one of the most notable achievements of German medical chemistry, is due to Oscar Liebreich. Local anaesthetics were inaugurated by Carl Koller (subsequently of New York), an ophthalmic surgeon, who first made use of cocaine for this purpose. Similarly, the cold light apparatus for internal operations was invented by Isaac Michael. The list must here end, but it might well be continued to much greater length.

5

The Jewish practitioner of the Middle Ages seems to have been especially interested in ophthalmology, a branch of medicine in which the writings of Isaac Judaeus once enjoyed a great reputation. The most renowned ophthalmologist of the period, in fact, was the Jew, Benvenutus Grapheus, or Rapheus,[1] of Jerusalem, whose *Practica oculorum* was widely used at the time; it was translated into Hebrew, Provençal, Old French, and Middle English, and numerous Latin editions appeared.

In the later Middle Ages, the Jewish oculist enjoyed great renown; one, for example, operated for cataract on King Juan of Aragon in 1468. In modern times the interest has continued. One of the earliest writers on astigmatism was George Hartog Gerson of Hamburg, who had served under Wellington in the Peninsula Campaign and superintended the Hôpital des Visitandines during the Battle of Waterloo. The first Atlas of Ophthalmology was published by Liebreich; Javal of Paris attained fame through his studies in physiological optics; Ludwig Mauthner of Vienna and Julius Hirschberg are recognized among the greatest authorities on the subject. The investigations of Herman Cohn, of Breslau, father of the more famous Emil Ludwig, the essayist and historian, laid the foundation of school hygiene for the eyes. Carl Koller, of New York, as we have seen, discovered the use of local anesthesia for ophthalmic operations.

Other names in the history of ophthalmology are those of Joseph Aub of Cincinnati, who first used the electric magnet for removing foreign bodies from the eye; Julius Jacobson, who improved the surgical treatment of cataracts and originated the operation for trachoma; and John Zachariah Laurence, perhaps the greatest English ophthalmologist of the first half of

[1] *Rophe* = Physician (Hebrew). This is however problematical.

the last century. It is of interest that the two greatest authorities on the history of the science of ophthalmology were August Hirsch and Julius Hirschberg, both Jews.

The particularly deep Jewish love of children is perhaps responsible for the Jew's bent towards pediatrics, the factual answer to the infamous ritual murder charge. This branch of medicine was, indeed, in large measure the creation of German Jews. One of the founders of the science was Eduard Henoch; Abraham Jacobi, a fiery German patriot, who was forced to take refuge in exile after 1848, introduced the science into America, where he founded the first children's clinic and was at the time of his death one of the most honored figures in American medicine. Until recently the outstanding German pediatrician was Heinrich Finkelstein, who discovered new principles in infant feeding. Adolf Baginsky, co-founder with Virchow of one of the greatest Berlin hospitals, the Kaiser-und-Kaiserin-Friedrich-Krankenhaus, was a pioneer in the clinical and scientific study of child life and a voluminous writer on the subject. Alois Epstein, founder of the world-renowned Foundling Hospital at Prague, initiated various antiseptic measures in infant hygiene by means of which the mortality in foundling asylums was reduced from 30% to 5% in the course of fourteen years.

The current medical insistence on vitamins is in itself homage to the genius of the Polish Jew, Casimir Funk, born at Warsaw in 1884, who, while working at the Lister Institute in London in 1912, named certain substances which he had succeeded in isolating "vitamins" because he thought that they belonged to a group of chemical substances which he called *amines* and which were *vital* for life. A good deal of modern medical treatment is based upon this discovery. Again, it was a German-Jewish physician, Kurt Huldschinsky, who in 1919 first used artificial sunlight to cure rickets, then very prevalent in Berlin.

In neurology and allied branches of the medical profession, Jews have also been particularly important. Moritz Heinrich Romberg is regarded as the founder of the science in the modern sense. Robert Remak, who discovered the cells which initiate the heart-beat and thus has an important place in the history of embryology, described a type of nerve-fibre which has been named after him and evolved the electrical treatment of nervous diseases. It was Moritz Schiff who first attributed cretinism or its converse to the action or inaction of the thyroid gland. Cesare Lombroso, an Italian, described the nervous relationships of pellagra, a skin-affectation then widely prevalent in Italy, which often ended in insanity.[1] His discovery had no immediate result except that he was compelled to resign his chair, but his opinion has since been universally accepted. In addition, he wrote *The Man of Genius*, one of the famous books of the century, and opened up fresh vistas by his theories on criminology. His ideas by their positive approach

[1] Joseph Goldberger made the most fundamental contribution to the understanding of pellagra prior to the recent isolation of the active vitamins, lack of which is responsible for this disease.

played a decisive role in the transformation of penology and criminal law.

But towering above all others is the commanding figure of Sigmund Freud, "The Columbus of the Subconscious World," founder of psychoanalysis. There have been excesses in the development of this science, due more to Freud's disciples than to himself. Yet there can be no question but that it has proved of inestimable value to countless sufferers, not only those from ostensibly nervous complaints. This, however, is only one aspect of its importance. No theory of modern times since that of Darwin has affected human thought so deeply, and every branch of intellectual life today, philosophy and literature, art and music, even daily speech, is profoundly influenced by the theories advanced by the Viennese Jewish psychiatrist.

To quote an English authority: "Sigmund Freud's name is as cardinal in the history of human thought as Charles Darwin's. Psychoanalysts, under his leadership, have created a new and dynamic psychology, one that thinks in terms of activities and strivings, of impulses and conflicts, in the place of a flat and lifeless picture of mental states." [1]

It must be added that very many of the outstanding exponents of Freudian psychology and psychiatry from the beginning have been Jews—Alfred Adler, Karl Abraham, Hans Sachs, Joseph Breuer, and so on.

[1] Wells, Wells and Huxley, *Outline of Science*. A psychologist who by no means accepts all his teachings writes of Freud: "He has done more for the advancement of psychology than any student since Aristotle." (McDougall, *Outline of Abnormal Psychology*, 1926, p. viii.)

Antiquarians, on the other hand, trace the whole conception back to a remote Jewish pioneer, Hibatullah ibn Jami, physician to the great Saladin.

6

The essence of the foregoing pages has been summed up in an amusing statement by Dr. Lukatchewsky, a non-Jewish medical man, depicting the quandary of a conscientious anti-Semite who refuses to avail himself of any remedy invented by Jews:

"A Nazi who has venereal disease must not allow himself to be cured by salvarsan, because it is the discovery of the Jew, Ehrlich. He must not even take steps to find out whether he has this ugly disease, because the Wassermann reaction which is used for the purpose is the discovery of a Jew. A Nazi who has heart disease must not use digitalis, the medical use of which was discovered by the Jew, Ludwig Traube.[1] If he has toothache he will not use cocaine, or he will be benefiting by the work of a Jew, Carl Koller. Typhoid must not be treated, or he will have to benefit by the discoveries of the Jews, Widal and Weil. If he has diabetes he must not use insulin, because its invention was made possible by the research work of the Jew, Minkowski. If he has a headache he must shun pyramidion and antipyrin (Spiro and Filehne).

[1] [This is not quite correct. Digitalis was introduced into medicine by the Englishman, William Withering, in the eighteenth century. A few other details in the statement have been corrected.]

Anti-Semites who have convulsions must put up with them, for it was a Jew, Oscar Liebreich, who thought of chloral-hydrate. The same with psychic ailments: Freud is the father of psychoanalysis. Anti-Semitic doctors must jettison all discoveries and improvements by the Nobel Prizemen Politzer, Bárány, and Warburg; the dermatologists Jadassohn, Bruno Bloch, Unna; the neurologists Mendel, Oppenheim, Kronecker, Benedikt; the lung specialist Fraenkel; the surgeon Israel; the anatomist Henle; and others."

It has been suggested that the proportion of Jews engaged in the practice of medicine is too high. In 1895, it was reckoned in Italy that eminent Jewish physicians amounted to 64 per 100,000 of the population, whereas non-Jews amounted to only 34. In Germany in 1932, of a total of about 52,000 physicians, 8,000 were Jews; in Berlin, the proportion was higher. For some incomprehensible reason, this is regarded as a "problem." But every person is at liberty to choose his own physician, as he is to choose his own lawyer, and if in these callings the number of Jews is particularly large, it can prove nothing other than their ability, devotion, and the manner in which these qualities are recognized by their clients. The foregoing pages have demonstrated that the Jew has shown a continuous devotion to the art of healing for the past thousand years or more, and that some of the most notable contributions to medical science have been due to him. If skill and understanding can be enhanced by generations of devotion, study, and practice, the Jew of today must be better qualified than most men to engage in the practice of medicine. To exclude or discourage him on the grounds of a numerical calculation is certainly a crime against the individual; it may be one against humanity.

CHAPTER X. *The Economic Sphere*

I

ABOUT the year 847, the Postmaster of the Caliphate of Bagdad, ibn Khordadhbeh, compiled a way-book for the guidance of travellers and couriers. A section is devoted to "the routes of the Jewish Merchants called Radanites." [1] Well known though it is, it deserves to be quoted here once again, for no source conveys more strikingly the part played by Jews in commerce at that period, when other international intercourse was relatively slight:—

"These merchants speak Arabic, Persian, Roman [i.e., Greek], the languages of the Franks, Andalusians and Slavs. They journey from West to East, from East to West, partly on land, partly by sea. They transport from the west eunuchs, female and male slaves, silk, castor, marten and other furs, and swords. They take ship in the land of the Franks, on the Western Sea, and steer for Farama (Pelusium). There they load their goods on the backs of camels and go by land to Kolzum (Suez) in five days' journey, over a distance of

[1] It is believed that this term is derived from Rhodanus (the Rhone), the estuary of which river was the base of these merchants, or else from the town of Rhaga in Persia.

twenty-five parasangs. They embark in the East Sea (Red Sea), and sail from Kolzum to el-Jar (port of Medina) and Jeddah (port of Mecca); then they go to Sind, India, and China. On their return they carry back musk, aloes, camphor, cinnamon, and other products of the Eastern countries to Kolzum, and bring them to Farama, where they again embark on the Western Sea. Some make sail for Constantinople to sell their goods to the Romans; others go to the palace of the King of the Franks to place their goods.

"Sometimes these Jew merchants prefer to carry their goods from the land of the Franks in the Western Sea, making for Antioch (at the mouth of the Orontes); thence they go by land to al-Jabia, where they arrive after three days' march. There they embark on the Euphrates for Bagdad, and then sail down the Tigris to al-Obolla. From al-Obolla they sail for Oman, Sind, Hind, and China. All this is connected one with another.

"These different journeys can also be made by land. The merchants that start from Spain or France go to Sous al-Akza (Morocco), and then to Tangiers, whence they march to Kairouan and the capital of Egypt. Thence they go to al-Ramla, visit Damascus, al-Kufa, Bagdad, and Basrah, cross Ahwaz, Fars, Kirman, Sind, Hind, and arrive at China. Sometimes they likewise take the route behind Rome, and, passing through the country of the Slavs, arrive at Khamlif, the capital of the Khazars. They embark on the Jorjan Sea, arrive at Balkh, betake themselves from there across the Oxus, and continue their journey toward

Yurt and Toghozghor, and from there to China."

This classical passage is one of many which indicate the importance of the Jews in the mercantile life of the Dark Ages. The Roman Empire and its magnificence had crumbled to pieces, so far as the West was concerned. The amenities of life which it had introduced were forgotten by the Nordic and semi-Nordic states which had sprung up on its ruins. On the other hand, a new civilization, that of Islam, had come into existence in the Middle East, opening a new gateway to the ideas and the commodities of China and India. The new inhabitants of Western Europe had little knowledge of, or interest in, what lay beyond their own borders; and it was natural for the Jews to step into the breach in the role of intermediaries. Thus they contributed largely to the process by which the harshness of the Dark Ages was mollified, and various refinements of life, later to be considered necessities, were introduced to the countries of the bleak north.

According to one authority [1]:—"Europe owes to the Jewish Radanites the introduction of oranges and apricots, sugar and rice, Jargonelle pears, and Gueldre roses, senna and borax, bdellium and asafoetida, sandalwood and aloes, cinnamon and galingale, mace and camphor, candy and julep, cubebs and tamarinds, slippers and tambours, mattresses, sofa, and calabash, musk and jujube, jasmine and lilac. There is also evidence that some of the more important items of foreign trade came in with the Radanites, as was perhaps natural. Thus the word 'douane,' for custom

[1] Jacobs, *op. cit.*, pp. 203–4.

house, 'tariff,' 'bazaar,' 'bale,' 'fondac,' or factory, and 'baggage,' all occur early, as well as 'barge,' 'barque,' and 'sloop.' There is also probability that the royal breed of horses in France known as limousin, introduced in the ninth century, was due to these Jewish merchants. . . ."

Yet more can be added to this list. The Jews are a people "endowed by divine grace with special aptitude for handicrafts," wrote Cosmas Indicopleustes in the sixth century, and, so long as Christian intolerance permitted, it was as artisans rather than capitalists that they were distinguished. Various branches of manufacture were associated with them almost exclusively. In the early centuries of the Christian Era and long after, the Jews were recognized as the most skilled workers in glass; indeed, in the Dark Ages, Greek artisans in France boasted that they had mastered the Jewish methods of work. Throughout the Middle Ages, particularly in South Italy and Greece, the Jewish communities had almost a monopoly in dyeing and silkweaving, and it is probable that much of their production was exported to Northern Europe. There was one yellow, of which they alone had the secret, and which was known by their name. A remarkable contrast, this, to the other shade of the same color called Isabella to commemorate that arch-persecutor of the Jews, who vowed never to change it until Granada had been captured from the infidel!

The tradition of silk manufacture, above all, had a continuous history among the Jews. When Benjamin of Tudela travelled in the Eastern Mediterranean at

the close of the twelfth century, he found this to be
the mainstay of the Jewish communities everywhere.
In Sicily and Southern Italy, they enjoyed all but a
monopoly, until Christian competitors from Genoa
and Lucca secured their expulsion from the coastal
towns. But the struggle was not yet over. In the sixteenth century, a Venetian Jew named Meir Magino
wrote a book on his improved method of silk-manu-
facture, which he attempted to introduce into both
Italy and Lorraine. It was about the same time that
the silk industry was first established in the Low
Countries by Antwerp Marranos. Later, they transferred it with them to Holland; but even in this generally tolerant milieu, once their trade secrets had been
learned, they were officially excluded from the industry by the jealous burghers, whose subsequent
decline may not be altogether a coincidence. Precisely
the same took place at Padua, where the Jews, after
having introduced the industry and practiced it undisturbed for generations, were driven out at the close of
the eighteenth century. As though to compensate, the
silk manufacture was first established in Berlin almost
simultaneously by a Jew, David Hirsch.

In all these cases, the function of the Jews was not
merely that of *entrepreneurs;* they were also the technicians and, so far as was permitted, the laborers. It
has been worth while recounting this case in some
detail as an illustration of the manner in which the
broadening of the basis of Jewish economic work was
consistently impeded.

The story may, however, be duplicated with regard

to many other branches of industry, especially the textile industry, with which the Jews of Spain in particular were long associated. They possessed above all the secret of certain methods of embroidery, such as the famous *Point d'Espagne,* which was much used for Christian ecclesiastical purposes. It has been pointed out that even the pomp and glitter of the autos da fé was in part the product of Jewish skill! As goldsmiths and silversmiths, too, Jews were famous, especially in the Mediterranean countries, throughout the Middle Ages and after. It is noteworthy that it is precisely with these callings that they have remained associated down to our own day; there is thus no question of a sudden, and competitive, incursion.

2

At a later stage, there were four commodites, the introduction or popularization of which in Europe had a considerable influence on social life, and indeed on economic organization. They were sugar, tobacco, coffee, and tea. In the distribution of all these the Jews were deeply interested.

It is believed that sugar was introduced to the European of the Dark Ages through the medium of the Radanite Jewish traders. The commodity continued to be an object of special interest for the Jews. Towards the close of the Middle Ages, it was exported by those of Crete as far as Austria, and treacle, the principal by-product of sugar, was, it appears, first made by them.

The industry entered upon a new phase after the

maritime discoveries of the fifteenth century, when sugar became one of the necessities of life instead of a luxury. In this process, the part played by the Jews was of great importance. In 1548, Portuguese Marranos transplanted the sugar-cane from the island of Madeira to South America, thus initiating what was for a long period one of the staple industries of the New World. In 1654, when the vast majority of Jews emigrated from Brazil rather than imperil the religious liberty laboriously achieved under Dutch rule, they transferred their activity to the West Indies, establishing the commercial prosperity of these islands on a new basis.

It was Benjamin da Costa, one of the refugees, who set up the industry in Martinique, while others brought it to the Dutch (at that time English) colony of Surinam. They were very prominent in this branch of activity also in Barbados, Jamaica, and the other islands. It was a Marrano, too, who introduced the first sugar-cane mill into the West Indies. Long after, in the nineteenth century, it was a certain Aaron de Pass who introduced the sugar-cane to Natal. Upon this industry, to so great extent of purely Jewish origin, the prosperity of the West Indies long rested, and the livelihood of a large number of the inhabitants still depends.

With regard to coffee, the most interesting sources of information at our disposal relate to England. The first recorded use dates from the Commonwealth period, and the place is Oxford. "This year," writes Anthony Wood, *sub anno* 1650, "Jacob, a Jew, opened

a Coffee House in the Parish of St. Peter in the East,
Oxon; and there it was by some, who delighted in
noveltie, drank." This Jacob may or may not have
been identical with another person mentioned by
Wood, "Cirques Jobson, a Jew and Jacobite, born near
Mount Libanus, who sold coffee in Oxon, in a house
between Edmund Hall and Queen Co. corner." Subsequently, according to the same authority, Jacob
left Oxford and transferred his business to London,
"in old Southampton Buildings in Holborne." He was
still alive in 1671. The whole question calls for further
investigation; what, however, seems to be quite clear
is that coffee was first introduced to England by
Levantine Jews, who already had a considerable interest in the commodity in their own country. In Egypt,
indeed, coffee was already so much associated with
the Jews that it was generally termed "Jews' Drink."
Tea plantations were first introduced into Ceylon by
the Dr. Worms family, who thus assisted, not only in
making an important contribution to the welfare of
the island, but also in making the beverage a popular
one in the fullest sense of the term. Similarly, it was
by Jewish agency that chocolate was introduced to
France in the eighteenth century.

More important was the case of tobacco. When,
not long after the first landing in the new world, the
ship's doctor on Columbus' expedition, Mestre Bernal,
who was of Jewish birth, and had indeed figured as a
Judaizer in an auto da fé returned to the Admiral's vessel, his companions were surprised to see him breathing
smoke out of his mouth—a procedure which appar-

ently had something to do with an imperceptibly-fuming tube which he held in his hand. This was the first recorded use of tobacco by any European or by any man whose name has been preserved to history. From that time on Jews have been closely associated with the tobacco industry; and they contributed thereby, incidentally, to a considerable degree, in laying the foundation of American economic prosperity.

The rabbis, though they questioned the permissibility of smoking on Sabbaths and Holydays, took neither the attitude of the Christian clergy, who considered it "offering incense to the devil," nor of James I of England, who devoted a special treatise against its use. They considered smoking, rather, an aid to sobriety. Jews were engaged at an early date in the tobacco monopolies in Italy; it was a Jew who first introduced the use of snuff to Venice; and in Spain, in the seventeenth century, persons engaged in the tobacco trade figure with significant frequency among the Marranos punished by the Inquisition. In Holland, tobacco was unknown until 1611. In that very year, a Jew named David Abendana sold a barrel of tobacco to a merchant in Hoorn, and from that date, tobacco-importing and tobacco-working played a very important part in the economic structure of the Amsterdam community. In the seventeenth century, a good part of the tobacco consumed in Germany was imported through the Spanish and Portuguese community of Hamburg. The Jewish interest in the tobacco industry, therefore, is not a recent development: Jews have been interested in it from the first.

Besides tobacco and sugar, other American products owe their introduction in the first instance to Marranos. Thus the first grant to export grain and horses to America was made by Ferdinand and Isabella to Columbus' "New Christian" patron, Luis de Santangel, to whom is hence due the genesis of two of the greatest American industries of today.

Vanilla, too, is said to have owed its introduction into general use to Jews. This report finds confirmation in the fact that when in 1684 a certain Salamon de la Roche died in the Dutch colony of Essequibo, the secret of preparing the vanilla-bean for the market died with him. Indigo was also a staple article of Jewish commerce, and its cultivation was introduced by Jews into North America. This links up with their participation in the dyeing industry in the Mediterranean world in the Middle Ages in the one direction, and in the establishment of aniline dyeing in Northern Europe in modern times in the other. As early as the thirteenth century, under the Emperor Frederick II, African Jews were given Crown lands to develop indigo plantations in Sicily. Five hundred years later, a certain Dr. Nuñes first introduced the growth to Georgia, while Moses Lindo, coming from London in 1756, invested a fortune in fostering it in South Carolina. In the nineteenth century, synthetic indigo was discovered (as we have seen on p. 159) by a half-Jew, Adolf von Baeyer. This is a striking example of the continuity of Jewish interest in certain types of industry for many generations.

It was perhaps fitting that Europe owed to the Jews

some of its cleanliness as well as godliness. A great center for the manufacture of castile soap in the Middle Ages was Marseilles; here, it was introduced in 1371, it is said, by the Jew, Crescas Davin, known as *sabonarius*. But the story does not end here. Four centuries later, in 1761, a similar incident took place in America, when the General Assembly of Rhode Island empowered James Lucena of Newport to manufacture castile soap according to the process which he had learned in Spain. At the same time, Jacob Rodrigues Rivera introduced to the colony the spermaceti industry and candle-making. It was because of this that Newport became the great whaling center in the middle of the eighteenth century, when its importance almost exceeded that of New York.

The diamond industry was another in which the Jews played a conspicuous part throughout the ages. Here, the reason is plain. In the Middle Ages, dealing in precious stones was one of the few callings, other than moneylending, in which Jews were allowed to engage. Moreover, because of their insecurity, it was desirable to have their property in easily transferable form; their international connections and their pawnbroking business gave an additional impulse. From dealing in precious stones they naturally became interested in working them. In the seventeenth century they were regarded as the best gem-polishers in Venice, though the protectionist policy of the *Serenissima* subsequently excluded them, to the great loss of the city, as was subsequently realized. Possibly, it was by the refugees from Venice that the craft was established in

Holland, where its introduction is associated with the Portuguese Jews. The latter were engaged in gem-working in Amsterdam as early as 1612. From that date on, this has been one of the mainstays of the Jewish community of that city, still the greatest center of business, where the proportion of Jewish workers employed has never been less than 70 per cent. When, in 1748, their Gentile competitors petitioned for legislation to exclude the Jews from the industry, the government refused to take action on the grounds that "the Jews have established the diamond trade in this city."

A natural outcome of this interest was that Jews, proficient in gem-cutting, became expert seal-engravers. In the seventeenth and eighteenth centuries they worked in this capacity in many Central European courts, and attained a high degree of skill and reputation. Similarly, we find them active under more humble conditions in various English provincial centers. Thus engraving and art in general (see above, p. 150) were introduced.

Meanwhile, they retained their prominence in the surveying of gems. Just as in the Middle Ages, as early as the time of Charlemagne, Jewish jewellers made perilous voyages over land and sea to the East to bring back gems for the courts of Europe, so at a later date they went to India with the same objective, this being the earliest settlement there of European Jews. Similarly, when Brazilian diamonds came on the market in the seventeenth century, they were brought to Europe largely by Marranos. It was not surprising

that Jews played such a large part in the development
of the diamond industry in South Africa at the close
of the nineteenth century; indeed, it was a new experience when they were subsequently ousted from
their previous almost dominant position by the immensely superior financial genius of Cecil Rhodes.

3

It is with the field of finance that Jewish economic
achievement is usually associated. This conception,
already widely held, was popularized by Sombart
in his ponderous and, in many ways, impressive
volume on the Jews and Modern Capitalism. In this he
maintains with a wealth of learning that the Jews, by
the circumstances of their history and of their intellectual bent, are particularly qualified to participate
in modern capitalism, and are largely responsible for its
evils. Indeed, according to him, all the predominant
features which distinguish modern capitalism from
medieval trade and industry are directly due to Jewish influence. "Thus, the economic form of the modern
state was due to the activities of the Jews as purveyors
and financiers, in providing the state with capital for
war and development. They helped considerably in
the foundation of modern colonies, which has determined the policy and controlled the development of
modern states, and quickened international trade by
the large scale of their trade, the variety of their wares,
and the introduction of new commodities. As a consequence, we find the centers of trade changing from
one country or center to another according as Jews

were expelled or found shelter; Sombart gives as examples the transference of trade from Spain to Holland, from Antwerp to Amsterdam, from Augsburg to Frankfort and Hamburg. Above all, Jews have transformed economic life in commercializing it by creating credit instruments and introducing the custom of buying and selling securities, which supplied mobile capital for industrial undertakings. They thereby introduced their capitalistic point of view into modern trade, with its competitive (against 'just') prices, its advertisements, adulterations, payment by installments, utilization of waste products, and general efficiency." [1]

This is a remarkable catalogue of achievement; and whatever its original object and whatever its present utilization, it is a record which does not necessarily call for apology. Sombart's theories, however, as has been shown by Jacobs, Hofman, Steckelmacher, Waetjen, and others, are based upon an arbitrary selection of facts. Isolated data are taken as representative; strange names are assumed without justification to be Jewish; theories are built upon a basis of assumptions. A more careful inquiry results in a very different picture.

The Jew was forced by the unfortunate circumstances of his history to be predominantly a townsman. He had to seek an outlet, despairingly, in every branch of urban economy. Yet even here he found himself hampered at every turn by repressive legislation, whether in buying, selling, or manufacturing.

[1] For this analysis I am indebted to Jacobs, *op. cit.*, pp. 247–8.

Hence he made an intermittent appearance in every branch of industry, but invariably before long he was ejected. The situation was much the same in finance, which he was supposed to dominate. It was only for brief periods, perhaps once or twice in history, as will be seen, that his influence was really considerable. At other times, he filled only minor functions. However, his quasi-exclusive association with finance conveyed the general impression that he monopolized it, while the fact that in the Jewish quarter there were invariably one or two wealthy householders gave rise to the popular delusion which identified all Jews with wealth. Actually, as is pointed out elsewhere, one-third of the Jews of the Ghetto Age were dependent on charity, and as many more lived on the verge of the minimum subsistence-level.

One simple fact shows how slight Jewish influence in finance really was. For the consistent exercise of an important role in economic life, a certain stability of fortune, like that which carried the Fuggers or the Medici through from generation to generation, is essential. But the Jew generally lacked this. There were in the Middle Ages some Jews of great wealth. But seldom did this wealth pass from father to son. Generally, it was strictly personal, and the confiscatory measures which followed the death of a wealthy Jew, whose fortune legally passed to the Crown, prevented his son from enjoying it. Hence, though in the Middle Ages we know of several wealthy Jews, it is difficult to trace any wealthy dynasties of the type which exist today; the children of an Aaron of Lincoln and the like enjoyed at the best a modest competence. Wealth, moreover, bred jealousy; and time after time Jewish financial magnates, such as Samuel Abulafia of Toledo, minister to Pedro IV, who built what is now called the House of El Greco, were hounded to a shameful and penurious death. Not until the time of the emancipated communities of enlightened Holland, in the seventeenth century, did the Jewish capitalist in the real sense come into being. In the countries where the Ghetto still prevailed, Germany and Italy, Jewish wealth remained strictly personal until the close of the eighteenth century.

There were two periods only when the Jewish financier played a part of real importance. One was at the height of the Middle Ages; the other at the height of the Industrial Revolution. Both were periods of change, and each, moreover, called for special qualities which the Jews, as it happened, could at that time provide.

The first of these two periods was between the eleventh century and the thirteenth, when the Jews, ejected from commerce and industry through the jealousy of the guilds, were seeking another outlet for their capital. At the same time the Papacy with an impracticable idealism was endeavoring to suppress the institution of interest among Christians (*supra*, pp. 29–31). Hence, for a short period the Jews, by no means the wealthiest persons in Europe (those whose property was measured in terms of land were more wealthy by far), were in certain parts the sole capitalists. They possessed their capital, in short, in mobile form, and it is mobile capital which is all-important in economic development. Europe's transition from a barter-economy to a money-economy in the two and a half centuries which succeeded the First Crusade was certainly facilitated by their presence. The ready money which they could provide made possible the development of the system of "scutage," whereby the baron acquitted himself of his obligations to the Crown by a monetary payment instead of personal service. Incidentally, the process meant that the hands of the central government were strengthened against the centrifugal powers of the nobility. Thus the dissolution of the feudal system was facilitated—itself no negligible factor in the development of civilization.

Moreover, for the two characteristic occupations of the Middle Ages, fighting and building, Jewish aid was at this time indispensable. The Crusades, fatal as they were to the Jews, would not have been possible on the same vast scale had it not been for the capital which Jews had to provide. Even ecclesiastical foundations had recourse to them when any important undertaking was contemplated; thus Aaron of Lincoln, the great Anglo-Jewish financier of the twelfth century, is thought to have assisted in the construction of no less than nine of the Cistercian monasteries of England as well as of the great Abbey of St. Albans and even Lincoln Minster.

This period of prominence, however, did not last long. The recurrent massacres which accompanied the Crusades and followed them, the competition of Christian usurers operating under the highest patronage, and finally the great expulsions at the close of the Middle Ages, drove the Jews into the position of mere pawnbrokers. From the thirteenth century to the eighteenth, their importance in the world of finance was, generally speaking, negligible.

The second period of the Jews' real significance in the world of finance began in the eighteenth century, and reached its climax in the nineteenth, after the Napoleonic Wars. It was a period of growing industrialization, of rapidly increasing manufactures, of rising exports. National economy gave place to a world economy, and it became necessary to perfect a method for the balance of payments without the laborious and superfluous process of transporting bullion. This need gave rise to the great international banks, which played so important a part in the economic life of Europe in the first half of the nineteenth century.

It was not remarkable that the Jews, newly released from the Ghetto and ebullient with a pent-up spirit of enterprise, played a prominent role at this stage. The circumstances of their recent history had forced them to finance: petty finance it was true, but not essentially different from large-scale operations. Their adaptability enabled them to devise fresh methods to cope with fresh problems. Above all, their mobility and the international connections which resulted from it provided them with potential agents and agencies in every commercial center. This was the secret of the prominence of the Rothschilds, the Worms, the Sterns, the Bischoffsheims, and the other international banking houses which played so prominent a part in European finance a century ago. The Jews of Frankfort were particularly to the fore, for Frankfort was the traditional financial center of the continent of Europe, and now for the first time its Jews were able to enjoy the advantages of their position to the full. On the other hand, the treatment of the Jews in Germany even at this period was not such as to encourage them to remain, and the constant emigration which resulted strengthened the international connections and outlook of those who remained. But the fact must not be overlooked that the success of these firms was ultimately dependent on their reputation for integrity. As far back as the seventeenth century, an Elector Palatine, grandson of James I of England, was advised to entrust his treasure to the keeping of a Frankfort Jew, as it would be safe in his hands as in those of the Almighty. The legendary account of the foundation of the fortunes of the House of Rothschild, as a result of a quixotic honesty in their dealings with the Elector of Hesse, has in it at least an element of truth. Nor should it be forgotten in this connection that none of the Jewish financiers of the nineteenth century ever earned anything approaching the obloquy which attached (for example) to some great non-Jewish American capitalists of the period.

One is accustomed to hear these nineteenth-century captains of finance designated as "bankers." It is very important therefore to realize that in the strict sense of the term (that is, "maintaining an establishment for the custody of money, which is paid out on the customer's order"—Oxford English Dictionary) the part played by Jews has been very slight, and in England particularly almost negligible. On the other hand, there was an old form of Financial House which used to be styled "merchants." Their business was international, and their principal occupation was to finance trade and industry—either on short terms, by bill-discounting, or on long terms, by means of loans. It was with this type of banking only, together with bullion-dealing and transactions in foreign exchange, that Jews were at one time (and in a modified degree still are) prominently associated.

It is true that the Jewish bankers, like their non-Jewish colleagues and competitors, operated for their own advantage.[1] Yet their services for the economic development of Europe and of the world were incontestable. It was not that they provided the capital. But they made it mobile. They perfected the delicate machinery by which it was brought together and rendered available for industry, and they transferred it from country to country as and when it was needed. If during the course of the nineteenth century communications improved to such an extent that what had previously been a week's journey could be accomplished in a few hours, if what had previously been the luxuries of the rich became familiar to every class, if the outposts of Europe overseas were developed to such an extent that they were able to absorb vast numbers of Europe's teeming millions, the new financial

---

[1] There are exceptions even to this elementary generalization. The Beit Bridge-building bequest to South Africa, though it happens to have achieved an outstanding material success, was intended as a pure benefaction.

machinery alone made it possible, and the Jewish financiers should share the credit, just as they are made to shoulder almost the entire blame.

Yet, contrary to popular belief, this period of quasi-hegemony lasted only for a very short time. The Revolution of 1848 involved the decline of the House of Rothschild in France, where its influence had previously been greatest; and simultaneously, the introduction of public subscription for state loans cut off what had formerly been a steady source of income. Above all, in the middle of the century, the great joint-stock banks began to flourish. This was largely due, as will be seen later, to the equalitarian initiative of the brothers Péreire in France and to the support of men like Sir David Salomons in England. But their rise inevitably implied the decline of the private banks, a great part of whose business they henceforth absorbed. The Jewish private banks which had in many cases meanwhile become less Jewish, both in personnel and in sympathies, suffered especially for precisely the same reasons which had previously brought about their rise.

The process of decline, which had already begun in the later Victorian Era, received an additional impetus with the outbreak of the European War in 1914, which violently disrupted the traditional structure of international finance. The Jews had introduced the new methods; but the machinery they constructed and the technique they developed were by now absorbed into the common stock.

This applies above all to England where the number

of Jewish private bankers was always small and the
Joint-Stock bank, in which Jewish participation is
slight, has especially flourished. Elsewhere the importance of the private bank is, of course, greater, but
nowhere is the influence of the Jew preponderant. In
the United States after the recent legislation by which
financial houses were compelled to choose between the
issuing or the banking sides of their business, Kuhn-
Loeb & Co. chose the former. It may now be said that
Jewish banks and banking, in the accepted sense of
the term, have practically ceased to exist in this country. In Germany, the influence of such well-known
private firms as Bleichröder, Mendelssohn, and Warburg, all of which boasted more than a hundred years
of existence, was even before the Nazi Revolution
very small in comparison with that of the big joint
stock banks, where Jewish directors were few.

On the Stock Exchange, contrary again to the general impression, matters were much the same. At
Ghent, where so far as is known, the "Bourse" first
assumed prominence, and at Bruges, where the name
originated, there was never a Jewish settlement of
any significance. In Antwerp, where what was to become the prototype of the European "Exchange" was
constructed in 1531, only a handful of Marranos
lived. The same applied to London in 1566 at the
period of Sir Thomas Gresham's epoch-making experiment.

The establishment of the Dutch East India Company, in 1602, marks what is generally regarded as the
beginning of the modern joint-stock method of trad-

ing. It has been alleged that the part taken in this by the Jews was overwhelmingly important. Actually, their contribution to the original capital was trivial—4,800 florins out of a total of 6,500,000, or less than one-tenth of one per cent—approximately proportionate, that is, to their actual numbers in relation to the general population. Moreover, Jews were rigorously excluded from the administration of the company until the Age of Emancipation. It was only long after the original establishment, when the institution had passed its climax and the Amsterdam Jews had lost their pioneering spirit, that they began to invest their funds in its stocks on a large scale for the sake of security. This step was almost fatal to the community as a whole at the time of the great slump in the eighteenth century, when the shares fell to one-tenth of their previous level, never to recover. Similarly, in the establishment of the Dutch West India Company in 1621–3, the original Jewish contribution to its capital was no more than one-half per cent, rising to four per cent half a century later.

It is true that a Dutch Jew of Portuguese origin, Joseph Penso de la Vega, wrote in 1688 the first handbook on the theory and practice of the bourse, which is still the best description, both in form and substance, of dealings in stocks and shares. Similarly, Isaac de Pinto's remarkable *Traité de la circulation et du crédit*, of 1771, has been described as standing at the beginning of the modern era, in which joint-stock enterprises have become the center of economic activity. But from these isolated illustrations of theoretical comprehension it is absurd to draw any far-reaching conclusions regarding actual participation.

The Stock Exchange in London was organized only at the close of the eighteenth century; the number of Jewish members being originally restricted to twelve. There was a time, in the height of nineteenth-century expansion, when Jews were perhaps prominent in this organization out of proportion to their numbers. This period, however, was short-lived. Today, the Jews on the London Stock Exchange number only some five per cent, and include no house of first importance, while of the thirty members of the Stock Exchange Committee only one is a Jew. In New York, too, the Jews, numbering some 25 per cent of the total population, are represented by only 15 per cent of the members on the Stock Exchange.

4

This is not to suggest that the Jewish share in modern capitalistic development was negligible. In view of the circumstances of their history, it was inevitable that Jews should have played a part of some importance in the evolution of the present financial system. From the simple moneylending, to which they were driven in the Middle Ages by religious prejudice and restrictive legislation, sprang commercial moneylending. This developed into anonymous lending, i.e., the purchase of bonds from States and issuing them to the general public. Hence, arose stock-dealing and, finally, stock-broking and bill-broking. And in all these various stages of development the part played by the Jews was of considerable, though not decisive, importance.

It is generally stated, for example, that the Letter of Credit was a Jewish invention. Hardly a particle of evidence can be found to confirm this assumption. Yet the theory is not unlikely. Though the Jews may not have been familiar with the institution of "credit" in the technical financial sense, they knew it as a social reality. If a talmudic scholar resident in London, at the end of a scholastic communication to a rabbi of Marseilles, requested him to oblige a client on his way to Palestine with an advance, he could rest assured that the other would carry out his wishes, realizing that a similar service would be performed for him in London should the necessity arise. Thus, too, in medieval England or Germany or France, a bond of indebtedness to a Jewish financier in one part of the country, duly endorsed, was equivalent to a draft or a letter of credit in the hands of the person who held it. The network of Jewish friends, relatives, and correspondents, spread throughout Europe and the Mediterranean world, had therefore in it the germ of a highly developed financial system. It is even suggested, though on slender authority, that the Bill of Exchange owes its origin to the exigencies of the Jewish refugees expelled from Spain in 1492.

In view of all this, it was natural for Jews to share in the genesis and development of banking, the cornerstone of modern economic organization. As early as the tenth century their activity is associated with the beginnings of the banking system in the Islamic world at Bagdad. The famous Venetian Bank, the Banco Giro, founded in 1619, owed a great deal to the financial acumen of Abraham del Banco. In the same year the Marrano community of Hamburg took a prominent part in the foundation of the Bank of Hamburg, forty of its members being included in the earliest roll of shareholders. Towards the close of the century, a Jew named Jacob Henriques, if the petition subsequently presented by his son is to be believed, played some part in the establishment of the Bank of England.[1] It is remarkable, though, that while the Jews collaborated in the establishment of these institutions both with advice and with capital, they played only the smallest share in their administration. The Banco Giro, in Catholic Venice never, of course, admitted a Jew to any responsible post, while there was no Jewish director of the Bank of England until the election of Alfred de Rothschild in 1868, the only Jew who has ever figured on the board.

The case was different with the private banks, which flourished in the period following the Napoleonic Wars. Their influence, we have seen, dwindled with the growth of the joint-stock banks in the middle of the century, which gave rise to present-day banking. By a coincidence the great impetus in establishing these institutions, which undermined the position of the Jewish private banks, came from the brothers Péreire, grandsons of that Jacob Rodrigues Pereira who in-

[1] To these earlier instances may be added the participation of Bernhard Eskeles in the foundation of the Austrian National Bank in 1816, and the great work of Ludwig Bamberger for the establishment of the German Reichsbank in 1870.

vented the system of teaching deaf-mutes. Among Saint-Simon's earliest and most devoted disciples, they felt that the management of credit should be controlled by those for whose benefit credit was intended, and that consequently the banking system should no longer be concentrated in private hands. Following this theory they founded first the Crédit Foncier and then the Société Générale du Crédit Mobilier, the first modern joint-stock banks. The former was the proto-type of the Agricultural Mortgage Banks, which have continued to do good work for one hundred years, are still being imitated with beneficial results and play an important part in the financial mechanism of mod-ern states. As bankers they were drawn inevitably into other interests, and a good deal of the railroad development of modern France was due to them. In this, their principal competitor was the House of Rothschild. This fact, combined with the disaster which the establishment of the joint-stock institutions brought upon many Jewish bankers, is yet another outstanding instance of the complete absence, con-trary to the anti-Semitic allegation, of unity of aim among the Jewish capitalists.

On more than one occasion, indeed, financiers who happened to be Jews (to speak of "Jewish Financiers" is to make an invidious and unjustifiable distinction) have done a great deal to restore public confidence at times of strain, and sometimes to uphold public credit in a crisis. The work of the House of Rothschild in this connection has been continuous. In 1886, the head of the English branch was raised to the peerage

in recognition of his courageous assistance to the
Egyptian Exchequer at a critical moment under circumstances which elicited cordial recognition in both
Houses of Parliament. "Egypt was in imminent danger
of bankruptcy," stated the Chancellor of the Exchequer. "In fact, it was saved only by monthly advances made by Messrs. Rothschild upon no legal security, but simply on the security of a private note
from the late Foreign Secretary." The firm enhanced
its reputation by its conduct during the Baring crisis
in 1890, when the difficulties of that great house produced a Black Friday in the City, and every effort
was needed to stave off a catastrophe. It was the Rothschilds who took the lead in measures to save their
rivals from disaster. So, too, in 1913, Paul M. Warburg
successfully carried through the reorganization of the
American banking system at which he had been working, together with Senator Aldrich, since 1911, thus
thoroughly consolidating the currency and finances
of the United States.

5

It is too often overlooked that the vision and courage
of the financial magnate, not necessarily altruistic in
intention, but essential to the working of the economic
system as we know it, are frequently responsible for
achievements which may be of enormous benefit to
the public. Failure does not win him sympathy, while
success may arouse envy and obloquy. Only one instance will be cited here: it was Sir Ernest Cassel, who
financed one of the most gigantic and most beneficial

mechanical enterprises of modern times, the construction of the Assuan Dam. While it may have secured its sponsors great profits, it has saved all Egypt from the specter of famine.

The part which Jews played in the great maritime discoveries has already been described. More than this, to be sure, was needed to open the ocean highways of the world to travellers and commerce—the enterprise of those who made international shipping the wonderfully organized thing that it is today. In this, too, Jews played their part. The first ship which sailed to the Western hemisphere under the Venetian flag, at the close of the eighteenth century, was dispatched by the firm of Treves de' Bonfili. Joseph Henry was the first person to build ships in Canada for the transatlantic trade, thus founding the Canadian Mercantile Marine, while the earliest service between Montreal and Antwerp was established by Jesse Joseph. Emile Péreire, of Paris, took part in the organization of the first French transatlantic steamboat service. The German Mercantile Marine was raised to the remarkable position which it enjoyed before 1914 by the genius of Albert Ballin. He was the only German in a prominent position who found the disgrace of his country's defeat too great to bear, and died by his own hand. Yet notwithstanding these services Jewish influence in the world's shipping today is negligible, and even the Hamburg-Amerika Line, which owes its existence to Jewish genius, is now *Judenrein*.

Part of Sombart's thesis states that while the Jew's part in the distributive trades has been disproportion-

ately large, he has played an insignificant role in the
so-called "heavy" industries. This is by no means justified by the facts. Many Eastern European Jews are
coal-miners, like their neighbors, while the development of the mining industry in Germany, for example, owed a good deal to the Friedlaender-Fuld family.
Similarly, Frankfort's pre-eminent position as a manufacturing city is largely due to the fact that it had an
intelligent and industrious Jewish population. Nothing
in its earlier history marked it as a manufacturing
center: but today the ring of factories that surrounds
it owes its origin in a majority of cases to Jewish effort.
A secondary result was that for a long time Frankfort
led Europe in social welfare work.

Another section of this work dealt with the participation of the Jews in establishing the chemical industry. Adolf Frank in Germany and the Mond family
in England have done particularly important work in
this connection. The development of the electrical industry, with its far-reaching results on social as well
as economic life, owed an enormous debt to Emil
Rathenau, founder of the German Allgemeine Elek-
trizitäts Gesellschaft, who today has his counterpart
in England in the person of Lord Hirst.

This type of activity may be paralleled all over the
world, but a few illustrations will suffice. One of the
staple South African products today is mohair. This
was originally exported only from Asia Minor, where
breeding Angora goats was jealously controlled by the
Turks. Numerous experiments had been made to introduce the industry to South Africa, where climatic

conditions were not dissimilar from those in Anatolia, but without success. At last, after the Crimean War, Adolph Mosenthal, a brother of the Austrian dramatist Salomon von Mosenthal, managed to bring to the Colony via England a consignment of Angora goats, purchased with great difficulty in Turkey. The monetary loss on this original enterprise was considerable. Nevertheless, it was demonstrated that the Angora goat could not only survive the long sea voyage from Turkey, but could also flourish in Cape Colony. Thus, one of the great South African industries was established.

Participation in the South African mining industry followed the same tradition. When in 1885 rumors of new discoveries of gold arrived in Kimberley, they were not taken too seriously; they had been only too common before. However, Alfred Beit optimistically put £25,000 at the disposal of the Englishman Joseph B. Robinson; this was the beginning of the Rand mining industry and of Johannesburg. The work of Jewish financiers in the subsequent development of the South African mining industry is well known. Yet it is not so widely appreciated that they did much also to increase the amenities of the territory and to make the city of Johannesburg what it is today. It was "Barney" Barnato who started the waterworks —an impossible and, indeed, chimerical venture it then seemed. Samuel Marks provided the means for damming the Vaal River and planted orchards, while, with his brother-in-law, Isaac Lewis, he invested vast sums in collieries, breweries, glass, steel, brick and tile works, and in this manner founded the industry of the country. Johannesburg and the Rand are in a way a monument to Jewish enterprise.

Or let us take another of the "new" countries which has provided refuge, livelihood and happiness to untold thousands of the surplus population of Europe. The part played by the Jews in the development of the American Middle West has never yet been properly investigated, but it is of incalculable importance. The territory involved was vast. Hundreds of miles divided city from city. Communications were primitive; roads were non-existent; travelling was dangerous. The pioneer from the Atlantic coast or the European immigrant who settled in this area cut himself off from civilization. It was the travelling peddler who brought the amenities of life to him and made his life bearable. And, in most cases, these peddlers were Jews —to a large extent, Jewish refugees from the intolerant policies of Central Europe. When after some time conditions improved, these peddlers settled down in the urban centers, where they opened the first primitive general stores. It is a significant fact, though its importance must not be exaggerated, that the first brick house in Chicago was built by a Jew. Sombart, indeed, avers that the Jewish traders constituted one in twenty of the pioneers who went out to conquer the American wilderness. This is a palpable exaggeration. But the fact remains that in the process which carried America forward from the Atlantic to the Pacific and gave the Middle West its prosperity and established the great urban centers of the area, the work of the Jewish petty trader was of supreme importance.[1]

6

Much is said about the power of the financier—the Jewish financier, for some reason, above all—in deciding war. Less, incomprehensibly, is said about his power in deciding peace. Yet his influence in the latter direction is the more usual, for the financier is more capable than most men of realizing the terrible waste of war and the permanent impoverishment which almost invariably succeeds an international conflict.

This fact is brought out very clearly in the most authoritative history of the House of Rothschild, written by Count Corti, a non-Jew, in a spirit which on the whole is not over-friendly. There is no instance in this of encouraging or even financing a war on the part of this most famous of international banking houses, but there are several instances of the reverse. At the height of its power in the early nineteenth century, this famous banking house threw its weight, which was at the time very considerable, on the side of peace; and it seems that the intervention was sometimes decisive. This was so particularly during the crises of 1830 and 1840. In 1831, when the Austrian troops intervened in North Italy, James de Rothschild "did everything to allay the indignation which was flaring up in Paris and to prevent any hasty action being taken." When, in 1839, the Belgian government

[1] It may be pointed out that in medieval Poland the Jews performed a very similar function, being largely instrumental in opening up the country to Western civilization.

applied to the House for an advance on the security
of Treasury Bills, with a view to rearmament in preparation for hostilities with Holland, it encountered a
point blank refusal. "Our goodwill necessarily stops
short of the point of providing the rod with which
we are to be beaten, that is to say, providing the money
wanted to make a war, which would destroy the credit
that we are applying all our energies and resources to
maintain," wrote the head of the Vienna branch. At
the time of the Russian crisis in 1854, Von Hübner,
the Austrian Ambassador, found James de Rothschild
of Paris "positively demoralized" by fear of war. In
1866, the House did its best to avert the Austro-
Prussian conflict, and three years later its heads were
expressing "absolute panic" at the possibility of
Franco-Prussian hostilities.

In the period before 1914, the international influence of the House had dwindled, yet it continued to
throw its influence on the side of peace. "If ever the
archives of this period should be made available to the
public, it will probably be possible to show by documentary evidence, too, what we can now deduce only
from the consistency of the Rothschild policy during
a century, as shown by various indications and the information derived from certain responsible persons,
that immediately before the World War the Rothschilds . . . did everything possible to avert the catastrophe," writes Count Corti. A little is known of
the part played by Alfred de Rothschild at this time
to improve the prospects of world peace. It was he
who succeeded in arranging the friendly encounter be-

tween Joseph Chamberlain and the German Ambassador, which took place under his roof, to discuss various points of friction between England and Germany without the encumbrance of diplomatic formality. His efforts were nobly seconded by two other Jews, Sir Ernest Cassel, who did everything possible to smooth the way for Haldane's despairing visit to Berlin in 1912, and, on the other side, Albert Ballin, head of the Hamburg-Amerika Line and founder of the German Mercantile Marine.

The classical example, constantly repeated, of the method in which hostilities can be exploited for the private benefit of the "financier" is the Waterloo fable, which, notwithstanding the fact that it has been so ruthlessly exposed, continues to be repeated at intervals even today. The story goes that in order to deceive the Stock Exchange, Nathan Meyer Rothschild followed Wellington to the field of Waterloo, that when he saw which way the battle was going he posted to London, depressed the market with hints of disaster and secretly bought the depressed stock. Thus, he contrived to clear several millions of pounds sterling when the official intelligence arrived. An alternative account tells how the news was carried by pigeon-post, first used by the House.

In point of fact, Nathan Rothschild was nowhere near the field of battle, remaining in London throughout these critical days, and leaving for Belgium, under instruction from the British Treasury, only on June 20th—two days after Wellington's overwhelming victory. It was true that, owing to his admirable news-service, he had learned the result of the great encounter before anyone else in England. But, far from keeping it to himself or profiting by it, he hastened to communicate with the Prime Minister, Lord Liverpool, who refused to believe him. As for the allegation that he had depressed the market by hinting at a British disaster, the truth is that from the first, as the reports in the contemporary press show, he had bought openly and largely, in the face of an incredulous and falling market.

An episode of English history more glorious than the Battle of Waterloo was the abolition of slavery, "among the three or four perfectly virtuous pages in the history of nations," as Lecky called it. This culminated in the Bill of 1833 for the abolition of slavery in the British dominions, especially, of course, in the West Indies. A sum of £20,000,000 was needed to compensate the slave-owners. It is significant that Nathan Meyer Rothschild's last great operation before his death in 1836 was to advance this amount.[1]

[1] It may be added that one of the few planters in the British West Indies who anticipated government action by freeing his slaves was Isaac Simon, father of the late Sergeant Sir John Simon, the eminent lawyer and philanthropist. This was not unnatural, for the slave legislation of the Bible, itself remarkable for its humanity (cf., Exodus 21:26f.; Deuteronomy 23:16), had been yet further developed by Jewish tradition. Thus the precedent of the English "Somerset Case," which liberated any slave who arrived in England, was anticipated at least fifteen centuries earlier by a rabbinical decision, that an escaped slave, whether Jew or Gentile, automatically regained his freedom on touching Palestinian soil.

Philo of Alexandria was centuries in advance of his age when he proclaimed (Spec. Leg. II, 69), "Servants are free by nature, no man being naturally a slave."

His son, Baron Lionel de Rothschild, inherited no small share of his business acumen and more than his public spirit. He achieved a "particularly honored position" in the financial life of Great Britain when in March, 1847, he offered the government his financial assistance for dealing with the miserable condition of Ireland. The Irish Famine Loan of £8,000,000 was subsequently raised without any view to profit through his agency, in collaboration with his greatest competitors, the house of Baring. Baron Lionel, who in 1858 became the first Jewish Member of Parliament, will be permanently remembered in the history of the British Empire for the public-spirited manner in which he came to the assistance of Lord Beaconsfield in 1875, when he advanced the money for the purchase of the Suez Canal shares, and took all risks pending the approval of Parliament. But for this action it is doubtful whether Beaconsfield's *coup* could have succeeded.

7

The most important economic function of the Jews in our day has been in a field very far removed from that of finance. In various branches of industry, they have played an important part in mass-production and improved distribution, which have wrought in our day a profound sociological change. Time was—and not so very long ago—when the rift between the rich and poor was far greater than it is at present, and when even the lower middle classes had to be content with the coarsest and barest necessities of life. The environ-

ment of the laboring classes was even more drab.
Luxuries were completely out of the poor man's reach;
his amusements were primitive; his clothing was coarse
and shapeless and could seldom be replaced; the rift
between the "classes" and "masses" was deep and un-
bridgeable.

In the course of the last generation this situation
has been altered fundamentally. The poor man, and to
an even greater extent the poor woman, dresses in the
same manner as the rich, even though the cut and the
materials may be inferior. His household amenities are
not dissimilar. His diversions are much the same, even
though he may have to wait a little longer until his
local place of resort brings within his reach for a few
pennies what has been available elsewhere at higher
prices some weeks before. The radio provides the same
entertainment for all. Even the methods of transportation which were once a sign of distinction are now
within the reach of the humblest purse.

In this profound social revolution Jews have played
an intimate part. It is the Jewish tailor, for example,
who has broken down the sartorial gap between rich
and poor. The persecutions in Russia at the close of
the last century first reduced to beggary, and then
drove into exile, large numbers of Jews without resources, and for the most part without a trade. In the
Anglo-Saxon countries a very high proportion of the
refugees entered the tailoring industry, for which they
had a certain bent and in which Jews were already
engaged to some extent. The influx of cheap labor,
coupled with an intensive organization (the so-called

"Boston System" of division of labor), completely
revolutionized the tailoring industry. The sewing machine became a scientific instrument of mass production; minute subdivision of labor was organized; the
cost of manufacture was immensely reduced; and in
consequence, the price of clothing was brought down
to a fraction of its previous level, coming for the first
time within the reach of every artisan's pocket. The
old clothes dealer, mainly Jewish heretofore (incidentally, there was no question of ejecting non-Jews
from employment), lost his importance. No longer was
it necessary for the workingman to wear the recondi-
tioned garments of his social superiors; for the same
amount, or less, he could periodically purchase a new
suit. The reduction in the cost of women's clothing
was even more striking. The process was repeated in
the boot-making and furniture-making industries.
What had previously been the greatest distinguishing
mark between the various social strata disappeared,
and the beneficial effect on the morale of the laboring
classes was incalculable. This epoch-making change
was assisted by great development in the distributive
trades, and the growth of the single-price store, in
which also the Jews played a considerable part, though
not perhaps as great as is often alleged. By this means,
prices in all commodities were vastly reduced, and
one time extravagances came to be considered necessities of existence in every class.

In other respects, too, Jews collaborated solidly in
this far-reaching change. A generation ago, their participation in the catering industry in England brought

the "restaurant" within the reach of the modest pocket and was a remarkable boon to city workers of that generation. More important was the part which they played in what is termed the "entertainment industry." The function which Jews have filled in the development of the motion-picture industry, as actors, inventors, technicians, producers and exhibitors, is enormous. They realized its implications when it was generally regarded as no more than an amusing novelty; and it was to a large extent under Jewish guidance that it became the great institution, and the universal amenity of life that it is today.[1]   Of the great levelling agencies of our time, it is only in the automobile industry that the part of Jews has been negligible.

The implications of this change are enormous, though hardly appreciated as yet. The *sansculotte* has disappeared. It is no longer possible to regard the upper classes and the lower as divided by an insurmountable barrier in quite the same sense as in the past. The social life of the two, at least, is now conceived on very much the same lines, differing in scale rather than in character. Through these recent developments, in short, the last generation has witnessed a sociological change unexampled in history. It is the

---

[1] In this connection, it is worth while to bear in mind the fact that, on the technical side fully as much as on the administrative, the modern motion-picture industry is indebted to Jewish genius. It is sufficient to recall that Levi ben Gershom was a pioneer in the development of the camera (*supra*, p. 197); the younger Herschel in the evolution of photography (p. 197); Berliner was the inventor of the microphone (p. 211); Lieben of the amplifier (p. 212); Lippman of color photography (*ibid*).

great peaceful revolution of our time and among the greatest stabilizing forces in the modern world. In helping to bring this about, rather than in a fictitious financial predominance, lies the real importance of the role of the Jew in modern economic life, and one of his most significant contributions to civilization in recent times.

APPENDIX: *The Jews in Agriculture*

THE rapidity of the Jewish economic readjustment, once external pressure was removed, has been remarkable. True, the effect of fifteen centuries of repression cannot be shaken off in one or two generations. But a beginning has been made, and its progress has been striking.

In the Hanoverian period, the majority of the Jews in England, as on the Continent, were probably engaged in petty trading, peddling, and old-clothes dealing. Scores of caricatures, engravings, and popular songs are sufficient proof. On the other hand, Jews were excluded almost completely from the professions, and the opponents of Jewish emancipation held that until Jews showed a greater interest in these more polite and useful callings, they would not justify their claim to be considered good and useful citizens.

A couple of generations were sufficient to destroy this reproach. Nowadays, the positions are reversed. The Jewish peddler is today non-existent, or almost so, in the areas in which he was previously best known.

The itinerant Jewish old-clothes dealer, formerly a characteristic figure in city streets, is completely extinct. At the same time, the range of Jewish economic activity has broadened, and the influx into the professions has grown to such proportions that great-grandchildren of those critics referred to above are now complaining of too great a tendency in this direction. One point, however, is overlooked in this criticism; a man employs a doctor, a lawyer, or a dentist, not because of his race or his creed, but because it is anticipated that he has the best qualifications and will give the most conscientious service.

The case of agriculture illustrates even more strikingly the progress which has been made in the economic readjustment of Jewish life. An urge to till the soil has invariably manifested itself in Jewish history, as soon as external pressure has been removed. There were Jewish agriculturalists in Russia under the old regime, though under the May Laws of 1882 they were uprooted from their holdings. There were Jewish farmers long established in South Germany, indistinguishable from their neighbors except for their religion; but the Nazi regime made life impossible for them. In free lands, however, the process continues.

Jewish agricultural settlements exist today all over the world, in Russia, Poland, Bessarabia, Roumania, even Siberia. In Canada, for example, there are a number of settlements, under the guidance of the Jewish Colonial Association; and 500,000 bushels of wheat are produced each year by the Canadian Jewish farmers. In the Argentine, there are whole areas covered by Jewish agricultural settlements, with their own vigorous community life. In the United States, at least 100,000 Jews look to agriculture for their livelihood and "more Jews are thinking today in terms of the farm than in any other period in the whole of American history." Above all, the return to Palestine, under the inspiration of the Zionist movement, is coupled with the ideal of the return to the land. Lack of funds and local obstructionism are responsible for the fact that the process has not been so complete as was at one time hoped; but, even so, some 15% of Palestinian Jewry is established on the soil. In England, it may be mentioned for the purpose of comparison, only 7% of the general population is thus engaged. The total number of Jews throughout the world who look to agriculture for their livelihood is now nearly 700,000, and the number is increasing almost daily. The phenomenon is unique in the world today, where the general tendency is not towards, but away from, the land.

It is curious, in view of the Jew's long exclusion from the soil and his comparatively recent re-association with it, that outstanding contributions to agricultural science should have been made by Jews. One may start at the commencement of the alphabet with Aaron Aaronson, one of a devoted family who rendered conspicuous service to Great Britain during the conquest of Palestine in 1917–18. (His sister, Sarah Aaronson, was killed for that reason by the Turks.) Aaronson, who founded the Agricultural Experimental Station near the ruins of the Crusading castle at Athlit, discovered in Palestine "wild wheat," which has been used extensively in the United States and elsewhere to strengthen the cultivated plant. More sensational were the discoveries of Fritz Haber, the chemical genius whose investigations notably assisted Germany between 1914 and 1918, but whom an ungrateful Fatherland compelled to die in exile after the advent of the Nazi regime. His greatest service to mankind was his discovery of the method of the fixation of nitrogen, the production, that is, of synthetic ammonia from the nitrogen in the atmosphere. From this, nitrates for fertilization could be extracted and were hence made available to the world in unlimited quantity. Thus was obviated the risk which serious thinkers, such as Sir William Brookes, once voiced, that when the deposits of natural fertilizers were exhausted, the world would be faced with starvation.

It must be added that the use of potash for agricultural purposes was due in the first instance to the activity of the German Jew, Adolf Frank. He collaborated in his later years with the young Nicodem Caro, whose discovery of cyanamide; the first synthetic nitrogenous fertilizer, and new methods for the production of hydrogen are similarly of considerable importance for the development of scientific agriculture.

These discoveries were carried a stage further by Jacob G. Lipman, Dean of the Faculty of Agriculture at Rutgers University, whose principal work was centered upon the determination of the nature of the chemical action produced by bacteria in making both organic and inorganic components of soils available for food. The bacteria which he has turned loose on the farms of the world, it is said, have more than made up for the Jews' failure (not of their own making) to work on the land.

Finally, mention should be made of that idealistic Polish-American businessman, David Lubin, who, after various adventures and travels, gained a competence by inventing a device for the extremely prosaic purpose of rivetting buttons on overalls. He was thus enabled to fulfil his ambition of engaging in fruit-farming. But he found a complete absence of organization in agriculture in all its branches. Every man worked for himself; experience was never pooled; and as a result there was a shocking degree of waste. After studying and comparing agricultural methods in Europe, Lubin published in 1900 his work, *Let There Be Light*, based upon Maimonides' *Guide to the Perplexed*, in which moral and practical idealism are curiously mixed.

Then he began to work out the solution of the agricultural problem from the standpoint of the farmer as well as of the producer. He laid his views before the U. S. Department of Agriculture, but received no encouragement; he travelled about Europe trying to interest official circles, but met with opposition and indifference at every turn. At last, he obtained an interview with Luigi Luzzatti, the Italian-Jewish statesman, at that time a member of the cabinet. The latter realized the practical importance of the suggestions implied in Lubin's idealistic approach, and secured him an audience with the King of Italy. In an hour's conference, Vittorio Emmanuele was won over to Lubin's theories and called an international conference to consider his plans. In 1905 the representatives of forty governments, excluding the United States, met in Rome, and the International Agricultural Institute, which has since done untold good and without which the state of agriculture in the world today would be even more chaotic than it is, was established. In October, 1934, fifteen years after Lubin's death, tribute was paid to his memory by delegates from the sixty-three nations then represented in the institute; and the name of this Polish-Jewish immigrant is commemorated, not only by a tablet in the institute which he founded, but also (at least until the triumph of racial intolerance in Italy) by a street in Rome.

Future inquirers may attach importance not only to the reconstruction of Jewish agricultural life in Palestine, but also to the type of the life that is emerging. The self-sacrificing devotion of the pioneers; the influence of the ideas of A. D. Gordon, that national regeneration can come only from personal labor and physical contact with the soil; the enthusiasm for social justice which inspires the new type of settlement such as the co-operative colony, the *Moshav*, and the communal settlement, the *Kvutzah*, which have realized such outstanding triumphs; are all developments whose significance is by no means restricted to Palestine. Above all, the new settlers have demonstrated for the first time in history that a peasantry can attain as high a level of cultural life and expression as the most sophisticated urban dweller. It is possible to discern in all this the kernel of a future contribution to rural, perhaps even more important than the past contribution to urban civilization.[1]

[1] It should perhaps be pointed out that an inclination toward physical activities is by no means a new thing among Jews. Even in the Ghetto period, there was a definite proclivity to, and sometimes even superiority in various fields of sport. A rabbi of the third century maintained that it is a religious duty for a man to teach his son to swim. Later, fencing-masters were commonly Jews. Modern students are becoming interested in a medieval rabbi's account of tennis as it was played by his co-religionists in Mantua. Jews took part in athletic contests at Rosenau in the fifteenth century, in the foot-races, jumping, weight-lifting, and so on. A particularly notable figure was the Jew, Ott, champion wrestler in Germany under Frederick III (1440–1493), who even wrote a handbook on the art, as also did one Andreas Jud Liegnitzer. It is clear from all this that even before the days of the great Anglo-Jewish boxers of the 18th century, Mendoza and the rest, and the champions in tennis, etc., in our own day, the intellectualization of the Jew was not exclusive of other interests.

CHAPTER XI. *Public Life*

I

EXTERNAL circumstances are responsible for the fact
that the Jews' participation in public life began only
at a comparatively recent date. For centuries Church
and State had combined to inveigh against the occupation by Jews of any position of authority, and the
exclusion remained effective until a hundred and fifty
years ago. The first breach in the theory was made by
the Declaration of Independence in 1775; it was introduced into Europe with the Declaration of the Rights
of Man in 1789, followed by the formal emancipation
of the French Jews in 1790. The following eighty
years saw the gradual imitation of this example in
Western Europe. Thus, in England, municipal rights
were conceded in 1831–1835, and Jews were first admitted to the House of Commons in 1858 and to the
Lords in 1886. After 1870 emancipation was established, in name at least, in all the so-called "civilized"
world. The only exception was Russia, where persecution continued in an exaggerated form, accompanied by frequent outbreaks of violence, as long as the
authority of the Czars was maintained.

For this reason, any examination of the part played

by Jews in public life after 70 A.D. must necessarily
be restricted almost entirely to very recent times. In
the Roman Empire, of course, exclusion was by no
means complete, and we find Jews participating amply
in municipal life, and the late Judean rulers honored
as benefactors by Athens and other centers of Greek
culture. In Moslem Spain, Jews occasionally rose to the
rank of vizier, directing the affairs of state, and even
under Christian rulers Jewish physicians, scientists,
or fiscal experts sometimes enjoyed considerable influence. The same was the case in Turkey at the
height of its power in the middle of the sixteenth century. Converted Jews, too, occasionally rose to positions of authority. But, broadly speaking, it was not
until the nineteenth century that the Jew had any
opportunity for political self-expression.[1]

This fact should be kept in mind in considering the

[1] There was, indeed, in France, at the close of the sixteenth
century a little group of men of Jewish origin who profoundly
influenced the course of political thought. Best remembered today
is Michel de Montaigne, whose mother, as has been indicated elsewhere, belonged to a crypto-Jewish family settled in France. His
contemporary, Jean Bodin, one of the most remarkable of French
political thinkers, was reproached in his lifetime for his Jewish
affinities and associates, and his mother, too, apparently belonged
to a Marrano family. His great work, *Six livres de la République*,
written as a reply to Machiavelli's *Principe*, champions the idea of
a monarchy tempered by the States General, and is the outstanding
vindication of the constitutional monarchy of its day. Noteworthy,
too, is the generous toleration in matters of religion, which he expresses in his *Heptaplomeres*. More in the public eye than either
of these was Michel de l'Hôpital, who, as Chancellor of France,
exerted himself to the utmost to bring about a more generous
spirit in questions of faith and to stop the bloodshed which had
so long been the scourge of the country. He, too, was of Jewish

irresponsible theory which has been summed up in
the phrase, "The Jews as revolutionary leaven"—that
is, that every upheaval in the history of the modern
world may be traced to the action of this one section
of the population. The prototype of the modern
revolution was the "Great Rebellion" in England, but
when this took place there was in that country only
a handful of Marrano merchants, unable to profess
Judaism and too timid to meddle in public affairs. One
of the few Jewish comments upon the situation that
has survived is that of a Marrano of Rouen, who expressed the conviction that "none of his religion would
ever adventure themselves among such bloody traitors
as had murdered their own King."

The myth of the Jew as revolutionary leaven takes
as its serious point of departure the French Revolution. Whether Jews would need to apologize for any
share in it is a question upon which there is no need
to express an opinion, in view of the fact that their
role was almost entirely passive. In Paris, always the
nerve-center of the Revolution, no Jewish community
was yet tolerated, and the few individuals living there
played a part barely worth mentioning. Indeed, the
only French Jew who enjoyed the slightest prominence at the period was a moderate—Abraham Fur-
tado of Bordeaux, a close friend of the Girondin

---

origin, being descended from an Avignonese Jewish family. Thus
the three chief intellectual voices of the party known as the
"politiques," who opposed religious fanaticism, wished to suppress
party faction and endeavored to set up a strong monarchy to save
France from further tribulations, were in part of Jewish blood.

leaders, who narrowly escaped the guillotine. Others of his co-religionists were less fortunate, nine of them being executed during the Reign of Terror. Meanwhile, during the supremacy of the Goddess of Reason, synagogues were pillaged, Jewish observances were forbidden, the Sabbath had to be publicly desecrated, and Jewish ministers of religion were dragged to the Temple of the new state Deity to do homage.

There was one place, indeed, where the Jews enjoyed considerable influence during the Terror—St. Esprit, the Ghetto suburb of Bayonne, renamed Jean-Jacques Rousseau by the extremists. Here, Jews were so numerous on the Comité de Surveillance as to be almost in control. It is significant that, while heads were rolling across the river at Bayonne in an intermittent blood-bath, not a single capital sentence was passed in the suburb, where there were tokens of a humanity and moderation hardly to be found elsewhere in France.[1]

That the Jew traditionally nourishes a feeling for equality needs neither argument nor apology. An observer who cannot be charged with pro-Jewish sympathy, Hilaire Belloc, has indicated what he considers to be the foundation of this Jewish democratic instinct (*The Battlefield*, p. 134): "The Jew today in the slums of our great cities has kept intact this sense of equality which is coincident with the feeling of human dignity—for human dignity is a product of re-

[1] So, too, it was Lange Cohen, a Jewish silk-merchant, guillotined in 1794, who saved the sacred relics of the Cathedral of Cavaillon from destruction.

ligion where religion binds the individual to a supreme
god; and the Jewish millionaire does not, like *our* rich
men, mistake his wealth for excellence, nor do his
fellow-Jews think him the greater for it, but only
more fortunate."

If there exists a Jewish point of view in politics, it
cannot be better illustrated than from the views of
Don Isaac Abravanel, the Spanish scholar-statesman
of the fifteenth century, who assisted in financing Columbus' first expedition and was perhaps the only
Jewish author of the Middle Ages to deal explicitly
with political problems. In his commentaries on Deuteronomy and Judges, he formulates a well-rounded
political theory. Monarchy is, according to him, a
human, not a divine, institution. His personal leanings
were in favor of the constitutional form of government such as he saw and admired in Venice, Florence,
and so on. Yet he denied the right of subjects to rebel
even against the most obvious grievances, and he maintained this position on more than one occasion at
Court in conversation with Christian thinkers who
held the opposite. "The law of the land is our law,"
taught a talmudic authority sixteen centuries ago, and
this has ever since been a cardinal principle of Judaism.

A review of the biographies included in the *Encyclopaedia Britannica* emphasizes the point. Among the
statesmen of first importance who are accorded entries
in that work fifteen only are of Jewish origin. Of these,
nine are reformers, including some revolutionaries,
while six may be classed as conservative. This con-

clusion is all the more remarkable if one bears in mind the fact that this particular survey excludes the United States and England, in which the conservative element is noticeably greater.

For it is perhaps only in these and one or two other politically advanced countries that the Jewish political genius has been able to find its natural level and direction. Where the Jew has been oppressed, deprived of economic opportunity, and excluded from public life, it was inevitable for him to throw his weight on the side of those parties endeavoring to effect a modification in the existing regime. Hence the activity of Jews in all the national movements of the nineteenth century, in which they imagined that their salvation lay. Hence the fact that in pre-war Russia, Jews were active in all the parties of the Left; though less by far among the Bolsheviks than among the moderates, the Constitutional Democrats and Menshiviks. Similarly, in countries where the clerical movement is strong, Jews have inevitably thrown themselves into opposition to those parties whose policies must necessarily, though not perhaps intentionally, add to the difficulties of the Jewish position.

2

The political movements with which the Jews have been associated out of proportion to their numbers have hence not been in general revolutionary but constitutional and national. Thus, they were particularly prominent among the fighters for American freedom, for German unity, for Italian independence, for Hungarian self-government, at the close of the eighteenth century and in the middle years of the nineteenth.

At the time of the great struggle between England and its revolted colonies, out of which the United States was to emerge, there were in the whole of North America barely 2,000 Jews. The part which they played was absolutely disproportionate to their insignificant numbers. For the first time in modern history, they had been permitted to participate in the political strivings of their neighbors, and they showed by their devotion and self-sacrifice how much they appreciated the privilege. It is a thrice-told tale how five Jews signed the Non-Importation Agreement of 1769, how numerous Jews served with the armies in the field and how some of them fell, how the community of New York virtually disbanded itself rather than continue to exist during the British occupation, how Hayim Salomon suffered and was ruined by reason of his financial services, never properly recognized. Yet this overwhelming preponderance of sympathy with the patriot cause did not imply that the Jewish community was blind to the other point of view. Perhaps the most typically Jewish of all was Abraham Wagg, who strove in his humble way for peace and even at the height of the conflict looked forward to the day when the mother country and her former colonies would live side by side in peace and amity.

In Europe it was in the great national movement of 1848, when throughout Europe the forces of democracy shook off the shackles of absolutism, and the peoples insisted on their natural right of self-government, that the Jews first had the opportunity to prove that they were prepared to shoulder the responsibilities of the citizenship of which they claimed the rights. Everywhere, they took a leading share in the struggle and in the sacrifice. In France, where the movement began, Adolphe Crémieux was a member of the Provisional Government. In Germany, Johann Jacoby, who was subsequently to raise an almost solitary voice in opposition to the annexation of Alsace-Lorraine, had dared to ask the King of Prussia for a constitution as early as 1841, and now, after a term of imprisonment, was once more to the fore. Several Jews were killed in the street fighting in Berlin. Jews were prominent, too, in the *Vorparlament* of Frankfort, which anticipated German unity. Here, the convert, Eduard von Simson, later President of the Reichstag and Reichsgericht, was president; the Austrian poet, Moritz Hartmann, was one of the most striking figures; and one of the vice-presidents, Gabriel Riesser, a stalwart champion of Jewish emancipation, was appointed with Simson among the delegation which offered the crown of a united Germany to Frederick William IV.

In the March Days in Vienna, Jews were similarly active. The dare-devil Adolf Fischhof was at the head of the popular movement, which was inspired by Moritz Hartmann, the poet, and the famous journalist, Ignaz Kuranda: and several more were among the martyrs to the cause of liberty. It was noteworthy, however, that the detested Prime Minister, Baron Doblhoff, owed his life to another Jewish leader of the popular party, who smuggled him away at considerable personal risk to a private house. In Hungary, a Jewish regiment fought under Kossuth, and many Jews followed their leader into exile. From every part of Central Europe Jewish refugees emigrated when the popular movement was suppressed, and it became evident that 1848 brought no more than a false dawn. The United States benefited especially; it is hardly an exaggeration to say that the great Jewish community of that country is a monument to the liberty-loving enthusiasm of Central European Jewry during those years of reaction.

In Italy, in particular, the part of the Jews in the *Risorgimento* was remarkable. In every part of the peninsula, they took the lead in the movement to shake off the hated Austrian yoke. There were at least nine Jews among Garibaldi's *Thousand*. For many years Cavour's closest collaborator was Isaac Artom, of whom he wrote, "He has a remarkable, mature mind, indefatigable zeal, golden character"; he was subsequently to take a prominent share in the public life of the united Italy for which he had worked. In exile, Mazzini had no friends more devoted than the Nathan family of London.

For a time the dramatic center of the whole movement was Venice, where for a few months in 1848–9 the pale ghost of the Serenissima was revived in Victorian costume. The London *Times*, an unfriendly critic at that period, paid eloquent testimony to the spirit which infused the leaders. On September 1st, 1849, it wrote that from February, 1848 onwards, "there has been no popular movement conducted with so much dignity and maintained with such unswerving decision as that of Venice."

Nor, even in that year of patriotic fervor, was there a movement in which the Jewish element was more prominent. The leader of the movement was Daniel Manin, one of the purest of Italian patriots, who bore the same surname as the last Doge. The coincidence was, however, merely accidental; he did not belong to an old patrician family, but was the grandson of a converted Veronese couple, Samuel and Allegra Medina, who had assumed the name of Manin in honor of their sponsor at baptism. There are few figures in the whole of nineteenth-century history so pure and noble as this last Venetian hero. Declared Jews followed him eagerly, including several who were subsequently to play an illustrious part in the history of United Italy. In the National Guard, which fought bravely for the defense of the city, there were a dozen Jewish officers and privates in proportion, one of whom was among the first to fall. Among the members of the National Assembly were three Jews, the number subsequently rising to seven: and they included two rabbis, one of whom introduced into it one of the most dramatic motions in favor of liberty. Leone Pincherle, who had played a prominent part in the events of the past heroic days, was Minister of Agriculture and Commerce in the Provisional Government, while Isaac Pesaro Maurogonato was Minister of Finance, his meticulous administration calling forth the grudging admiration of the Austrians themselves after the recapture. He was subsequently Vice-

President of the Italian Chamber of Deputies, and in 1884, when the government recognized the Venetian loans of 1848, he turned over his claims to the municipality of Venice. The "Forty" who were exiled from the city with Manin for their share in the revolution included a number of members of the group to which he traced his origin. This one case is recounted here in detail, but the tale may be duplicated for every part of Italy and Europe during that heroic period.

Contrary to what might be imagined, the case was the same even among the hyper-orthodox Jews of Poland. Here, as early as 1794, they had participated in Kosciusko's revolt. A certain Berek, who held the rank of colonel, had raised among them a troop of light horse, which was almost wiped out by Suvarov's troops during the siege of Warsaw. During the revolt against Russian misgovernment in 1830, Berek's son, Joseph Berkovitz, took the lead and summoned his co-religionists to arms, with the result that a special "bearded" section of the Metropolitan Guard was formed in Warsaw, comprising 850 Jews. So also in the revolution of 1860–1863, the Jews of every school of thought took their place by the side of their fellow-Poles, and two rabbis were sent to prison for daring to march in the funeral procession behind the coffins of the demonstrators who had been cut down by the Cossacks. The artificial distinction between Jewish and Catholic Poles had not yet been crystallized.

Adolphe Crémieux was perhaps the most typical as he was the most brilliant Jewish statesman of the Age of Emancipation. From the days of the First Empire

to the reign of Louis Philippe, he was one of France's
great orators and lawyers. In 1848, he became Minister
of Justice, and it was due to his assiduity that the royal
family left Paris unscathed. From that date almost to
his death, thirty-two years later, he was one of the outstanding figures in French public life. An old man of
over seventy at the time of the fall of the Second Empire, he was, nevertheless, forced by public opinion to
take part in the Government of National Defense,[1]
and at this time offered a great part of his property to
pay the war indemnity imposed and ruthlessly exacted
by the Germans. But his name is associated above all
with humanitarian achievement. On writing to con-
gratulate the American people on the emancipation
of the slaves, he prided himself on the fact that he had
been a member of the government of 1848 which had
proclaimed the abolition of slavery in the French dominions, and perhaps the most important measure for
which he was himself responsible as Minister of Justice
was the abolition of the capital penalty for political
offences.

The instances which have been assembled in the
foregoing pages are by no means exhaustive. Illustrations of the sort may be multiplied to an almost wearisome degree. What has been said is, however, sufficient
to demonstrate the participation of the Jews in the national, as distinct from nationalistic, movements of the

[1] He was a colleague in this of his former Secretary, Gambetta.
There is no ground whatever for believing that the latter was a
Jew, as is so often said, but there would be no reason for apologiz-
ing were this indeed the case.

last century. The same was true in the popular governments which were set up all over Central Europe at the close of 1918, as in governments of National Emergency generally, such as those of 1870 in France, of 1931 in England, and so on. In settled periods, Jews have found a more catholic outlet for their political sympathies, which have in no other circumstances been confined to one party.

3

One of the most prominent figures in German public life in the middle of the last century was Ferdinand Lassalle, whose influence is traceable in the political conceptions of all Western countries. He began his public life in the battle for liberty in 1848, but in prison he came to the conclusion that the wrongs of the masses lay more in the economic than in the political sphere. From 1861 to his premature death in a duel in 1864, he swept Germany with his campaign of economic democracy. In 1863, he founded the first Workers' Party, the General German Workingman's Association, out of which grew the party of the Social Democrats or Socialists. In return for the franchise and social welfare legislation, he was prepared to support even Bismarck. On the Continent his was perhaps the first authoritative voice of the nineteenth century to assert, notwithstanding the angry resentment which his views aroused, the right of the masses to a voice in the government. He was barely forty years old at the time of his death, but he had prepared the ground for a new attitude in Europe.

Lassalle's views seemed extreme in his day. After him, the political interests of German Jews, if generally inclined to the Left, were predominantly moderate. When, in 1890, the ban on Socialism was removed and it came once more into the open, it had lost its revolutionary character—mainly owing to Eduard Bernstein, the theoretician of the movement as a reformist doctrine. The revolutionary ardor had clearly disappeared.[1]

Thereafter, the tendency of the emancipated Jew in public life throughout Europe was predominantly liberal. In Germany the mass of the Jewish population, now that its rights were, as it thought, won, inclined to the National Liberal Party. The founder of this party, indeed, in the teeth of Bismarck's frenzied opposition, was the Jew, Eduard Lasker, who was ably assisted by

[1] Elsewhere Jews contributed during this period a few important names, but not many leaders, to the Left wing in politics. In France, Olinde and Eugène Rodrigues, with their banker cousins Péreire, were among the earliest and most fervent supporters of Saint-Simon, and a few others, such as Gaston Crémieux and Alfred Joseph Naquet, were prominent in the troubled period which succeeded the Franco-Prussian war. Later, the aristocratic Léon Blum was to be France's first Socialist premier. In Holland, there was Henri Pollack, one of the organizers of the Trade Union movement in that country; in Austria, the Adlers, father and son; in the United States, Morris Hillquit, one of the organizers of American Socialism, and Samuel Gompers, creator of the American Federation of Labor, who was for nearly half a century the dominant and moderating influence in the working-class movement. England can furnish the names of several liberal leaders during this period, but none of real prominence belonging to the Left wing in politics. To the German names mentioned above should be added that of Moses Hess, who was unusual in that he retained his enthusiasm for Judaism.

Ludwig Bamberger and others. This tendency in politics continued to attract the sympathies of the average German Jew. Lasker's greatest title to fame was achieved in a non-partisan role on that memorable occasion in 1873 when from the tribune of the Reichstag he thundered against the "promotion swindle" and misleading the public by printing great names on the prospectuses of new ventures. This speech, one of the strongest ever delivered in the German Parliament, became historical and had wide repercussions.

In England, Jewish emancipation had been opposed by the Conservatives and supported by the Liberals. It was therefore inevitable that the earliest Jewish members of Parliament were all adherents of the latter party. But at the time of the Liberal Unionist split, Jewish public opinion veered round, and some of the outstanding representatives of English Jewry accompanied Chamberlain into the Conservative camp. From that period the distribution of the Jews in politics reflected more evenly the general political tendency of the country. Thus, while after the political landslide of 1906 the Liberal members of Parliament who were Jews outnumbered the Conservatives by three to one (12 to 4), the numbers four years later were approximately equal (8 to 7).

Jewish ministers of the Crown have been appointed by Prime Ministers of all political complexions. If the Conservative party can point to no great public servants who belonged to the Jewish community of the caliber of the Marquess of Reading or Viscount Samuel, this does no more than accentuate the natural tendency pointed out above, while, on the other hand the Liberal party can provide no parallel to Benjamin Disraeli.

So completely impartial a distribution was perhaps confined to the English-speaking world, in which effective emancipation has gone furthest and where for a long time no reactionary party in the Continental sense has existed. Elsewhere, the Liberal and Left tendency is perhaps stronger; yet nowhere has it been exclusive. Indeed, everywhere it is possible to point to conservative leaders of great influence who were of Jewish extraction.

In the opinion of some competent observers, the most influential statesman of Jewish birth in the nineteenth century was Disraeli's German contemporary, Friedrich Julius Stahl. His was a fairly commonplace career in the Germany of those days. Brought up as a Jew, he found the inevitable difficulties in his path and was baptized at the age of seventeen. He became one of the best known German jurists of his day, devoting himself especially to the philosophy of law, his great *Die Philosophie des Rechts nach geschichtlicher Ansicht* running into several editions. When, in 1845, the revolutionary agitation broke out in Germany, Stahl, unlike the majority of Jews, threw himself whole-heartedly into politics on the conservative (perhaps it is more correct to say reactionary) side. In the Revolutions of 1848, his was the most active, most biting and most effective pen on the side of the Government, and he was rewarded by appointment as a life member of the Upper House.

Throughout the following decade, he was recognized as the leader of the reactionary party, and he lost his power only with the fall of the Manteuffel ministry. No less an authority than Lord Acton regarded his influence in German conservatism as more dominant than that of Beaconsfield in England. He is described in the *Cambridge Modern History* as "the intellectual leader of the conservative aristocratic party and the most remarkable brain in the Upper Chamber. . . . He largely supplied the ruling party with the learning and wealth of ideas on which to found their claims." Bluntschli describes him as being "after Hegel, the most important representative of the philosophical theory of the state." His influence on Bismarck, in the latter's formative period, was very strong. So, incidentally, was that of Professor Emil von Friedberg (brother of that Heinrich von Friedberg who was Minister of Justice in Prussia from 1879 to 1889), the great authority on ecclesiastical history, who was the Chancellor's principal adviser during the Kulturkampf and was also of Jewish birth.

One of the heirs to Stahl's spirit, in the days when the Prussian *junker* had taken a slightly more liberal attitude, was Karl Rudolph Friedenthal, nephew of a well-known Hebrew writer. Converted like Stahl in youth, he was a member of the Reichstag from 1867 and one of the founders of the Free Conservative Party. He it was whom Bismarck invited in 1870 to formulate the constitution of the German Empire which was promulgated at Versailles, in collaboration with Blankenburg and Bennigsen; subsequently, he became Minister of Agriculture. The constitution which Friedenthal framed continued to function until the revolution of 1918. It was then overthrown in favor of the Weimar Constitution, one of the principal framers of which was the Berlin jurist, Hugo Preuss. Hence the Weimar Constitution could no more be described as Jewish than the Versailles Constitution could. Both were the work of patriotic Germans, among whom there happened to be persons who were Jews by birth.

Austria provides a further illustration of the participation of Jews in formulating the ideology of the conservative element in Central European politics, in Heinrich Friedjung, who has received mention as perhaps the greatest Austrian historian. Born in Moravia of Jewish parentage, he was by conviction a passionate German Austrian, equally proud of the great traditions both of Germany and of Austria. In 1880, in collaboration with George von Schönerer (later the leader of the extreme Pan-Germans in Austria) and the Jew, Victor Adler (subsequently founder of the Austrian Social Democratic Party, and Foreign Secretary in the first Republican Cabinet of October, 1918), he produced the Conservative Linz program as a basis for the future policy of the German Austrians.

In short-lived liberal Germany, contrary to what is generally believed, the participation of Jews in public life was not particularly great. Thus in the twenty cabinets which ruled the country from the downfall of the monarchy to the Nazi Revolution, there were some 200 different ministers in all. Of these, only seven were of Jewish descent—Preuss, Rathenau, Landsberg, Schiffer, Gradnauer, Hilferding, and Dernburg (who was only half-Jewish). In the German federal states there were still fewer Jewish ministers. Between 1920 and 1932 neither Prussia, the largest state, nor Bavaria, second in size, had a single Jewish minister. The same was the case in most of the smaller states. In the Reichstag of 1930 there was only one Jew among about 600 members, and 20 members of known Jewish descent; the Socialist Party comprised 143 members, of whom none were Jews and only 14 of Jewish blood. In fact, the only outstanding Jewish statesman in Germany in recent years was Walther Rathenau, whose essential work lay in his courageous effort to rehabilitate Germany, both morally and economically, after her shattering defeat in 1918. Nor can he, a capitalist by birth and training, be regarded by any stretch of the imagination as an exponent of extreme political principles. He was, however, quick to realize that his class had left the era of privilege and entered that of responsibility, and wisely endeavored to bridge the gap which divided the proletariat from the bourgeoisie.

4

"His German extraction gave him an objective view of the British Empire not always obtainable by an Englishman," said a contemporary writer with reference to the late Lord Milner. A similar fact perhaps explains the enduring influence of Disraeli in English politics. His exuberant imagination made it possible for him to realize not only the romance, but also the potentialities of the empire. At a time when the majority of Englishmen regarded the "colonies" as a home for younger sons, he had more than a glimmering of what has subsequently come to be termed the "Commonwealth of Nations," composed of equal partners who might perform an important function in maintaining a balance among nations.

More important still, perhaps, was his conception of conservatism, not as the party of privilege and hence of a perpetual minority, but as the representative of historic instead of radical development. It is hence remarkable but not astonishing that of the statesmen of the last century Disraeli alone is a living force and a source of political inspiration in England.

There are many persons who consider Luigi Luzzatti, Prime Minister of Italy from 1909–11, the greatest Italian of modern times. His work was, of course, greater in the economic than in the political sphere. From early manhood he devoted himself to the task of raising the economic status of the people. His ideal was to abolish the monopoly of wealth through other means than those advocated by the socialists, whose remedies were in his opinion ridiculously inadequate to the unhealthy state of affairs which they criticized. Long before the union of Italy was an accomplished fact, he toured the country advocating the foundation of people's banks and cooperative societies. In pursuance of this policy he founded the Banco Popolare of Milan and started the first cooperative store in Italy. His influence is stamped upon the cooperative movement in Italy as strongly as is that of Schulze-Delitzch in Germany or that of the Rochdale pioneers in England. As Cabinet Minister, even before he became Premier, he advocated this same policy. It was Luzzatti, in D'Annunzio's happy phrase, who spiritualized the power of gold.

An analysis of the Jewish participation in American public life is not easy, if only by reason of its complete naturalness, impartiality, and lack of constraint. On the whole, it may be said that whereas in local and in state politics Jews have played a prominent and honorable part—witness, for example, Governor Herbert H. Lehman of New York State, and Governor Henry Horner of Illinois—in national politics their participation has barely been in proportion to their numerical importance. Thus, though a succession of American presidents have considered that the Jew may have a range of sympathy and knowledge which peculiarly qualifies him to represent the country abroad (instance after instance will readily come to mind) it was not until the appointment of Henry Morgenthau, Jr., to the post of Secretary of the Treasury in 1934, the second Jew to hold office in a presidential cabinet, that any administrative position of the highest importance was filled by a Jew. The total number of U. S. Senators up to 1937 who were Jews was only eight—a very modest figure. It is only in the sphere of law, in which Jews have always been particularly distinguished, that their participation may be said to be outstanding. In its political alignment, American Jewry has simply reflected, naturally and faithfully, its social and economic position.[1]

5

The instances adduced above are sufficient to show that the identification of the Jews with extreme opinions in politics rests upon slender evidence, and that even their dominant liberal sympathies are by no means exclusive. They have been identified with every party; and it is as easy to quote instances of conservatives or even reactionaries as it is to cite exponents of extreme left principles. It is certainly significant that the champions of conservatism both in England and in Germany were of Jewish birth.

Karl Marx was to be sure, like them, of Jewish extraction. His affiliations are, however, needlessly exaggerated, both by his admirers and by his detractors. His father, Hirschel Marx, a typical Rhenish lawyer of the assimilationist period, was baptized some time between the midsummer of 1816 and the spring of 1817, some time, therefore, before his famous son was born. Karl himself was received into the Evangelical Church at the age of seven and was brought up as a Christian. Not only was he ignorant of Judaism: he was, unlike Disraeli, bitterly antagonistic to it. The story of his association with Zunz and Heine in the

[1] We may also mention Sidney Hillman, who has worked out many original solutions to the problems of both laborer and manufacturer and was awarded the Harmon medal; and Bernard M. Baruch, who founded the Williamstown Institute of Politics, a genuine contribution to the understanding of national and international problems.

Verein fur Cultur und Wissenschaft der Juden is an obvious fable, as that institution was founded when he was less than three years old and disbanded before he was ten! Nor was there anything especially Jewish about his teaching, an intellectual product of the characteristically Teutonic doctrines of Hegel and Feuerbach.

In point of fact, the whole of the Marxian theory, far from being fundamentally Jewish, is a reaction against (though he himself inferred that it was a logical consequence of) the decorous conclusions drawn by another theorist who, like Marx, happened to be a Jew by birth. Orthodox economics are to a large extent the creation of David Ricardo, the illustrious English economist of the nineteenth century and founder of the science of political economy. He was, indeed, rather more Jewish than Marx, as he had been born and bred in the faith of his fathers, which he left only after attaining manhood. Unlike Marx, moreover, his attitude towards Jews and Judaism was friendly to the end. It may be remarked that Nassau Senior, the most distinguished English economist of the ensuing age, was also of Jewish descent, his ancestor, Aaron Senior, having emigrated from the West Indies at the beginning of the eighteenth century.[1]

Ricardo's Theory of Value dominated English and,

[1] For some other outstanding Jewish economists, see above, p. 273. Among the pioneers in this sphere was the Jewish astronomer Mashaala (*supra*, pp. 57, 114), who composed in the eighth century one of the earliest works on the subject, a dissertation on prices, as well as a remarkable political treatise on communities, faiths, and nations.

in fact, European thought in the sphere of political
economy until the end of the nineteenth century, and
still constitutes the core of accepted economic theory.
But his conclusions ran counter to the whole of the
social and humanitarian preconceptions of Karl Marx,
who thought only in terms of human suffering and
upheaval. The two attitudes are clearly expressions of
the temperaments of the two theorists. It is therefore
highly unfortunate that to the Jews should be ascribed
the sole responsibility for one whose connection with
them was so slight, and whose attitude so unfriendly
—a misconception all the more unjustified in view of
the fact that Engels, to whom Marxism owes hardly
less than to Marx himself, had no Jewish connections
or affiliations whatsoever. But perhaps time has dealt
no less unkindly with Marx himself, whose name has
been associated in Russia and the world with the
Bolshevik form of autocracy.

In fact, the persons responsible for the translation
of Marx's theories into the amalgam which is associated
with the term "Bolshevism" were mainly Russians,
such as Herzen and Bakunin. Russian Bolshevism lies
deep in the root of the Russian nature and in the
politico-economic structure of the Empire of the
Czars. To conceive it merely as a variant of the prole-
tarian socialism of the Marxist school would be to dis-
regard its distinctively national character. The Russian Jew of the period before 1917 was essentially
bourgeois. In 1918, the Lenin government issued a
manifesto violently attacking the Jewish workers for
their anti-Bolshevik attitude. That same year, in the

Jewish National Assembly of the Ukraine, no less than 63% of the representatives were affiliated with bourgeois groups, while among the fiercest opponents of the Bolsheviks was the General League of Jewish Workers, known as the Bund, subsequently suppressed by the new regime. It is hence more preposterous to ascribe the triumph of Bolshevism in Russia to the Jews than it is to ascribe it to the Germans, who sent Lenin in a sealed carriage across Germany in 1917 with the express purpose of inculcating communist ideas into the Russian masses.

On the other hand, since the Jews were the only portion of the Russian proletariat who were as a rule highly educated, it was inevitable that the Bolshevik government drew a considerable number of its instruments from their ranks. The proportions, however, have been distorted. Out of 48 persons who constituted Lenin's administration in 1919, only eleven, or some 20% (not 90%, as is sometimes alleged) were of Jewish birth. The attitude of this group to Judaism, moreover, may be gauged from the reply of Trotsky to a representative Jewish delegation which begged him to resign: "Go home to your Jews. I am not a Jew, and I care nothing for the Jews or their fate."

6

Is it possible, nevertheless, to find any common factor in those Jews who were active in public life and some of whose names have been mentioned above? There is the instinctive anti-Semitic reply: that all were a disruptive influence in the state. This, in the face of the names of the reactionaries, the conservatives, and the very moderate liberals which may be marshalled on the other side, is absurd. Nor among the members of this group, so far removed from one another in background, in object, in character and in policy, is there discernible any singleness of purpose.

One bond of union only may perhaps be observed. There seems to have been among them all a broad sympathy with the under-dog. The people who had suffered for two thousand years could not fail to feel sympathy with those who suffered in their own day. The children of those to whom the prophets had addressed their message could not but retain some inkling of the ideal of social justice. And so the Jewish statesmen, whether elaborating plans for Young England like Disraeli, or endeavoring to institute a new order on earth like Karl Marx, all appear to have been actuated by that wide sympathy with suffering humanity which is, one may hope, part of the Jewish heritage.

The foregoing pages are contributory to an objective consideration of the part played by Jews in European and American political life. They imply no criticism of the systems involved. There are circles in every country in which the fancied responsibility of the Jews for the triumph of Bolshevism in Russia is even now considered a high compliment; the name of Disraeli is nearly as unpopular in some groups as is that of Karl Marx in others. In the interest of veracity, however, it is necessary to remove the current misunderstanding. Individual Jews have played some part in politics at all times; "the Jews," never—save perhaps, (and there were exceptions even then) in the heyday of the national revival in the middle of the last century. And, though it is possible to discern a certain propensity on the part of Jews to that side in politics which was formerly termed "liberal," that tendency has never been exclusive. All parties and outlooks have found their response in the Jewish community, and in nothing does its representative character show up more clearly. Western civilization has, however, been permanently enriched by the Jew's devoted, and sometimes heroic, participation in the cause of self-government, of humanitarianism, and of social reform.

APPENDIX: *Jews and Western Law*

ANY evaluation of the part of the Jews in the legal development of modern Europe must necessarily take account of the Bible. For, while European law traces its origin, in the main, to Rome, the influence of Hebrew ethics on the mind of legislators and on the growth of customary law cannot be overlooked. Moreover, the medieval Canon Law, based to a considerable extent on the Old Testament, could not but exercise a profound influence upon the Civil Law with which it was studied contemporaneously.

In accordance with one theory which has been advanced, the Jewish influence on European law was far more profound and far-reaching than is usually believed. It has been maintained in a recent study, with a wealth of learning and great force of argument, that talmudic law deeply affected Syrian law, which in turn (it will be recalled that Berytus, now Beyrout, was the seat of one of the most famous Imperial schools of jurisprudence) had a great influence on the Byzantine codes and the Roman law as it was formulated by the great legalists of the Eastern Empire. If this theory is correct, the exclusive claims of the Roman jurists and the German folkways to the paternity of the European codes must be modified.

It is indisputable that the parallels between European and talmudic law go beyond a few vague general principles. There is rabbinic, but not Roman, precedent for the principle *qui facit per alium facit per se,* "he who acts through another acts through himself." The medieval rabbis evolved a law of copyright which probably preceded the practice among their neighbors. The Jewish system of tenant-right, or right of possession, became familiar in general circles through the *Jus Gazaga,* miserably evolved through force of circumstances in the Italian Ghetto, and may not have been a barren example. The suggestion has even been made that one or two institutions and formulae of English law, such as the Writ *Eligit,* the mortgage, and the phrase *cuius est solum eius usque ad coelum usque ad inferos,* are derived from Jewish deeds, which were familiar to medieval lawyers. The "universal code" based on the Bible, termed by the rabbis the laws of the Sons of Noah, is paralleled by the *jus naturale et gentium,* or Natural law, recognized by medieval jurists; this in turn was the formative principle at the base of the English Equity law and of the Continental legal philosophies upon which the nineteenth-century codifications depended. The great jurists of the seventeenth century, Grotius on the continent, Selden in England, were positively soaked in Hebraic lore—biblical, rabbinic, and contemporary—traces of which may be discerned throughout their writings.

The God of Israel is the God of Justice; and it is not remarkable that, since the Age of Emancipation, the profession of law has exercised a powerful attraction on the Jewish mind. There can be no doubt as to the importance of the part played by Jewish lawyers in modern jurisprudence. Even before the period of emancipation, a few eminent Jewish lawyers emerged, such as the Austrian humanitarian, Joseph von Sonnenfels, who was responsible for the abolition of torture in Austria (*infra*, p. 343). The nineteenth century saw the beginning of a series of notable Jewish jurists and advocates in every country. Pre-eminent in England, above all, was Sir George Jessel, one of the great lawmaking judges of his time, generally recognized as the founder of the court of chancery as it exists to-day. His judgments were models of clarity and learning and were seldom reversed on appeal.

Jessel was in his prime when Judah Philip Benjamin, the eminent Southern statesman called "the Brains of the Confederacy," found refuge in England at the conclusion of the American Civil War. The latter was admitted to the bar and for some years enjoyed a practice which even now has seldom been surpassed. He wrote the *Law of the Sale of Personal Property*, which remained a classic to the present day. It is believed that his elevation to the bench, an honor for which he was more than qualified, was prevented only by deference to American public opinion.

In France, among many Jewish lawyers of high repute, the outstanding name is undoubtedly that of Adolphe Crémieux, one of the most brilliant of advocates and a great Minister of Justice, who did much to abolish the many cruel penal punishments which still persisted even in his day. Holland owes its code of judicial procedure to an equally great lawyer and friend of his coreligionists, Michael H. Godefroi, Minister of Justice in that country in 1866, while Aaron Adolf de Pinto was part-author (1886) of the Dutch penal code. J. L. Simonsen was for many years the outstanding lawyer in Denmark.

Germany, in the course of a single generation, produced a host of Jewish jurists of high distinction— Eugen Fuchs, Herman Staub, Max Hachenburg, Eduard von Simson (*supra*, pp. 134, 305), Heinrich Dernburg, Eduard Gans, Joseph Unger, Georg Jellinek, Heinrich von Friedberg, at one time Minister of Justice, Hugo Preuss (*supra*, p. 315), and a vast number of others. With Hans Kelson of Geneva, they were virtually the creators of the science of the philosophy of Law, in which Germany was long preeminent: and Friedrich Julius Stahl's great *Die Philosophie des Rechts nach geschichtlicher Ansicht* is still a classic. So also is Levin Goldschmidt's great history of commercial law, one of the triumphs of German scholarship of the nineteenth century.

In Italy, one of the earliest Jewish lawyers to achieve a high reputation was Gioacchino Basevi, who had the courage to defend the German-Austrian hero, Andreas Hofer, during the Napoleonic domination. Later, the contributions of Cesare Vivante, the founder of the new school of Italian commercial law (with Leone Bolaffi and David Supino), of Vittorio Polacco, one of the most important Italian legalists, and of Ludovico Mortara, the great systematizer of the procedure of Italian Civil Law, were of the utmost importance. Federico Cammeo, a recognized expert in administrative law, played a part of some distinction in negotiating the recent treaty with the Vatican.

While Jews are largely represented in the legal profession in America, two in our own day achieved a particularly high reputation, and were members of the Supreme Court: Louis Brandeis for the liberal spirit which won him before his elevation to the bench the title "the People's attorney"; and the late Benjamin Nathan Cardozo, the philosopher of American jurisprudence. Both were notably liberal in their sympathies, and it is significant that they were elevated to their high positions by Presidents of opposite political tendencies. Another outstanding contemporary American is Professor Felix Frankfurter, one of the most eminent legal theorists in the country, author of a number of standard works on political and constitutional problems, Professor of Law at Harvard University, and now Justice of the Supreme Court.

That Jews have been exceptionally active in the field of international law might be anticipated. A great part in the development of the modern system was taken by the Dutch jurist, Tobias Michael Carel Asser. The name of Albrecht Mendelssohn-Bartholdy was particularly prominent in the same field in Germany. In England, Leone Levi, primarily an economist, was largely responsible for the codification of international commercial law. He was the author of several important works on this subject, in one of which he anticipated the modern view as to the disastrous consequences of any war, victorious or otherwise.

CHAPTER XII. *"The Greatest of These Is Charity"*

I

IT is natural in a work which deals with the Jewish contribution to civilization to devote a section to beneficent activities, for, if there was any quality which the Jew was able to enhance even during the age of persecution, it was the spirit of charity.

Research upon this subject is still necessary in order to bring out fully the distinctive quality of this Jewish contribution. For it had certain specific characteristics of its own. The degree of destitution among the Jews was enormous at the time when Ghetto deprivation was at its height. In the eighteenth century it is computed that one in three of the Jewish population in Germany, England, and Italy was dependent upon his coreligionists for relief and as many more were living upon the borderline of penury. Yet the cry for assistance was never made in vain, and relief was given in such a manner as to facilitate the maximum self-reliance and to avoid pauperization. It is significant that the most bulky work on charity ever published, with the exception of Lallemand's four-volume *Histoire de la Charité* is the *Meil Zedaka*, written by an eighteenth century Jewish author, Elijah Cohen of Smyrna.

330

Some of the outstanding characteristics of post-biblical and medieval Jewish philanthropy deserve cursory mention. It was realized from the beginning that the poor have rights, and the rich have duties. This principle, explicitly laid down in the Mosaic code, was extended and crystallized in talmudic practice. From the period of the fall of the Jewish state the charity overseer was part of the recognized institutional system of every community. It was expected of the medieval Jew that he should devote a tithe of his income, at the very least, to philanthropic objects, and this ideal has been preserved to our own day. Even the pauper, who lived on the charity of others, was expected to contribute his mite to the relief of those more needy than himself.

A series of voluntary associations took care of the indigent from birth to death. The mother could expect assistance in child-birth, the ailing on their sick bed, the mourners in their hour of affliction, the prisoner in his dungeon, the slave in captivity. Another charitable activity which was particularly highly esteemed was the dowering of poor brides. In Rome in the Ghetto period not less than thirty of these benevolent associations existed, in a population which did not exceed five thousand souls.

Every Ghetto had its lodging house for indigent strangers, which was also used as a hospital (the institution is found at Cologne as early as the eleventh century); every community had its salaried physician, so that medical care was available for all. There was, too, (supra, pp. 43–44) a free educational system, supported by voluntary subscriptions and open to every child. A town without its proper charity organizations, it was laid down in the codes, was no proper residence for a self-respecting Jew, any more so than if it lacked its place of worship. Yet, at the same time, it was a cardinal principle that the poor should not be put to shame by the method of administering relief. As early as the fourth century, the Emperor Julian, when he ordered the institution of hostels for strangers in every city, referred with admiration to the example of the Jews, "the enemies of the gods," in whose midst no beggars were to be found.

It should be noted, in this connection, how catholic is the Jewish conception of charity. It is man's duty, we are informed in the Talmud, to relieve the Gentile poor, to visit their sick, and to bury their dead, just as with a coreligionist. This principle was not inculcated for the sake of appearances or of policy, but on a purely ethical basis, being deduced from the verse of Psalm 145, which tells how the tender mercy of the Lord is over *all* His creatures.   Moreover, the principle was taken over in the Ghetto period and reiterated in such intimate ethical treatises as the *Mesillat Yesharim* of Moses Hayim Luzzatto. It is illuminating to compare this with the spectacle which horrified the world at the time of the expulsion from Spain in 1492, when zealous friars wandered among the groups of starving Jewish refugees on the quay-side in Genoa, loaves of bread in one hand and a crucifix in the other, offering food in return for a recognition of the spiritual pre-eminence of Christianity.

2

With this tradition in the background it was natural that Jews played a conspicuous part, once they were given the opportunity, in every modern humanitarian movement. It is impossible to give a detailed account in these pages of their record in this field, but an attempt will be made to outline some of the more significant achievements.

It has been pointed out above that the Jewish ideal in charitable relief was to avoid pauperization and do all that was possible to render the beneficiary self-supporting. Scientific charity, in a word, took the place of indiscriminate giving. This ideal was adopted by the Jews in their general philanthropic work, as soon as the breach in the walls of the Ghetto enabled them to assume their natural place in such activity.

The wealthy Jews who took the lead in this process, at the beginning of the last century, made it a rule to employ their almoners, to investigate the cases which they were called upon to assist. This simple beginning developed into the rudiments of a scientific and constructive system of charity administration, which replaced the haphazard alms-giving which had previously been the general rule. In the present state of knowledge upon this point, it is impossible to say that the Jews took the lead in this, but they were certainly among the pioneers, and they continued to develop the new ideal.

One of the most remarkable illustrations of this comes from the United States. It was perhaps because

he himself belonged to a misunderstood and persecuted group that Julius Rosenwald directed his attention to the amelioration of the condition of the American Negro. The total of his benefactions has been
estimated at some $62,000,000; and a good part of this
sum was devoted to Negro welfare. Eighteen Negro
Y.M.C.A.s and no less than 3,433 Negro rural school
buildings were the result of his interest. The method of
his giving, above all, marked an epoch in philanthropy.
It was not only scientific; it was also impersonal. He
organized a staff of experts and consultants to advise
him, and to ensure that his benefactions were expended
to the utmost advantage. He made it a rule, moreover,
to give conditionally, that is, provided that certain
further amounts were raised or certain local conditions
fulfilled. He had a rooted objection to having his name
associated with his donations. So little did he look for
eleemosynary immortality, indeed, that he took steps
to ensure that his benefactions should be expended
within a comparatively short period of years. The
spirit of his charities was thus even more important
than their extent. It was a contribution not to one cause
or another but to the common store of humanity.

The Rothschild family is today taken as the outstanding exemplification of the Jew in high finance.
It is less generally realized how unselfishly they made
use of the riches which they amassed. If any family
has regarded its accumulated wealth as a public trust,
it is this one. For a period of several generations, the
name is repeated with impressive regularity in every
beneficent enterprise and endeavor in over half of

Europe; and, up to the war of 1914–18, their firm figured at the head of the subscription list of almost every charitable fund raised in London. To recount their benefactions in detail would be an endless task, but it is impossible to touch upon this subject without making specific mention of their liberality in some directions.

They were among the foremost to recognize that housing conditions are the key to many other social problems, and they led in the attempt to cope with the abuse. Betty de Rothschild of Paris, widow of Baron James de Rothschild, founder of the French house, showed her interest in the timid spirit of unscientific benefaction when, on her death in 1886, she left 600,000 francs to the public charities to assist poor laborers in paying their rents. Her three sons, advancing beyond this elementary conception, subscribed 10,000,000 francs in 1904 for the erection of inexpensive dwelling-houses, and for the general amelioration of the condition of the working classes. And one of the most remarkable achievements of practical philanthropy, before the time when the government had begun to interest itself in the housing question on an enormous scale, was the first Lord Rothschild's organization of the 4% Industrial Dwellings, which replaced some of the most notorious London slums with model tenements. Jews took the lead in the movement for housing reform at Mulhouse, which in turn set a model for the whole of France, and indeed of Europe.

Other initiatives, too, reflected an understanding of the interaction between economic and social problems, and of the desirability of leavening the law of supply and demand with a modicum of humanity. Witness Maud Nathan, who founded the Consumers' League of America, which has done a great deal to improve conditions of labor in the United States. Another great American figure, whose merits are likely to be increasingly recognized, was Edward Filene, founder first of the Boston, then of the American, and finally of the International Chamber of Commerce. His greatest title to fame was, however, his unflagging advocacy of higher wages, shorter hours, and comprehensive social insurance, and his leading share in the establishment of the Credit Union Extension Bureau, with its thousands of branches.

No account has hitherto been given of benefactions for specifically Jewish purposes. Yet there are certain instances of this, the significance of which is more than denominational. In his day, there was no greater or more objective philanthropist than Baron de Hirsch, who, in addition to his multifarious activities, endeavored to solve the problem of Russian Jewry single-handed by diverting it to the agricultural colonies which he founded in America. He maintained a regiment of supervisors and almoners, in the hope of achieving a scientific approach to the question. The total of his charities at the time of his death was estimated at more than twice the fortune which he left. Actually, he was unable to do more than touch the fringes of the problem which he had endeavored to solve, but his work is a landmark in the history of scientific beneficence.

The Baroness de Hirsch worthily seconded all her husband's charitable endeavors, in the non-Jewish as well as the Jewish sphere; and she figures by the side of the famous philanthropist, Madame Boucicaut, founder of the Bon Marché in Paris, in the monument which faces that institution. Incidentally, of the seven women to whom statues have been erected in the French capital, three were Jewesses; besides the Baroness de Hirsch, there are also Rosa Bonheur and Sarah Bernhardt.

The founders of two of the greatest English philanthropic agencies happen to have been of Jewish blood, though in neither case were they Jews by religion. One was Thomas John Barnardo, who established in 1867 the first modest nucleus of Dr. Barnardo's Homes, which by the time of his death, forty years later, had given homes to 250,000 poor children and has continued the work since on an expanding scale. According to his official biographer, J. M. Bready, the "Father of the Fatherless" was the son of John Michaelis Barnardo, a Hamburg *Sephardi* who, settling in Dublin, lost all connection with his coreligionists. Even greater than this institution in the extent of its work for the relief of human misery is the Salvation Army which, in addition, introduced a new spirit into religious life in England in the middle of last century and awakened Church circles to a sense of their wider social responsibilities. The founder of this organization, "General" William Booth, was the son of a Nottingham woman named Moss, and it is generally assumed, rightly or wrongly, that he owed to her his rabbinical appearance, his prophetic enthusiasm, and his burning sympathy for the poor.

3

The people who originated the adage that the whole universe is poised on the breath of school children, who were sneered at by Greek and Roman writers for considering child-murder a sin and whose family life remained a model for the world, naturally showed a particular interest in children's welfare. A curious illustration of this comes from Leghorn in Italy. Here, in the eighteenth century, when the death of children through "overlying" was shamefully common, the community passed a regulation, enforced by the severest religious sanctions, forbidding mothers to take their infant children to sleep with them in the same bed. Such devoted regard for infant welfare, coupled with the hygienic regulation of the traditional Jewish life, had its consequence in a greatly reduced death-rate among Jewish children. In Czarist Russia the death-rate for infants under one year among Jews was 13.21 per cent, among non-Jews 25.96 per cent. In Vienna at one period the death-rate for infants under one month was among Jews 8.3 per cent, among non-Jews 16.1 per cent. These figures are reflected in other parts of Europe, though the contrast is not always quite so striking. Even in New York Jewish infant mortality in 1915 was 78 for each 1,000 births while that for the remainder of the population was 105; and the infant death-rate among Palestinian Jewry today is almost the lowest in the world.

It was natural, therefore, that Jews took a prominent part in infant welfare work on a large scale, when they were allowed to become part of the general community. In another connection (*supra*, p. 212) mention has been made regarding the Jewish contribution to the science of pediatrics. Here, a few details will be added which illustrate that same interest from a different angle.

One of the most remarkable philanthropic endeavors of our day was that of the American philanthropist, Nathan Straus, who, appalled at the waste of child-life through the inroads of tuberculosis, devoted his energy entirely to an attempt to grapple with the problem at its source. In 1890, he installed a system for the distribution of sterilized milk to the poor of New York. A greatly reduced infant mortality showed that the experiment was more than justified. He then set about installing this same system and providing pasteurized milk in various other cities of the United States and abroad, maintaining his own laboratory for this purpose. It was through his efforts that the relationship of bovine tuberculosis to the spread of the disease was finally demonstrated at the Eighth International Tuberculosis Conference at Stockholm in 1909. Immediately afterwards, he established the first tuberculosis preventorium for children. During one period of his life, he gave away more than his income to charity; he sold his yacht, and his wife sold her jewels, so that the proceeds could be devoted to more useful purposes. But the aged philanthropist retained his greatest treasure, a slip of paper which he carried about in his pocket to his last day, and on which were shown the number of infant deaths in New York before and after he introduced his scheme.

Another American philanthropist who did work in this direction, though not on so large a scale, was the inventor, Emil Berliner, who was a foremost advocate of milk pasteurization, besides doing much to popularize preventive medicine. It is noteworthy that a similar system was set up in France by another Jew, Henri de Rothschild—a rare instance of the heir to wealth who has devoted his whole energy to science and philanthropy—who founded the first Infant Consultations in Paris and was instrumental in establishing milk-stations for the poor in that city. Emile Deutsch de la Meurthe, during the war of 1914–18, organized the Franco-American Brotherhood, which ultimately took care of 286,000 orphans.

In England, Ernest Abraham Hart, founder of the *British Medical Journal*, was responsible for the Infant Life Protection Act, which eliminated the hideous old type of baby farm, as well as for the act which established the Metropolitan Asylums Board. In the following generation, Herbert Samuel, as Home Secretary, was to pilot the Children's Bill, a notable step in social reform, through the House of Commons.

In the United States, the Child Study Association of America, which has done splendid work, was started by Jews, while the Federal Children's Bureau was originated in 1908 by Lillian D. Wald, who six years earlier had organized school nursing in New York. She is better remembered, however, by the famous

Henry Street Settlement which she founded in 1893 in the face of considerable opposition, but which originated a new era in welfare work in America. Later she was responsible for the beginning of the district nursing system throughout the United States. In Germany, Lina Morgenstern, who later convened the first International Women's Congress, was the most sedulous advocate of the kindergarten system, her *Childhood's Paradise* of 1860 being one of the epoch-making publications in this sphere. The earliest kindergarten in Italy was established by Adolph Pick, the pioneer of Froebellian methods in that country. Similarly, it was Albert Neisser who founded the first society in the world to combat venereal disease and safeguard maternity.

By a coincidence, Jews have played an important role in removing the calamities of another common affliction of infancy. At one time, a child born deaf was necessarily considered dumb, and generally semi-idiot also for, unable to hear what was said to it, it could not understand any language or express its thoughts. It was only in the eighteenth century that this horror was averted. The pioneer was a certain Jacob Rodrigues Pereira, a Marrano returned to Judaism, and grandfather of the famous bankers of the Second Empire. After long study of anatomy and physiology and numerous experiments on congenital deaf-mutes, Pereira perfected a system for instructing them which received official recognition from the Académie des Belles Lettres of Caen in 1747. Unfortunately, his religion and origin were against him, and the Abbé de l'Epée's method, not greatly dissimilar from his own and to some extent based upon it, was officially adopted. Nevertheless, Pereira's work as first teacher of deaf-mutes in France remains a perpetual title to the gratitude of posterity.

4

The Hebraic abhorrence of capital punishment is to be traced throughout the centuries. In the Second Jewish Commonwealth, it was virtually abolished; so much so, that a court which passed a capital sentence once in seventy years was stigmatized as one of murderers. This, incidentally, is one of the many indications that the execution of Jesus of Nazareth was the outcome of the sentence of a Roman, not a Jewish, court. What was more natural than that in England Sir Moses Montefiore, the Jewish philanthropist, was among those who led the opposition to capital punishment. He was overjoyed when he secured the remission of the sentence of the only person sentenced to death during his term as sheriff of the city of London; it was symptomatic of the times that Lord John Russell, when approached, took no interest in the subject, while Marshal Soult, then on a visit to London, showed nothing but astonishment at these humanitarian views. Indeed, Montefiore received his main encouragement from another Jew, Sir David Salamons, who was whole-heartedly opposed to the savage penalties which had survived Peel's reforms.

Similarly, in France, Adolphe Crémieux procured the abolition of capital punishment for political offences. In the previous century it had been a baptized Jew, the jurist Joseph von Sonnenfels, who was responsible for the abolition of torture in Austria in 1776—a revolutionary step at that time, though in the Jewish tradition this perversion of the judicial system was never allowed. It was Uriah Phillips Levy, the first Jew to rise to high rank in the American navy, who brought about the abolition of flogging which had previously been one of its disgraces.

The record may be continued. In the field of prison reform, John Howard was preceded by Antonio Ribeiro Sanches, a Portuguese Marrano physician, who spent part of his time as a professing Jew in London. Elizabeth Fry, who continued Howard's work, had no more staunch supporter in England than Sir Isaac Lyon Goldsmid, the first Anglo-Jewish baronet; and in America, later on, Adolf Lewisohn was active in the same field. Similarly, in all the other humanitarian endeavors of the nineteenth century, Jews stood by the side of their fellow-citizens in every country, always seconding and sometimes directing them.

The origin of the movement for the humane treatment of animals is particularly significant, for in this a Jew was working in the oldest Jewish tradition. The simple humanitarianism of the biblical precept, "Thou shalt not muzzle the ox when he treadeth out the corn" (Deuteronomy 25:4) contrasts strangely with Paul's comment, "Doth God take care for oxen?" (I Corinthians 9:9). That all this is not a matter of twentieth century apologetics is made plain from Josephus (*Contra Apionem* II. 29), "So thorough a lesson has he

(Moses) given us in gentleness and humanity that he does not overlook even the brute beasts," a sentiment which Philo also echoes. Cattle and oxen and asses must be permitted to share in the Sabbatical repose (Exodus 20:10; Deuteronomy 5:14); Nineveh was spared on account of its dumb animals as well as the human beings (Jonah, last verse); the Psalmist praised God for preserving beast as well as man (Psalm 36:7).

This strain continues in the Talmud. Thus, from the verse, "And I will send grass in thy fields for thy cattle, and thou mayest eat and be full" (Deuteronomy 11:15), it was deduced that a man should not sit down to table until he had fed his domestic animals; and in a legend paraphrased by Coleridge, it was told how God marked out Moses as a fitting pastor for his people by reason of his devoted treatment of a lamb which had strayed. Even the much decried law of *Shehita*, or the ritual slaughter of animals, seems to have been dictated to a large extent by humane considerations.[1] This was in keeping with the rabbinical conception that cruelty to animals was a breach of the Divine law and of the Mosaic code. "The Jews never torment or abuse or put to any cruel death any brute beast," wrote a Venetian rabbi three centuries ago. It has been pointed out that, until the nineteenth century, cruelty to animals was nowhere illegal, except in Jewish law.

Who was responsible for the change in attitude? As much as any other man, it was a Jew, following the

[1] "I should be happy to think that my own end were likely to be as swift and painless as the end of these cattle killed in this [the Jewish] way undoubtedly is." (Lovat Evans, Professor of Physiology in the University of London.)

prophetical and rabbinical teaching. Lewis Gompertz belonged to a Jewish family established in London since the beginning of the eighteenth century. One of his brothers was a famous mathematician and another a much admired poet. Lewis, on the other hand, an active and successful inventor, devoted his energies to the cause of kindness to animals. In 1824, he recorded his views in a work entitled *Moral Enquiries on the Situation of Men and Brutes.* This attracted considerable attention and contributed greatly to the movement as a result of which the Society (subsequently Royal Society) for the Prevention of Cruelty to Animals was founded. Gompertz was associated with the institution from the first, revived it when it was in difficulties, acted for years in an honorary capacity as its secretary and nursed it back to life. Religious prejudice was not as yet dead in England. A dispute arose between the secretary and the executive committee, and the former's *Moral Enquiries* were denounced as hostile to Christianity. In consequence, he was compelled to sever his connection with the Society. He then formed the "Animals' Friend Society," which speedily outstripped the parent body. However, in 1846, he was obliged by ill-health to retire from public life; his society was disbanded, and the Royal Society for Prevention of Cruelty to Animals henceforth held undisputed sway, and became ultimately the parent body of a network spread over the civilized world. It has long since forgotten that it owes its very existence, as well as its inspiration, to a professing Jew, working in the talmudic and biblical tradition.

5

Visitation and relief of the sick was regarded as one of the cardinal Jewish virtues, and Jews have naturally taken their share in the endowment and support of hospitals.

This is true both in the countries of Europe as well as in the United States. Not only have Jews had a share in the endowment and building of general hospitals and dispensaries in various cities but most of the larger cities in the United States have their "Jewish" hospitals as well.

First should be mentioned the Touro Hospital in New Orleans, founded by Judah Touro. This is a non-sectarian institution which serves all alike and as a matter of fact treats more non-Jewish patients than Jewish. Incidentally, Judah Touro contributed to many philanthropies. Foremost among these was his gift to help in the erection of the Bunker Hill Monument. Both in Newport and New Orleans, streets named after him tell how dear his memory is to both these cities. Mt. Sinai Hospital in New York, originally known as the Jews' Hospital, was founded in 1857. The Michael Reese Hospital in Chicago was established in 1879. Then there are others not local but national in scope. The most outstanding are the National Jewish Hospital in Denver and the sanitarium in Los Angeles, both for the treatment of tuberculosis. A unique institution is the hospital for blood diseases in Hot Springs, Arkansas.

Nor should we, in considering the Jewish contribution to philanthropy, overlook the development of a whole network of institutions known by various names as settlements, Y.M.H.A.s, Y.W.H.A.s, and Jewish Centers, all of which aim at character development of young men and women and thus contribute not only to improving Jewish life but also to making better American citizens.

If these instances are derived from the United States only, it is merely because of the difficulty of drawing up and studying a detailed list in which every country of the world would require mention. It is sufficient to say that illustrations, certainly no less striking, could be assembled for England, France, and Germany, and for every other land in which Jews live.

6

The Jew of the Ghetto period was brought up to realize the supreme importance of rabbinic learning. Admitted to the general world, he translated this conception into general terms and became a munificent patron of scholarship and a pioneer in the establishment of educational institutions. Sir Isaac Lyon Goldsmid, for example, collaborated whole-heartedly with Joseph Lancaster in his great work of enlightening the masses and arousing public interest in education. It was he, too, who headed the group of Jews who worked fervently for the establishment of University College, London, the first non-sectarian British University, the site of which he purchased; and he was thus one of the fathers of the University of London. The library of the University of Liverpool is a monument to the munificence of Harold Cohen, just as a great public library in Frankfort commemorates the generosity of the House of Rothschild and long bore its name. Baron Edmond de Rothschild of Paris, in addition to his many other benefactions, endowed a foundation for scientific research with a gift of 40,-000,000 francs, one of the most princely endowments of that time. Emile Deutsch de la Meurthe, in 1922, established a group of buildings on the outskirts of Paris, the nucleus of the imposing Cité Universitaire, where 350 destitute students could live while receiving their university training. Joseph Pulitzer, as we have seen, founded the School of Journalism at Columbia University, the first institution of its kind in the world. These illustrations, too, could be extended almost indefinitely.

The case of the University of Frankfort-on-Main is an outstanding one. William Merton, a member of a Jewish family which had emigrated to England and anglicized its name, was a real prince of charity and a scientific benefactor as well. He established out of his own means the Academy for Social and Commercial Sciences, which flourished exceedingly and in 1914 was transformed into the University of Frankfort. This University had a special charter and a more liberal constitution than the other German seats of learning. It was a communal affair, the State making no contribution to its upkeep: and the significance of this in a city which contained many wealthy and open-handed Jews is obvious. George Speyer contributed the "Institut für experimentell-chemotherapeutische

Forschung" (Georg Speyer Haus), and so made it possible for Paul Ehrlich to discover salvarsan. Mathilde von Rothschild, the Sterns, and others made large bequests to it. Even Jacob Schiff in far-away New York remembered it. And today, no Jews are permitted to enter its lecture-halls.

More specialized benefactions include characteristically the foundation of Chairs for Industrial and International Peace by Sir Montagu Burton at more than one British university. The thirty Beit fellowships for medical research have done an enormous amount for the relief of human suffering, and, it is to be hoped, will do much more. In the United States, the John Simon Guggenheim Memorial Foundation, established with a capital of $3,000,000 for aiding scientists and artists in their education, without distinction of race, creed, or color, is one of the most munificent endowments for the encouragement of post-graduate research. To another member of the same family thanks are due for a princely endowment for the study of aeronautics.

Adolf Lewisohn donated the School of Mines to Columbia University and the Lewisohn Stadium, where New York hears its great summer concerts, to the College of the City of New York. Elkan Naumberg was another great musical patron, whose generosity was responsible for the erection of the Music Pavilion in Central Park. Jacob Schiff, previously mentioned, made munificent gifts to the New York Public Library, to the Library of Congress, and to Barnard College. What Otto Kahn did for American music, and above all for the opera, cannot easily be summarized in a single sentence. Lucius Littauer is one of the most liberal supporters of Harvard University. The Institute for Advanced Study at Princeton was the creation of Louis Bamberger and his sister. The first American Planetarium was a gift to the city of Chicago from Max Adler, but this was soon followed by a similar gift from Samuel Fels to the Franklin Institute in Philadelphia. James Loeb, another Harvard benefactor and formerly a partner in the famous American banking firm, established the Institute of Musical Art in New York, in addition to founding the famous Loeb Classics, which have placed the masterpieces of Latin and Greek literature within the grasp of the ordinary reader. On his demise, after the beginning of the Nazi regime, his residuary estate, amounting to over $1,000,000, was left to the Institute for Experimental Psychiatry in his beloved Munich.[1]

In 1927, Baron Edmond de Rothschild, mentioned so often in these pages, gave the princely sum of 30,-000,000 francs for the establishment in Paris of a Biological Institute to continue the research work of Claud Bernard, the digestive specialist. Similarly, one of the greatest benefactors of the Pasteur Institute, where so many Jews have done useful work, was the Jewish philanthropist Osiris Iffla. In the East, David and Albert Sassoon, father and son, did an enormous

[1] It may be added that as far back as the middle of the eighteenth century, when Brown University was founded at Newport, Rhode Island, contributions were forthcoming from Jewish magnates of southern cities, while the timber was provided by Aaron Lopez, a local merchant-prince.

amount to further education among all races and creeds in India, China, Turkey, Persia, and even Japan, while the Kadoorie bequests are applied for the benefit not only of the Jews but also the Arabs in Palestine.

The widespread connections of the Jew prevent his purview from being confined to a single country. The "international" outlook, however, has consistently worked to achieve a peaceful understanding between all peoples. It is only characteristic that Sir Ernest Cassel could think of no more fitting manner of commemorating his beloved friend, King Edward VII, than by his gift of £200,000 to found the Anglo-German Institute, for the promotion of English studies in Germany and German studies in England. It was in this tradition that the first public speech which was delivered by a German in England after the war of 1914–18, which did so much to clear away international misunderstanding, was that of Albert Einstein; and also that Rufus Isaacs, Marquess of Reading, became first President of the Anglo-German Fellowship, when it was organized at that period.

The same spirit is shown with regard to other countries. The London center of the *Institut de France* was established by Baron Edmond de Rothschild, while the Casa Velasquez in the University City at Madrid, which performed a similar function, owes its existence to the same noble philanthropist. The same ideal inspired the establishment of the Henry Traveling Fellowships, intended to foster closer relationships between England and the United States. In this connection, we have the justification in the acute comment made by Joseph Addison in the *Spectator*, over two hundred years ago: "They (the Jews) are, indeed, so disseminated through all the trading parts of the world, that they are become the instruments by which the most distant nations converse with one another and by which mankind are knit together in a general correspondence."

7

A chapter of this study has already been devoted to a consideration of some Jewish contributions to art. But the function of the patron and collector in this field should not be neglected. Their work is indeed imperfectly appreciated; yet it is through them that the artist exists, that works of art are preserved, and that collections are brought together.

The circumstances of their history made it impossible for Jews to figure conspicuously in this capacity in the Ghetto period. Nevertheless, there is evidence that they patronized Giotto, Bonifazio il Giovane, and other eminent painters for illuminating their liturgical and scientific manuscripts. The Roman community possesses ritual appurtenances ascribed to Cellini; the Florentine Jews appreciated the iron-work of Niccolo Grosso, "Il Caparra"; and it is certain that Rembrandt was supported by his Jewish neighbors, in whom he showed such great interest.

It was only in the nineteenth century that Jews had the opportunity to show their artistic appreciation freely. At once they stepped into the front rank of artistic patrons. Once more, it is inevitable that a beginning must be made with the Rothschild family, who patronized artists of every sort with a magnificence which recalled the Italian merchant-princes of the Renaissance. In volume after volume of recent reminiscences it is possible to read enthusiastic appreciation of their munificence and taste. But there were many more: the Bischoffsheims, the Sterns, the Wertheimers, and others. Of more recent memory is Henry Oppenheimer, whose collection of Old Master drawings was perhaps the most comprehensive ever brought together by a private individual. (His business associate, Marten Erdmann, not a Jew, built up a collection of mezzotints unequalled in their range of examples and discrimination of choice.) Mortimer Schiff's wonderful art collection, disbanded in 1938, defies description by reason of its astonishing versatility; but he was at the same time conspicuously generous in his donations to public collections.

The collector is of greater significance when he becomes a benefactor, and many are the Jews who have taken measures to ensure that the treasures in which they took delight during their lives should be accessible to a larger circle after their deaths. Most of the great art-centers of the world exemplify this fact. The Cà d'Oro, that magnificent, treasure-filled Renaissance palace on the Grand Canal at Venice, was bequeathed to the city by the Baron Franchetti. The Hertz collection of paintings was left to the Italian government and is now in the Palazzo Venezia at Rome. In Paris, there was inaugurated in 1936 the Nissim Camondo Museum of decorative art of the eight-

eenth century, founded in memory of a young French
Jew who died on the field of honor. This is not the
only memorial of the family in Paris, for another member, Isaac de Camondo, left his remarkable collection
of nineteenth-century art to the Louvre in 1911. At
the Louvre, too, as at the Bibliothèque Nationale, are
many other monuments to Jewish taste, including the
wonderful collection of French engravings of Baron
Edmond de Rothschild, whose munificence is commemorated on a marble tablet in the former institution;
here, too, is the Salle Rothschild, containing masterpieces of goldwork and enamel of the Middle Ages
and Renaissance, presented by Baron Edmond's
brother, Adolphe. And it was Daniel Osiris who,
among many other benefactions, presented to the
French nation the Empress Josephine's home, La
Malmaison.

In Germany, among a host of important donations
may be mentioned those lavishly made by James Simon
to the Kaiser Friedrich Museum in Berlin, and the
famous collection of antiquities given by Fritz von
Gans to the Altes Museum. The collection of pictures
which Jules Bache presented to the City of New York
in 1937, valued at some $10,000,000, is among the
most munificent gifts ever made to any city.

In England, Jews supported the British Museum
almost from its inception, and perhaps the most remarkable addition that the institution has ever received was the great Waddesdon Bequest. This gift, in
itself almost a complete museum of medieval and
renaissance art, was left to it by Baron Ferdinand de

Rothschild in 1898. Some of the greatest treasures of the National Gallery are included in the collection of Ludwig Mond and are maintained as a separate entity. Mention must be made also of the great Duveen endowments to the British Museum, Tate Gallery, and National Portrait Gallery, which transformed the last institution from an artistic mausoleum of patriotic interest into the palace of delight which it is today.[1]

8

From the point of view of the conforming Jew, it is perhaps regrettable that persons who were Jews by birth have taken so prominent a share in forwarding the interests of other religions. On the other hand, it is a remarkable commentary upon the religious genius of the Jewish people and a standing refutation of the preposterous idea (all the more preposterous in view of the notorious aversion of the Jews to proselytization) that a deliberate attempt is being made by persons of Jewish origin to establish the supremacy of Judaism in the world. One may for the moment overlook the fact that the founders of Christianity, many of the Church Fathers, including the first three Popes, and a goodly proportion of the Catholic saints were

[1] One of the most remarkable acquisitions which the Berlin Museums owe to James Simon (who has been mentioned above) is the famous bust of the Egyptian Queen Nephretiti, discovered, incidentally, by the Jewish archaeologist, Burchardt. Simon was also founder of the German Oriental Society and the most munificent supporter of the German archaeological expeditions to the Near East. Similarly, a collection of modern paintings was presented to the Berlin Gallery by Robert von Mendelssohn, and the German Academy at Rome was founded by Eduard Arnhold.

of Jewish birth. Coming down to a date when all suspicion of legend disappears one may mention Saint
Isidor of Seville, one of the most commanding and devout figures in Spanish church history of the Visi-
gothic period; or the family of Santa Maria, descended
from Rabbi Solomon Levi of Burgos, who contributed
to the Spanish Church in the fifteenth century several
prelates and ecclesiastical writers as well as one of the
most active spirits in the Council of Basle.

The tradition has continued to the present time
without interruption. Not many persons of our day
have influenced the Catholic Church to a greater extent than the brothers Ratisbonne, Jews by birth, who
founded the Order of Notre Dame de Sion in 1842.
This was given canonical existence by Pope Pius IX
and consists of societies of both priests and sisters, who
maintain schools, orphanages, and workrooms for the
poorer classes as well as secondary schools for the
well-to-do. Under the auspices of the Congregation
there has been established the Archiconfraternity of
Christian Mothers, which numbers nearly 2,500
branches in different parts of the world. Similarly, the
Catholic Church cherishes the memory of the venerable Francis Mary Paul Libermann, an Alsatian Jew
baptized at the age of 22. By his foundation of the
Congregation of the Immaculate Conception, since
merged in the Congregation of the Holy Ghost, he
initiated the modern movement for the evangelization
of the negroes, through which the Catholic Church
has been firmly established in Africa. The movement
for the beatification of this convert from Judaism has

already made very considerable progress, and it is anticipated that he will shortly be added to the list of officially recognized Catholic saints.

To take another instance, the Society of St. Vincent de Paul, an international association of Catholic laymen engaging systematically in personal service to the poor, was founded in the middle of the last century by Antoine Frédéric Ozanam, a distinguished jurist and historian, who desired, as he put it, "to insure my faith by works of charity." He belonged, according to the accepted account, to an old French Jewish family, and was a great-grand-nephew of Jacques Ozanam, the eminent French mathematician of the age of Louis XIV, whose *Recréations Mathématiques et Scientifiques* continued to be translated into foreign tongues 150 years after they first appeared. It is asserted, too, that St. Francesco of Paola, who founded the order of the Minims in 1436, was the son of a Jewess.

Turning to the Protestant Church, Sir Culling Eardley, a descendant of the Jewish financier, Sampson Gideon, was founder of the Evangelical Alliance, which secured the independence of the Bulgarian Church and the abolition of the penal laws against the Catholics in Sweden. Michael Solomon Alexander, formerly minister to the Plymouth Synagogue, was responsible for the Anglican missionary activity which established the influence of the Church of England in the Holy Land, and for the foundation of the Anglican Bishopric of Jerusalem, of which he was the first incumbent. Again, Dr. Isaac Capadose was associated

with the disciples of Irving in launching the Catholic
Apostolic Church; Felix Adler was the founder of the
Ethical Culture movement, and Maximilian Low
collaborated with Charles Annesley Voysey in the
foundation of the Theistic Church.

Finally, the father of Church history in the modern
sense is Johann August Wilhelm Neander, originally
named David Mendel, who embraced Christianity at
the age of seventeen. His impressive *Allgemeine Geschichte der christlichen Religion und Kirche*, which
required more than a quarter of a century to write, has
established his position as one of the greatest Church
historians of all time. Yet perhaps his Jewish upbringing was responsible for the spirit which inspired
his classical reply to the Prussian government, which
had asked his opinion as to whether Strauss' *Life of
Jesus* should be prohibited: "Scholarly works are to
be fought with the weapons of science, not by the
power of the State." [1]

9

"God knoweth no vessel so full of blessing for Israel
as peace," runs a well-known rabbinic dictum. It is

[1] It may be pointed out, incidentally, that not all the Jewish
benefactions to Christian objects have emanated from non-
professing Jews, for the traditional tolerance of the Jews has
often overlooked the difference of faith. Thus the Marrano magnate of the seventeenth century, Abraham Senior Texeira, supplied the copper roofing for the Church of St. Michael at Hamburg; several Jews subscribed to the completion of the Trinity
Church in New York in the eighteenth century; while the English
church was first erected at Rio de Janeiro through the efforts of
Denis Samuel.

not remarkable that a group, brought up under the influence of such an ideal, and aware that the Jewish masses must necessarily suffer disproportionately in time of war, should have made a practical contribution to the realization of this hope.[1] After medicine the greatest proportion of Jewish Nobel Prizewinners received the award for services to peace. They include Tobias Michael Carel Asser, the famous Dutch jurist and one of the great figures in the development of international law, and Alfred Hermann Fried, who worked passionately for the ideal of international peace for several decades. The latter, among his other achievements, founded the German Peace Society in 1892 and published a series of works dealing with the subject to which he had devoted his heart.

Lazar (Ludwig) Zamenhof labored for international understanding through a different medium. He felt that a universal language was the one certain means of removing the conflicts and misunderstandings and differences which separate nation from nation and create national rivalries. In the midst of his professional work as a physician he worked hard to propagate this ideal, signing his first essays by the *nom de plume* "Dr. Esperanto." The plan which he suggested achieved remarkable success. Within a few years the new international language had been created, an international Esperanto Congress had been held, an Esperanto literature had come into being. Though the high hopes

[1] It is not perhaps without its significance that Florence Nightingale's Swiss collaborator, Jean Henri Dunant, founder of the Red Cross, was also one of the great Gentile forerunners of Zionism.

which the movement once aroused have not been realized, it has achieved something at least in that direction, and its utility as an international instrument is incontestable.

More important by far was Jean (Ivan Stanislavovich) Bloch. He was the author of a weighty work, published in 1898, in which he maintained a thesis, now familiar, which was then strikingly novel. Technical progress, he declared, had made such strides that future war would mean the suicide of humanity, and it was vitally necessary to devise some other means for settling international disputes. This work attracted the attention of the Czar Nicholas II. Notwithstanding his anti-Semitic bent, the latter was so impressed that he took steps which led to the Peace Conference at The Hague in 1899 and ultimately to the establishment of The Hague Tribunal for International Arbitration. A prominent member of this body for some years was the American representative, Oscar Straus, subsequently Chairman of the League of Nations Peace Committee. And it was a Chicago Jewish lawyer, Salmon Levinson, who in 1927 first published the plan for the outlawry of war, which was the basis for the significant, though abortive Kellogg Pact.

Thus, in the present generation Jews have endeavored to merit the noble sentiment expressed by Azariah de' Rossi nearly four centuries ago (*Meor Enayim*, Mantua 1573, p. 169b):

All the peoples of the earth should know that while we, the remnant of Israel, live in dispersion, we are obliged, according to the words of the prophets and the tradition of the fathers, to pray for the peace and welfare of the state that rules over us. At the present time above all, when for our sins we are scattered to the four winds, it is our duty to supplicate Almighty God for the peace of all the inhabitants of the world that no people may lift up the sword against another . . . and that He may remove from their hearts all strife and hatred, implanting instead peace in the world: for in their peace we too have peace.

EPILOGUE

As this survey draws to a close, a final word is needed so that there shall be no misunderstanding as to the purpose or the conclusion. The names of a large number of Jews have been presented whose contributions to European culture and to human civilization as a whole have been of considerable importance. Yet it is not desired to exaggerate the share that these persons have had in the evolution of the modern world. Of the great names of human history, the Jews have not produced an unusual proportion, save in the religious sphere with Moses and Isaiah, Jesus and Paul. In modern times there have been no towering figures, excepting perhaps Spinoza in the seventeenth century, Disraeli in the nineteenth, Einstein in the twentieth. (I omit, of course, those whose essential work was performed within the bounds of their own religious community.) The proportion may be respectable; it is not abnormally large.

But it is not by the giants alone that civilization can be assessed. Great advances in human progress are the work, not of a single genius, but of scores of less-known pioneers, from whose work, experiences, and failures the genius profits. Civilization is a complex affair. There is constant action and reaction. More startling results would be in most cases impossible without the painstaking research of scores of humble,

unrecorded workers of a previous generation. The
battles may be won by the general; they are fought
by the private soldiers, and victory is a result of the
laborious plans of the staff. It is accordingly a more
solid contribution to progress on the part of any one
of the subsections of the human race if it has performed its duty consistently in the lesser functions
than if it has contributed one of the giants of discovery, whose intuition and good fortune enable him
to sum up the work and the tendencies of his generation.

The Jews have provided both. For centuries past,
they have formed an integral part of the culture of
Europe and have contributed to it incessantly—as
scientists, as men of letters, as translators, as explorers,
as pioneers, as physicians. Had Haber or Reiss or
Ehrlich not made his discoveries, it may well be that
someone else would have done so—a little later, perhaps—for those discoveries were in the air. It is of
even greater significance, then, to recall that in the
more remarkable achievement, the evolution of that
vibrant intellectual atmosphere in which these discoveries were made, the Jews also collaborated effectively—and not in the last century only. Western civilization would not stand where it does today without
that collaboration. The world could not afford to dis-
pense with it any more than with that of England, of
France, or of Germany.

There is a corollary, however. These Jewish investigators and discoverers had in almost every case
non-Jewish teachers on the one hand, non-Jewish

pupils on the other; just as many of the other great scientists and discoverers of modern times received their training partially from and transmitted it to Jewish experts. The resultant discoveries cannot be qualified as "Jewish" or "non-Jewish." The distinction is, from this point of view, arbitrary and ridiculous. If the term has been used in the foregoing pages it is simply as a convenient ellipsis, without any exclusive implication. Such contributions are human.

The Jew, in fact, is heir to a double tradition. There is the religious history of three and a half millennia, which fructified above all on the soil of Palestine and with God's help may fructify there again. And there is the political history of the past twenty centuries, which has been associated principally with the Western World, in whose civilization persons of Jewish birth have taken, not indeed a dominant, nor a disproportionate share, but a share which is worthy of study and respect.

The point gains in force from a glance at the map. Palestine, the cradle of the Jewish people, is a narrow, fertile strip on the eastern seaboard of the Mediterranean, between the Arabian Desert and the sea. Let us imagine for the moment that the geological upheaval which is responsible for the present configuration of that area had happened otherwise, that the desert had come down to the sea on the west of the Arabian Peninsula, as it now does on the east, but that instead, on the shores of the Indian Ocean, there were a tiny fertile area capable of human habitation, to which the Israelites had migrated from Babylonia and

Egypt. Palestine would thus have faced east instead of west, towards Asia instead of towards Europe.

It is difficult to imagine any slight geological change which would have influenced the history of mankind to quite the same extent. One may imagine that Europe would have remained pagan, divided between the immoral deities of Rome and Greece and the bloodthirsty gods of the Teutonic Valhalla. The Latin and Greek genius would not have been fertilized by Christian religious thought. It would have lacked the unity and the force which is based in the last instance upon Jewish monotheism. It would have lacked, too, the invigorating influence of the Jewish mind. Notwithstanding its fertility, its favored geographical position, its temperate situation, Europe might have remained in the condition in which it was left by the Dark Ages.

The Hebraic influence, on the other hand, would have radiated eastward. India and China, rather than Rome, would have received the Jewish message through Christianity. The unchanging East would have known those influences which set European thought, discovery, and progress in motion. The ingenious inventions of the Orient would have received just that impetus which they lacked. America might have been colonized from Asia instead of from Europe. One may sum the matter up thus: Palestine, though situated on the Asiatic seaboard, is to a large extent cut off from Asia because of the sea of desert which nearly surrounds it, and, facing west as it does, has always had a more important influence on Europe than on Asia and, reciprocally, has received more important

influences from Europe than from Asia, since it first
came into the orbit of the Greek world in the fourth
century B.C.

"There is," writes H. A. L. Fisher, in his *History of
Europe*, "a European civilization. . . . It is distinct;
it is also all-pervading and preponderant. In superficial
area Europe is surpassed by Asia, Africa, and America,
in population, by the vast stable peasantry of Asia.
Yet, if a comprehensive survey of the globe were to
be made, it would be found that in almost every quarter of it there were settlements of European men, or
traces of the operation of the European mind. . . .
The political influences of Europe are apparent even
where they are not embodied in direct European control. The ideas of nationality and responsible government, of freedom and progress, of democracy and
democratic education have passed from the west to the
east with revolutionary and far-reaching consequences.
It is, moreover, to European man that the world owes
the incomparable gifts of modern science. It is hardly
excessive to say that the material fabric of modern
civilized life is the result of the intellectual daring and
tenacity of the European peoples."

It would be foolish to contest the essential truth of
this passage. But one modification is necessary. The
term "Europe" is an arbitrary one. To the ancient
world, the differentiation would have been meaning-
less except as a mythological exercise. Hellenic culture
flourished nearly as much on the shores of Asia, and,
at a later date, of Africa, as it did in Greece proper.
Lasting contributions to the Roman heritage, whether

in literature or in law or in religion, were made by persons living on the southern and eastern seaboards of the Mediterranean. It is hence invidious and inaccurate to place too rigid an interpretation on the terms "Europe" and "European Culture." That civilization to which Mr. Fisher refers had its birth in the Eastern Mediterranean, not in the irregular peninsula and archipelago which we now term "Greece"; it subsequently moved westward, and finally, after the Renaissance, it moved northward and became world-wide.

The center of gravity of the Jewish people moved with it, starting in the East, moving gradually to Greece, Italy, France, and Spain, finally to Northern Europe and the Atlantic seaboard. Each stage of Western culture has affected the Jews profoundly; they, on their side, have, so far as they have been allowed, exercised a considerable influence upon it at every stage and in every land. There is in this nothing to boast of. Contemporary events have, however, shown that even in the twentieth century, it is necessary to emphasize the fact that in the tradition of Western culture, in all its branches and centers, the share of the Jew has been as it was proper that it should be, solid, continuous, and integral.

For two thousand years, then, the Jews have formed part of Europe. Throughout that period, though more intensively during the past century, since the gates of the Ghetto were broken down, they have made their contribution to the common heritage—sometimes as intermediaries, sometimes as pioneers, more often, if their activities were not curtailed, as participants. In the long run their contribution has become interwoven inextricably with the common stock by a thousand different strands. Disintegrate these, and the tree of Western culture would be mutilated. Allow them unobstructed growth, and it may bear in the future through this means fruit yet more splendid than in the past.

BIBLIOGRAPHY

THE nature of this work renders it impossible to give a detailed bibliography illustrating every statement made. The works listed below give guidance for the reader who desires to study the question more thoroughly in its general aspects. The utility of the volumes is not, of course, necessarily confined to those chapters in connection with which they are mentioned. A preference has been given to works in the English language. Those listed in the first group have proved particularly useful throughout.

It is the author's duty to acknowledge particularly the assistance which he has derived from Jacobs' *Jewish Contributions to Civilization*, *The Legacy of Israel*, and *The German Jew: His Share in Modern Culture* by Myerson and Goldberg.

GENERAL

BAECK, LEO, *The Essence of Judaism*, London, 1936.

BARON, SALO WITTMAYER, *A Social and Religious History of the Jews*, 3 vols., New York, 1937.

COHEN, ISRAEL, *Jews in the Modern World*, New York, 1929.

DAVID, ELIEZER BEN, *Gli Ebrei nella vita culturale italiana*, Cittá di Castello, 1931.

Encyclopaedia Judaica, 10 vols., Berlin, 1928–1934 (incomplete).

JACOBS, JOSEPH, *Jewish Contributions to Civilization*, Philadelphia, 1919.

Jewish Encyclopaedia, 12 vols., New York, 1901–1906.

KAPLAN, MORDECAI M., *Judaism as a Civilization*, New York, 1934.

L'apport des Juifs d'Allemagne á la civilisation allemande (ed. Cahiers Juifs), Paris, 1933.

The Legacy of Israel, planned by the late I. Abrahams and edited by Edwyn R. Bevan and Charles Singer, Oxford, 1927.

LEVINGER, LEE J., *History of the Jews in the United States*, Cincinnati, 1935.

MAGNUS, LAURIE, *The Jews in the Christian Era from the First to the Eighteenth Century, and Their Contribution to Its Civilization*, London, 1929.

MYERSON, ABRAHAM and ISAAC GOLDBERG, *The German Jew: His Share in Modern Culture*, London, 1933.

ROTH, CECIL, *A Bird's-Eye View of Jewish History*, Cincinnati, 1935.

SILBER, MENDEL, *Jewish Achievement*, St. Louis, 1910.

STERLING, ADA, *The Jew and Civilization*, New York, 1924.

CHAPTER I. *The Hebraic Heritage*

ABRAHAMS, ISRAEL, *Some Permanent Values in Judaism*, Oxford, 1924.

BERDYAEV, N., *The Meaning of History*, London, 1936.

BERTHOLET, ALFRED, *History of Hebrew Civilization*, New York, 1926.

FAIRWEATHER, WILLIAM, *The Background of the Gospels*, Edinburgh, 1908.

HERTZ, J. H., *A Book of Jewish Thoughts*, London, 1937.
———, *The Pentateuch*, 5 vols., London, 1929–1936. (The excursus to this commentary illustrate many instances of Hebraic influences in the modern world.)

JACKSON, F. J. FOAKES (ed.), *The Parting of the Roads. Studies in the Development of Judaism and Early Christianity*, London, 1912.

LAZARUS, MORITZ, *Ethics of Judaism*, Philadelphia, 1901.

MOULTON, RICHARD G., *Literary Study of the Bible*, London, 1895.

SANDS, P. C., *Literary Genius of the Old Testament*, Oxford, 1926.

SULZBERGER, MAYER, *The Am Ha-Aretz: the Ancient Hebrew Parliament*, Philadelphia, 1910.

TRÉNEL, J., *L'Ancien Testament et la Langue Française*, Paris, 1904.

CHAPTER II. *The Process of Degradation*

ABRAHAMS, ISRAEL, *Jewish Life in the Middle Ages*, London, 1932.

CARO, GEORG, *Sozial und Wirtschaftsegeschichte der Juden*, 2 vols., Frankfort-on-Main, 1924.

DITO, ORESTE, *La storia calabrese e la dimora degli ebrei in Calabria*, Rocca S. Casciano, 1916.

LOWENTHAL, M., *The Jews of Germany*, Phila., 1936.

MARCUS, JACOB R., *The Jew in the Medieval World*, Cincinnati, 1938.
———, *The Rise and Destiny of the German Jew*, Cincinnati, 1935.

MORRIS, NATHAN, *The Jewish School*, London, 1937.

PARKES, JAMES, *The Conflict of the Church and the Synagogue*, London, 1934.

ROTH, CECIL, *History of the Jews in Venice*, Philadelphia, 1930.

SESSA, JOSEPH, *Tractatus de Judaeis*, Turin, 1717.

CHAPTER III. *The Revival of Learning*

CASSUTO, UMBERTO, *Gli Ebrei a Firenze nell' etá del Rinascimento*, Florence, 1918.

GAMORAN, EMANUEL, *Changing Conceptions in Jewish Education*, New York, 1925.

GÜDEMANN, MORITZ, *Geschichte des Erziehungswesens und der Kultur der abendländischen Juden während des Mittelalters und der neueren Zeit*, 3 vols., Vienna, 1880–1888.

HUME, MARTIN, "Some Debts the World Owes to Spanish Jews," in *Transactions of the Jewish Historical Society of England*, Vol. VI, 138 ff.

MANOEL, KING OF PORTUGAL, *Catalogue of Early Portuguese Books*, London, 1929–1935.

NEWMAN, L. I., *Jewish Influence on Christian Reform Movements*, New York, 1925.

RENAN, ERNEST, *Averroes et l'Averroïsme*, Paris, 1866.

SCHLEIDEN, M. I., *The Importance of the Jews for the Preservation and Revival of Learning during the Middle Ages*, London, 1911.

STEINSCHNEIDER, MORITZ, *Hebräische Übersetzungen des Mittelalters*, Berlin, 1893.

CHAPTER IV. *The Great Voyages of Discovery*

BURGOS, F. CANTERA, *Eljudio salmantino Abraham Zacut*, Madrid, 1931.

DUFF, C., *The Truth about Columbus*, London, 1936.

HEPPNER, ERNST, *Juden als Erfinder und Entdecker*, Berlin, 1913.

ISAACS, A. LIONEL, *The Jews of Majorca*, London, 1936.

KAYSERLING, MORITZ, *Christopher Columbus and the Participation of the Jews in the Spanish and Portuguese Discoveries*, New York, 1894.

RONCIÉRE, CHARLES DE LA, *La Découverte de l'Afrique au Moyen Age*, Vol. I, Cairo, 1925.

SANZ, MANUEL SERRANO Y, *Origenes de la dominación española en América*, Vol. I, Madrid, 1918.

SCHÜCK, A., *Der Jakobstab*, Munich, 1896.

CHAPTER V. *The Jew in Letters*

ABRAHAMS, ISRAEL, *A History of Jewish Literature*, Philadelphia, 1899.

ASIN, MIGUEL, *La Escatologia musulmana en la Divina Comedia*, Madrid, 1919.

BLONDHEIM, D. S., *Les parlers judéo-romains et la Vetus Latina*, Paris, 1925.

CALÍSCH, E., *The Jew in English Fiction*, Richmond, 1909.

CASSUTO, UMBERTO, *Dante e Manoello*, Florence, 1921.

COTARELO Y MORI, E., *Cancionero de Anton de Montoro*, Madrid, 1900.

DEBRÉ, M., *Der Jude in der französischen Literatur*, Ansbach, 1909.

FLETCHER, H. F., *Milton's Semitic Studies*, Chicago, 1926.

———, *Milton's Rabbinic Reading*, Urbana, 1930.

GEIGER, LUDWIG, *Die deutsche Literatur und die Juden*, Berlin, 1910.

KARPELES, GUSTAV, *Jewish Literature and Other Essays*, Philadelphia, 1895.

KROJANKER, GUSTAV, *Juden in der deutschen Literatur*, Berlin, 1922.

LICHTENSTEIN, J., *Racine, Poéte Biblique*, Paris, 1934.

MANLY, JOHN M., and EDITH RICKERT, *Contemporary American Literature*, New York, 1929.

MANTLE, BURNS, *Contemporary American Playwrights*, New York, 1938.

MERSAND, JOSEPH, *Traditions in American Literature*, New York, 1939.

NOBLE, RICHMOND, *Shakespeare's Biblical Knowledge*, London, 1935.

PHILIPSON, DAVID, *The Jew in English Fiction*, New York, 1918.

STEIN, LEOPOLD, *Untersuchungen über die Proverbios Morales von Santob de Carrion*, Berlin, 1900.

WAXMAN, MYER, *A History of Jewish Literature*, Vols. I–IV, New York, 1930.

ZINBERG, ISRAEL, *A History of Jewish Literature* (in Yiddish).

CHAPTER VI. *Art, Music, Stage*

BERL, HEINRICH, *Das Judenthum in der Musik*, Stuttgart, 1926.

BUBER, MARTIN, *Jüdische Künstler*, Berlin, 1903.

COHN-WIENER, ERNST, *Die Jüdische Kunst*, Berlin, 1929.

COHON, A. I., *An Introduction to Jewish Music*, New York, 1923.

COLEMAN, EDWARD D., *The Bible in English Drama*, New York, 1931.

COLLMANN, SOPHIE M., *Jews in Art*, Cincinnati, 1909.

IDELSOHN, A. Z., *Jewish Music*, New York, 1929.

LANDA, M. J., *The Jew in Drama*, London, 1926.

SALESKI, GDAL, *Famous Musicians of a Wandering Race*, New York, 1929.

SAMINSKI, LAZAR, *Musicians of the Ghetto and the Bible*.

SCHWARTZ, KARL, *Die Juden in der Kunst*, Vienna, 1936.

ZWEIG, ARNOLD, *Juden auf der deutschen Bühne*, Berlin, 1928.

CHAPTER VII. *The Jew in European Thought*

BENSION, ARIEL, *The Zohar in Moslem and Christian Spain*, London, 1932.

GUTHMANN, JULIUS, *Die Philosophie des Judenbunds*, 1933.

GUTTMANN, JACOB, *Moses ben Maimon*, 2 vols., Frankfort, 1908–1914.

JACOBS, JOSEPH, *The God of Israel*, Cincinnati, 1880.

ROBACK, A. A., *Jewish Influence in Modern Thought*, Cambridge, Mass., 1929.

ROTH, LEON, *Spinoza, Descartes and Maimonides*, Oxford, 1924.

WOLFSON, HARRY AUSTRYN, *The Philosophy of Spinoza*, Cambridge, Mass., 1934.

CHAPTER VIII. *Scientific Progress*

CARLEBACH, JOSEPH, *Lewi ben Gerson als Mathematiker*, Berlin, 1910.

GERSHENFELD, LOUIS, *The Jew in Science*, Philadelphia, 1934. (Must be used with the utmost caution.)

MacCALLUM, T., and J. S. TAYLOR, *The Nobel Prize Winners*, 1901–1937.

MARX, A., "The Scientific Work and Some Medieval Jewish Scholars" in *Essays and Studies in Memory of L. R. Miller*, New York, 1938.

SCHLEIDEN, M. J., *Les Juifs et La Science au Moyen Age*, Paris, 1877.

CHAPTER IX. *Medicine*

CARVALHO, AUGUSTO DA SILVA, *Garcia D'Orta*, Coimbra, 1934.

CASTELLI, DAVID, *Il Commento di Sabbatai Donnolo sul libro della creazione*, Florence, 1880.

EPSTEIN, I. (ed.), *Moses Maimonides: Eighth Centenary Memorial Volume*, London, 1935.

FRIEDENWALD, HARRY, *The Bibliography of Ancient Hebrew Medicine* (n.d.), and various other writings by the same authority.

GRUNWALD, MAX (ed.), *Die Hygiene der Juden*, Dresden, 1911.

GUTHMANN, JULIUS, *Die Philosophie des Judenbunds*, 1933.

KAGAN, S. R., *Jewish Contributions to Medicine in America*, Boston, 1934.

KRAUSS, SAMUEL, *Geschichte der jüdischen Ärzte*, Vienna, 1930.

LEVINSON, DR. ABRAHAM (ed.), *Medical Leaves*, Chicago, 1939.

MUNZ, *Die jüdischen Ärzte im Mittelalter*, Frankfort, 1922.

NEUBURGER, MAX, "Die Stellung der jüdischen Aerzte in der Geschichte der medizinischen Wiessenschaften." *Mitteilungsblatt der vereinigung jüdischer Ärzte*, Vienna, April, 1936.

SIMON, I., *Asaph Ha-Iehoudi*, Paris, 1933.

CHAPTER X. *The Economic Sphere*

BLOOM, HERBERT I., *The Economic Activities of the Jews of Amsterdam in the Seventeenth and Eighteenth Centuries*, Williamsport, 1937.

COHEN, GEORGE, *The Jews in the Making of America*, Boston, 1924.

CORTI, COUNT, *The Reign of the House of Rothschild*, London, 1928.

———, *The Rise of the House of Rothschild*, London, 1928.

EMDEN, PAUL, *Money Powers of Europe*, London, 1937.

HERRMAN, LOUIS, *A History of the Jews in South Africa*, Johannesburg, 1935.

HOFFMANN, M., *Judentum und Kapitalismus*, Berlin, 1912.

LEWINSOHN, RICHARD, *Jüdische Weltfinanz*, Berlin, 1925.

RUPPIN, ARTHUR, *Jews in the Modern World*, London, 1934.

———, *Jews of Today*, London, 1913.

SOMBART, WERNER, *The Jews and Modern Capitalism*, trans. by M. Epstein, New York, 1913.

STECKELMACHER, M., *Randbemerkungen zu Werner Sombart*, Berlin, 1912.

VAN DIAS, A. M., *Over den vermogenstoestand der Amsterdamsche Joden in de 17e en de 18e eeuw*, in *Tijdschrift voor Geschiedenis*, Vol. LI, 165–176 (and other studies by the same writer).

WAETJEN, H., *Das Judentum und die Anfäenge der modernen Kolonisation*, Berlin, 1914.

WOLF, LUCIEN, *Essays in Jewish History*, London, 1934.

ZIELENZIGER, KURT, *Juden in der deutschen Wirtschaft*, Berlin, 1930.

CHAPTER XI. *Public Life*

ABBOTT, A. F., *Israel in Europe*, London, 1907.

BARON, H. S., *Haym Salomon*, New York, 1929.

GINSBURGER, ERNEST, *Le comité de surveillance de Jean-Jacques Rousseau*, Paris, 1934.

GOLDBERG, ISAAC, *Major Noah, American Jewish Pioneer*, Philadelphia, 1936.

HART, CHARLES S., *General Washington, Son of Israel, and Other Forgotten Heroes*, Philadelphia, 1936.

LEVY, BERYL H., *Cardozo, Frontiers of Legal Thinking*, New York, 1938.

LIEF, ALFRED, *Brandeis*, New York, 1936.

SCHAY, RUDOLF, *Juden in der deutschen Politik*, Berlin, 1929.

SEITZ, DON C., *Joseph Pulitzer, His Life and Letters*, New York, 1924.

STOKES, RICHARD L., *Leon Blum, Poet to Premier*, New York, 1937.

CHAPTER XII. *"The Greatest of These Is Charity"*

BOGEN, BORIS, *Jewish Philanthropy*, New York, 1917.

FELDMAN, WILLIAM MOSES, *The Jewish Child*, London, 1917.

FLEUGEL, MAURICE, *The Humanity, Benevolence and Charity Legislation of the Pentateuch and Talmud*, Baltimore, 1908.

FRISCH, EPHRAIM, *An Historical Survey of Jewish Philanthropy*, New York, 1924.

JOSEPH, SAMUEL, *The History of the Baron de Hirsch Fund*, Philadelphia, 1935.

INDEX

(Except for some contemporaries, vital dates are given only in the case of Jews and persons of Jewish origin.)

381

Commission on Jewish Education

of the Union of American Hebrew Congregations
and the Central Conference of American Rabbis

David Philipson, *Chairman*
Solomon B. Freehof, *Vice-Chairman*
George Zepin, *Secretary*

Bernard J. Bamberger	Jacob R. Marcus
Samuel M. Blumenfield	Samuel H. Markowitz
Barnett R. Brickner	Julian Morgenstern
Beryl D. Cohon	David Polish
Henry Englander	William Rosenau
Leon Fram	Samuel Schulman
A. N. Franzblau	Lawrence W. Schwartz
Roland B. Gittelsohn	Abraham Shusterman
B. Benedict Glazer	Abba H. Silver
Samuel H. Goldenson	Nathan Stern
Joshua L. Liebman	Louis Wolsey

Edited by Emanuel Gamoran, Ph.D.
Educational Director
Union of American Hebrew Congregations

Date